FIVE GROUNDBREAKING MOMENTS IN HEIDEGGER'S THINKING

Five Groundbreaking Moments in Heidegger's Thinking presents a fresh interpretation of some of Heidegger's most difficult but important works, including his second major work, *Beiträge zur Philosophie (Vom Ereignis)* [*Contributions to Philosophy (From Enowning)*]. The careful approach shows how, for Heidegger, the acts of reading, thinking, and saying all move beyond the theoretical/conceptual and become an ongoing experience.

In new translations of central texts, Kenneth Maly invites the reader to think along the way by reading, contemplating, and translating Heidegger's ideas into this context. An introduction to the field of philosophy and more specifically to Heidegger's thought, *Five Groundbreaking Moments in Heidegger's Thinking* asks the reader, in some manner, to actively engage in thinking.

KENNETH MALY is an emeritus professor of philosophy at the University of Wisconsin–La Crosse.

New Studies in Phenomenology and Hermeneutics

Kenneth Maly, General Editor

New Studies in Phenomenology and Hermeneutics aims to open up new approaches to classical issues in phenomenology and hermeneutics. Thus its intentions are the following: to further the work of Edmund Husserl, Maurice Merleau-Ponty, and Martin Heidegger – as well as that of Paul Ricoeur, Hans-Georg Gadamer, and Emmanuel Levinas; to enhance phenomenological thinking today by means of insightful interpretations of texts in phenomenology as they inform current issues in philosophical study; to inquire into the role of interpretation in phenomenological thinking; to take seriously Husserl's term *phenomenology* as "a science which is intended to supply the basic instrument for a rigorously scientific philosophy and, in its consequent application, to make possible a methodical reform of all the sciences"; to take up Heidegger's claim that "what is own to phenomenology, as a philosophical 'direction,' does not rest in being *real*. Higher than reality stands *possibility*. Understanding phenomenology consists solely in grasping it as possibility"; to practise *phenomenology* as "underway," as "the *praxis* of the self-showing of the matter for thinking," as "entering into the movement of enactment-thinking."

The commitment of this book series is also to provide English translations of significant works from other languages. In summary, **New Studies in Phenomenology and Hermeneutics** intends to provide a forum for a full and fresh thinking and rethinking of the way of phenomenology and interpretive phenomenology, that is, hermeneutics.

For a list of books published in this series, see page 237.

FIVE GROUNDBREAKING MOMENTS IN HEIDEGGER'S THINKING

Kenneth Maly

UNIVERSITY OF TORONTO PRESS
Toronto Buffalo London

© University of Toronto Press 2020
Toronto Buffalo London
utorontopress.com

ISBN 978-1-4875-0801-2 (cloth)   ISBN 978-1-4875-3738-8 (EPUB)
ISBN 978-1-4875-2563-7 (paper)   ISBN 978-1-4875-3737-1 (PDF)

New Studies in Phenomenology and Hermeneutics

___

Library and Archives Canada Cataloguing in Publication

Title: Five groundbreaking moments in Heidegger's thinking /
   Kenneth Maly.
Names: Maly, Kenneth, author.
Series: New studies in phenomenology and hermeneutics (Toronto, Ont.)
Description: Series statement: New studies in phenomenology and
   hermeneutics | Includes bibliographical references and index.
Identifiers: Canadiana (print) 20200281631 | Canadiana (ebook)
   20200281674 | ISBN 9781487508012 (cloth) | ISBN 9781487525637
   (paper) | ISBN 9781487537388 (EPUB) | ISBN 9781487537371 (PDF)
Subjects: LCSH: Heidegger, Martin, 1889–1976 – Criticism and
   interpretation.
Classification: LCC B3279.H49 M26 2020 | DDC 193 – dc23

___

This book has been published with the help of a grant from the Federation for the Humanities and Social Sciences, through the Awards to Scholarly Publications Program, using funds provided by the Social Sciences and Humanities Research Council of Canada.

University of Toronto Press acknowledges the financial assistance to its publishing program of the Canada Council for the Arts and the Ontario Arts Council, an agency of the Government of Ontario.

  Canada Council   Conseil des Arts
         for the Arts   du Canada

 ONTARIO ARTS COUNCIL
CONSEIL DES ARTS DE L'ONTARIO
an Ontario government agency
un organisme du gouvernement de l'Ontario

Funded by the   Financé par le
Government   gouvernement
  of Canada   du Canada

Dedicated to
Professor Friedrich-Wilhelm von Herrmann
with enormous gratitude

Do not seek to follow those who came before; seek what they sought.
— Basho

The task is, not so much to see what no one has yet seen; but to think what nobody has yet thought, about that which everybody sees.
— Erwin Schrödinger

We explore the ways that others have gone in creating their work, so that by becoming acquainted with their ways we ourselves get underway. This way of observing should protect us from construing the work as something rigid and firmly standing there as fixed and unchanging.
— Paul Klee

The *Gesamtausgabe* is meant to show several ways: being underway in an array of ways in the changing questioning of the polysemous question of being. Thus, the *Gesamtausgabe* should guide us to take up the question, to ask the question along-with, and above all then to ask the question more deeply … It is a matter of en-countering the question of the matter for thinking … and not of communicating the author's meaning and not of labeling the standpoint of the writer and not of classifying [what is written] in the sequence of other historically certifiable philosophical standpoints. Such is of course always possible, especially in the age of information. But they are totally extraneous when preparing the questioning access to the matter for thinking.
– Martin Heidegger (GA 1:437f.)

All words of thinking are *starting* words [*an-fangende Worte*, words that "start" thinking, that get thinking going on the way, i.e., words of the "second beginning"] ... As words that get thinking started, they remain unfailingly starting words – not *final* words, not definitive – rather they open up what is in question [as a question].

The unintelligible – letting go of intellect ...

Thinking means to honour [zeroes in on honouring, *heißt anerkennen*] the inconceivable as such. If one wanted to make it [the incomprehensible] conceivable-comprehensible and to take it *back* to something known, it would be destroyed. But how to honour this? And how is this honouring as a thinking?

Unintelligible [inconceivable] – not yet intellectually understood, or what is in contrast to all understanding = wanting-to-understand intellectually – something that is other.

Honouring [zeroing in on] ... *acknowledging* – letting it be said.
– Martin Heidegger (GA 89:623–4)

> "*Ereignis*" – the word that I used earlier – is too easily misunderstood, as if it only means "happening/event" [*Geschehnis*]. "*Eignen*" [*Eignis*] – glimpsing, letting-belong in the clearing of the fourfold – owning-crossing-over [owning-over-to, *übereignen*], – full owning [owning-all-the-way, *vereignen*].
> – Martin Heidegger (GA 81:47)

Contents

Preface   xv

Suggestions, Reminders   xvii

1 Setting the Stage   3

2 The Conditions in Which We Find Ourselves   7

3 Guideposts for This Work   13

    a. Heidegger's Thinking   14

    b. Different Languages, Different Worlds   14

    c. Not So Useful Ways of Reading Heidegger   15

    d. Thinking with and after Heidegger   16

    e. The Dynamic That Is No Thing Nowhere and in No Dimension of Time as Specific   17

    f. Revolutionizing Western Philosophy   19

    g. Dynamic Onefold   19

    h. The Richness of Possibilities   19

    i. Thinking as Always Underway   20

j. Possibility Changes Us 22

k. The First and the Other Beginnings – First Beginning "in Time" and the "Timeless" Start 23

l. The Inexhaustible, the Withdrawing, the Hidden, the Sheltered 24

m. Hermeneutics 24

n. The First Beginning in Dualist Metaphysics 25

4 First Moment: Heidegger and Non-Dual Thinking, Inseparable Phenomenon 29

a. The Dynamic of the Non-Dual 29

b. Thinking-Saying in the Non-Dual Crossing 33

c. Experiencing the Inseparable Onefold, Non-Dual and No-Thing 41

d. Some Examples from Heidegger That Say-Show the Non-Dual Dynamic 50

e. Heraclitus, Fragment 16 52

f. A Way of Gathering 53

5 Second Moment: Heidegger and Non-Conceptual Language as Saying 55

a. Traditional Understanding of Language 56

b. Experiencing "from" Language 57

c. From within a Dialogue from Language 60

d. Gatherings 73

6 **Third Moment: Heidegger and the Symbiosis of Translation and Thinking, from Saying** 79

   a. From Saying to Translation 81

   b. Hearing Heidegger's Words 84

   c. Who Are We, the Translators? 85

   d. In the Translator's Workshop 88

   e. Markings, in Closing 96

7 **Fourth Moment: Heidegger and Engaging in the Retrieval of Greek Thinking-Saying** 99

   a. Thinking When It Is Not "About" 102

   b. The Step Back … Re-trieving Greek Thinking 103

   c. Heidegger's Words on Translating the Greeks 109

   d. Retrieving the Words Λόγος and Φύσις 110

   e. Taking a Brief Look into the Saying of Anaximander 114

   f. Working through a Small Text by Heidegger on Ἀλήθεια in Parmenides 118

   g. Reading Aristotle on Δύναμις and Ἐνέργεια, Inspired by Heidegger 123

8 **Fifth Moment: Time-Space as Ab-ground – Ab-grounding and Timing-Spacing** 137

   a. Setting the Stage: Marking Time-Space in Heidegger's Thinking 138

- b. Word-Images Marking the Non-Conceptual Experience of Knowing Awareness (Knowing Awareness as Experience) of the Non-Dual Dynamic of Timing-Spacing as an Enriching Way of Saying the Truth of Beyng   144
- c. The Way and How to Go It   153
- d. Timing-Spacing as Way   165
- e. Thinking as Experience, Thinking-Experience   172
- f. Words, the Word, the "Speechless" Dynamic Stillness   176
- g. Interlude: A Gathering of the Non-Dual, Non-Conceptual Experience of Dynamic Emptiness   178
- h. Traditional Words to Say Traditional Conceptual Understanding of Space and Time   184
- i. Reading Heidegger's Words on Time-Space as Ab-ground   186
    1. *Reading and "the Word"*   186
    2. *Hinting as Hesitating Self-Withholding*   189
    3. *The Da- of Da-sein Here*   191
    4. *Truth as Ab-ground*   194
    5. *Reading Section 239*   196
- j. Fusing "Saying the Non-Dual Dynamic of Radiant Emptiness" with "Saying Timing-Spacing as Ab-ground" in Section 242   198

Notes   213

Index   233

Preface

The work presented here intends to open up the possibility of thinking Heidegger's question of being (which he pursued carefully and with fresh eyes throughout his lifetime of thinking) as the non-dual dynamic of radiant emptiness. This does not replace the words for being: *beyng, nonconcealment, Er-eignis, timing-spacing, physis, logos*. Rather it moves into a possible way of thinking-saying Heidegger's question, a way that comes "after" Heidegger did his thinking – and, I might say, with Heidegger's blessing.

This text tries to honour the inconceivable as such, leaping to what is own to it and not taking it *back* to something conceivable or known. Doing so, Heidegger says, would destroy it. But how to honour the inconceivable? And how to honour it as a thinking? Not by providing scholarly information to support what we already believe to know about Heidegger, but by opening up to the possibility that shows itself in the saying.

My intention is to *let be* shown how, within the words of Heidegger, there hovers the possibility of hearing and experiencing and saying the non-dual dynamic of radiant emptiness, which, I propose, is at the core of Heidegger's thinking throughout. "Throughout" *says* here the way on which Heidegger continued to press forward throughout his life and to break through barriers, methodically and honestly, in his thinking search for the "meaning of being." **That is, the matter/issue that calls for thinking can be named the no-thing non-dual dynamic of radiant emptiness that is at work and that we can experience: not a being, not dual, not conceptual, sayable**

but not definable, thinkable but not *intellectwise*, sayable but not propositional/logical.

My strategy is to carefully render Heidegger's words – unto what is being said and the letting thereof – so as to allow the insights and experience that I have to provide opening experiences, ones that will shine on and illuminate the texture of what emerges for the reader. In a sense it is a "Heidegger Reader" following a freshly emerging thread.

Suggestions, Reminders

Dear reader, the book you hold in your hands does not belong to the usual category of secondary literature, nor is it only a primary source. It is something else, for which I do not have a name. But given this unusual status, I offer some guidelines while you read and work with it.

*Reading. Some parts in the book are an intellectual exercise in reading. But many are not. I invite you to take your time, to hear the words as an opening to thinking awareness.

I invite you to think along the way, with patient, slow attention to what is being said. To enter into and go along with the spirit of the project. To take a slow pace, allowing for pregnant pauses to savour and experience what emerges for thinking awareness. To be actively patient.

This admonition applies as well to the several "lists" that you will find. Each list may look like a bunch of concepts. But they are always more than that and, rather than being read "past," are meant to goad your experience as a thinker.

*A gathering of conditions. Think of the way as a bunch of conditions. Nothing is anything by itself. Thus you cannot isolate this or that point in the text, for every point belongs to a set of conditions.

*Poi-etic saying. Whatever the thrust of this writing is, it is to a great extent elusive and poi-etic. If you seek a summary of what Heidegger finally means in the form of propositional sentences, you will be frustrated, and perhaps disappointed. The way of poi-etic saying calls for *doing thinking, along the way.* Having an experience with the thinking-saying.

*Repetitions. The many repetitions are deliberate. They belong to the poi-etic way of saying, which is central to the book. I urge the reader to take each repetition seriously – and to avoid being annoyed with them.

*Emptiness. The dynamic of emptiness is the key to the attempt of this book, and it gradually unfolds as the text proceeds. Emptiness is the key that opens this work of thinking and the thread that guides and holds it together. There is nothing outside emptiness (being or beyng or Ereignis as emptiness). All phenomena are the unfolding of emptiness, which is primordially no-thing and does not exist as any "thing." Along with Ereignis, being–beyng as emptiness is the key word-image that says the import of Heidegger's thinking. It names a dynamic, not a thing or a concept.

*The move of dualism within non-dualism. My mantra, if you will, is the non-dual dynamic of radiant emptiness. Along with radiant emptiness not being a thing – thus we cannot "find" it in the same way that we find "things" – the dynamic must be non-dual. This does not mean there is no duality anywhere. Dualism exists in our world and in thinking, and it is useful. But it does not encompass everything, every dynamic of the way things are. Even so, it is part of and ensconced in the non-dualism that is at issue here. Let me explain.

We traditionally think of two ways of thinking and doing. One is the dominant world of empirical, scientific methodology, which deals with the measurable, the empirical, the "objective" world of facts and data. The other deals with the more intuitive but just as significant world of meaning in living and in how we die, with aspects of life, like hope, grief, love, meaning, boredom, sadness.

The scientific method and logic are both at work in rational discourse as well as in scientific and technological discoveries. These are useful for improving the quality of our outer lives, for developing highly precise instruments in technology that are very useful in the physical world, for example, very precise technology used in medicine today, especially in surgery. It is a useful way to deal with empirical and measurable information. Just admire the development of hearing aids over the past ten to fifteen years.

But at the same time, we live and love and hate and find life's deepest meaning in the realm of the knowing mind, of intuition, of awareness. It is in this realm that what I am calling the "non-dual dynamic of radiant emptiness" comes to the fore.

There is a dualism in force in our world. And it is very useful. So what does it mean to think beyond this dualism? It means to think how dualism is in force within the non-dual dynamic. One of the things I try to show in this book is how this happens or is at work.

Here I try to elucidate the *question*. To find or enter into the dynamic itself and to come to know what is at work here – this takes some time and will hopefully unfold within this book. As a starter, let me try this: Think within duality (subject–object, subject–predicate, body–mind, I–world), conceptually. Go deep – all the way – into the concepts and into duality. Dwell there awarely, and the seed of radiant emptiness will show itself. Duality does not go away, but held within the full flourishing of the dual/conceptual is the emerging non-dual and non-conceptual. Heed the full blossoming of the non-dual dynamic of radiant emptiness.

In any case, stay with the question.

***An attempt, not an answer or solution.** Whatever the thrust of this writing is, it is elusive and poi-etic. This belongs to the core of thinking "after" Heidegger. And it is constantly tested, not by me or by Heidegger, but by your own response to the questions and by the leads that are offered.

*Viability, not propositional. Certainly the words are not reductive or always logical. Given this, it is possible that at times the words are not quite right. Do not let this hold you back in thinking the possibility that underlies everything.

*Coming back to the original. Quite often I have chosen to include the original German, alongside the English. Among other things, this is a reminder never to lose sight of the original German and how it necessarily informs the English translation. This is necessary – especially in the case of Heidegger's German – even if the reader does not know German.

These admonitions are gentle reminders, words of caution, pointers, guidelines, tips. You are your own guiding light.

FIVE GROUNDBREAKING MOMENTS IN HEIDEGGER'S THINKING

Chapter One

Setting the Stage

I have chosen five moments in Heidegger's work of thinking that are so groundbreaking that it will take some time for us to understand, to gather, and to own them. This amazing work is so important and essential that we cannot permit ourselves to get waylaid by the postmodernist deconstruction of Heidegger's thinking or by the current fad among some philosophers to let some passages in the *Schwarze Hefte* define the most essential thinking of the twentieth century. However the political issues of the *Schwarze Hefte* or deconstruction's way with Heidegger play out, they pale in comparison to what Heidegger's thinking provokes and enriches.

These five moments of Heidegger's thinking have revolutionized – and will continue to revolutionize – Western thinking so that there can be no turning back. These five matters for thinking (*Sachen des Denkens*) are so revolutionary that thinking has barely begun to plumb the depths of what they say/show. These five matters are:

- Heidegger and non-dual thinking, inseparable phenomenon
- Heidegger and non-conceptual language
- Heidegger and the symbiosis of thinking and doing translation, from saying
- Heidegger and the retrieval of thinking in Greek philosophy
- Heidegger and time-space as ab-ground

The introductory remarks (see Chapter 3) and the first three moments formed the basis of an article that appeared in the 2015

Ročenka pro filosofii fenomenologický výzkum (Czech Yearbook for Phenomenological Research). That text emerged from a lecture series I was invited to give in April 2015 in the Philosophy Department of Charles University in Prague. For their invitation to lecture, and for their warm support and collegiality while I was living in Prague, I am grateful to Professors Hans Rainer Sepp and Ivan Chvatik and Doctors Aleš Novák and Jiří Tourek.

The Fourth Moment was the thematic of a lecture titled "Carrying Out a Retrieval of Greek Thinking ...,"[1] which I gave at the University of Vienna in November 2016, in conjunction with a seminar sponsored by the Austrian Daseinsanalytical Institute.[2] For the invitation to give this lecture as well as collegial support at the University of Vienna, I am grateful to Professor Emeritus Günther Pöltner and Dr. med. Hans-Dieter Foerster, then director of the Institute.

Finally, here is a list of all the volumes of Heidegger's *Gesamtausgabe* that are mentioned in this work. Some of these volumes exist in earlier, separate editions. References in the text are to the various volumes of the *Gesamtausgabe*, followed by the page number – for example, GA 8:17. The *Gesamtausgabe* is published by Vittorio Klostermann Verlag, Frankfurt am Main, Germany. For all other texts quoted or referred to – including those volumes that exist in earlier, separate editions – bibliographical information can be found in the notes.

All the translations of Heidegger's German are my own. I have allowed myself a bit of freedom that I would not allow if I were doing an "official" translation to be published. For this reason – among others – you will often find the German words in the text, in brackets within quotations and otherwise in parentheses.

Within quotations from Heidegger, parentheses are his, while brackets are mine.

GA 1   *Frühe Schriften*, ed. F.-W. von Herrmann, 1978.
GA 2   *Sein und Zeit*, ed. F.-W. von Herrmann, 1977.
GA 4   *Erläuterungen zu Hölderlins Dichtung*, ed. F.-W. von Herrmann, 1981, 1996, 2012.
GA 5   *Holzwege*, ed. F.-W. von Herrmann, 1977, 2003.

GA 6.2	*Nietzsche 2*, ed. B. Schillbach, 1997.
GA 7	*Vorträge und Aufsätze*, ed. F.-W. von Herrmann, 2000.
GA 8	*Was heißt Denken?*, ed. P.-L. Coriando, 2002.
GA 9	*Wegmarken*, ed. F.-W. von Herrmann, 1976, 2000.
GA 11	*Identität und Differenz*, ed. F.-W. von Herrmann, 2006.
GA 12	*Unterwegs zur Sprache*, ed. F.-W. von Herrmann, 1985.
GA 13	*Aus der Erfahrung des Denkens*, ed. H. Heidegger 1983, 2002.
GA 14	*Zur Sache des Denkens*, ed. F.-W. von Herrmann, 2007.
GA 15	*Seminare*, ed. Curd Ochwadt, 1986, 2005.
GA 16	*Reden und andere Zeugnisse eines Lebensweges*, ed. H. Heidegger, 2000.
GA 19	*Platon: Sophistes*, ed. I. Schüssler, 1992.
GA 25	*Phänomenologische Interpretation von Kants Kritik der reinen Vernunft*, ed. I. Görland, 1977, 1987, 1995.
GA 33	*Aristoteles, Metaphysik Θ 1–3. Von Wesen und Wirklichkeit der Kraft*, ed. H. Hüni, 1981, 1990, 2006.
GA 40	*Einführung in die Metaphysik*, ed. P. Jaeger, 1983.
GA 51	*Grundbegriffe*, ed. P. Jaeger, 1981, 1991.
GA 54	*Parmenides*, ed. M. Frings, 1982, 1992.
GA 55	*Heraklit*, ed. M. Frings, 1979, 1987, 1994.
GA 59	*Phänomenologie der Anschauung und des Ausdrucks. Theorie der philosophischen Begriffsbildung*, ed. C. Strube, 1993.
GA 65	*Beiträge zur Philosophie (Vom Ereignis)*, ed. F.-W. von Herrmann, 1989, 1994.
GA 70	*Über den Anfang*, ed. P.-L. Coriando, 2005.
GA 73.1	*Zum Ereignis-Denken*, ed. P. Trawny, 2013.
GA 77	*Feldweg-Gespräche (1944/45)*, ed. I. Schüßler, 1995.
GA 81	*Gedachtes*, ed. P.-L. Coriando, 2007.
GA 89	*Zollikoner Seminare*, ed. P. Trawny, 2018.
GA 79	*Bremer und Freiburger Vorträge*, ed. P. Jaeger, 1994, 2004.
GA 97	*Anmerkungen I–IV*, ed. P. Trawny, 2013.

Chapter Two

The Conditions in Which We Find Ourselves

We Westerners are very good at technology. We have a highly developed scientific mind. We pride ourselves in our "rational" approach, even though it is often not as rational as we think it is. We have explored the external aspects of the planet. Western metaphysics has dominated philosophy for many years. As we value conceptual thinking, we value what we call empirical knowledge. That is, we value what we conceptualize and what we can measure.

But we are not so good at experiential knowing, knowing that goes beyond measurement and theoretical knowledge. It is the concrete knowing that comes through experience-based critical thinking, which goes beyond a working technology, that Heidegger's question of being moves toward. It is hermeneutic phenomenology, rather than reflexive phenomenology. This way of doing philosophy requires both concrete, experiential understanding and critical thinking. Today we are barely able to hear this call.

Heidegger's question of being thinks what is not a being, not a thing, no-thing whatsoever, even as all that is emerges from within this dynamic. As Heidegger's thinking unfolds, it stays with the central question of being, even as it strives to think – and then to say – this no-thing from within which all that is emerges and manifests itself. Thus he kept looking for the ways in which to say the dynamic that is no-thing. This became his pursuit, what made his life meaningful.

As the dynamic of being-beyng-enowning, that is nothing whatsoever, showed itself for Heidegger, the way of thinking-saying evolved; and new words emerged to say the question: *aletheia* = disclosure or unconcealment, beyng (German *Seyn*, over against *Sein*), Ereignis = enowning,[1] the fourfold (and especially the opening that sustains and starts and reveals the four, the dif-ference that is a non-thing), or the spacing that is in tension as the opening – a spacing that is no-thing whatsoever but a dynamic that holds open, works, and lets manifest. This dynamic of holding-open Heidegger calls rift (*der Riß*):

> This in-tension [*Streit*] is not a rift as ripping open a mere cleft, but rather it is the intimate belonging together of the dynamic in tension. This rift pulls together the dynamic that is in tension into the provenance of its [non-dual] onefold from within the joining ground. (GA 5:51)

Rift: an opening, an open spacing, a bursting open. Itself nothing whatsoever but a dynamic that shows/says beyng or enowning. It is empty of form and empty of concept. Thus it can also be called "emptiness" – what I call, then, "the dynamic of radiant emptiness." How this wording says-shows the matter to be experienced in thinking will become clear as we go along.

Can this thinking "after" Heidegger be sustained from within the call for thinking to which Heidegger responds? Is this a possibility that Heidegger's thinking can open to, one that the words and grammar available at the time could not grant? A thinking-saying that Heidegger's thinking made possible, for us (perhaps!) to pursue "after" Heidegger?

Because this dynamic is no thing whatsoever and cannot be thought conceptually, it remains strange and estranging – impenetrable. It is a paradox because, over against what we know in concepts and can distinguish about things, beings – "reality" if you will – the most fundamental bearing of being and of our being remains hidden, inaccessible, and unrecognized. To have theoretical knowledge of human being and of the world is very different from realizing in experience, concretely, this dynamic of the emptiness of being – or beyng, enowning, *aletheia*. We are called to experiential knowing, along with critical thinking within it. It emerges in awareness, not in concepts. It is something strange.

Heidegger's life-work of thinking is a relentless pursuit of this dynamic, from being to beyng as enowning (from *Sein* to *Seyn als Ereignis*). Given the inexorable difficulty of this pursuit, it is incumbent upon us who think "after" Heidegger to follow up on the path of this pursuit. Therefore, the craft that is called for is (a) to follow Heidegger's words, to listen closely and carefully to the said, and (b) to think the possible in the said, a possibility that Heidegger's words open up for us, to think within and beyond the said.

Following upon what Heidegger's words say, (a) I present quotations that open up this thread – I invite thinking into the possibilities of this saying for showing the way to thinking/saying this dynamic of radiant emptiness, and (b) with my own words, following from and after Heidegger, I try to think the "next step," the possibilities in what calls for thinking in Heidegger's words. Think of it as a path, with Heidegger's words as signposts along the way. My own words are a kind of thread, as Heidegger's words are meant to be contemplated and thought within possibility. As he wrote in *Sein und Zeit* and again at the end of his essay "My Way into Phenomenology":

> What is ownmost to it [phenomenology] does not lie in its being actual as a philosophical orientation. Higher than actuality is possibility. Understanding phenomenology lies solely in grasping it as possibility. (GA 2:51f.)

Here is his own way of thinking this "next step":

> For example, we have to translate Kant's *Critique of Pure Reason* every time anew, in order to understand it. That does not mean reducing the lofty language of the work into ordinary language. It means to translate [*übersetzen*] the thinking of this work into a dialoguing [*auseinandersetzend*] thinking and saying. With that, then, there sometimes arises the odd semblance that the interpreter "really" understands the thinker "better" than the thinker himself. For the empty vanity of minds that are merely clever, this semblance is dangerous. They conclude that in such a case Kant himself had not quite known what he really wanted and that now the interpreter who comes afterwards knows this precisely.

> But, that a thinker can be understood "better" than he understood himself – this is in no way a flaw [*Mangel*, lack] that could be attributed to him afterwards, but rather a sign of his greatness. For only the originary thinking hides in itself that treasure that can never be thought through completely – and can each time be understood "better," i.e., other than what the immediately meant wording says. In the run-of-the-mill situation there is only what is understandable – and nothing of that which constantly requires more originary understanding and interpreting and that might itself call forth [*hervorrufen*, evoke, call for] the times that are necessary to recognize again what was supposedly known long ago and to translate. (55:63–4)

I put emphasis on these words of the quotation:

> But, that a thinker can be understood "better" than he understood himself – this is in no way a flaw that could be attributed to him afterwards, but rather a sign of his greatness. For only the originary thinking hides in itself that treasure that can never be thought through completely – and can each time be understood "better," i.e., other than what the immediately meant wording says.

We need a kind of mirror. Words can point and show but they cannot "capture" the dynamic of radiant emptiness, also known as being-beyng-enowning. This being-beyng-enowning is no where and is indescribable. This no-thing whatsoever, however, can be said-shown, is at work, and we can experience it. A way of language is called for that is other than logical or propositional. It is the way of poi-etic saying. With poi-etic language we can learn to say-show, even as we cannot say-show what it *is*. That fits the dynamic named in being-beyng-enowning, which I name the nondual dynamic of radiant emptiness.

It is not about staying within the security and certainty of the known and conceivable, but rather moving to its edges and toward the experienceable but impenetrable. This experience of thinking takes place beyond the cognitive limit.

In this context I freely repeat things throughout this work. These repetitions do not belong to the normal flow of conceptual thinking. Here, they shine as word-images inviting us to an experience of thinking. Sometimes I just simply present Heidegger's words, *mirroring* what I want to say, sometimes with the addition of my own words. I hope Heidegger's words can be heard other than as a scholarly reading, heard more freshly and richly in the context in which they appear here.

Chapter Three

Guideposts for This Work

Before I turn to the first moment, I want to say some things that apply throughout all five moments. I share these, even though they may seem somehow clear and self-evident. I share them in the hope that something I say will be useful for the reader's own journey in philosophical thinking and in developing the mind.

As a kind of directive, I offer two word-images from Heidegger here: thinker and teacher. In *Anmerkungen*, Heidegger distinguishes philosophy scholars, philosophers who are metaphysicians, and thinkers (GA 97:57). And in *Was heißt Denken?* (GA 8:17–18), he tells us what a teacher does: A teacher "lets-learn" – is neither an authority who "knows a lot" nor a famous professor.

Always modest and always honest, Husserl addressed this same issue. To those who had prejudices or assumptions and apparently "knew in advance" how to interpret and critique his thinking, he had this response: "First hear and see what is presented, go along with and watch to see where it leads and what happens with it."[1]

Heidegger followed this maxim. Although he called Husserl's phenomenology "reflexive" over against his own "hermeneutic" phenomenology and showed how Husserl ended up in transcendental subjectivity – not where Heidegger himself went[2] – still Husserl's method and honesty paved the way. The point: it is not about defining and "always already knowing," but about following and going along with the phenomenon: seeing where it leads and what happens with and in it (the phenomenon) – being aware of what shows itself.

I invite you, the reader, to defer any temptation to find where you disagree or to focus on what you might find "incorrect" in what I say here. There is always time, later, to find mistakes or play with whether I am "right." For now I urge you simply to go along with, thoughtfully, and see where the path leads.

Let me say, then, that we face a challenge: not to let our normal ways of thinking and saying limit us, but "to say originarily and to build up what is essential in accord with its own law; but then to keep trying, 'ununderstood' and indecipherably, to release beyng [*Seyn*] once again for its arrival and to awaken a reminder of the sublime/noble"[3] (GA 97:7).

So, before I turn to the First Moment – Heidegger and non-dual thinking, inseparable phenomenon – let me make a few, sometimes simple, observations.

a. Heidegger's Thinking

The measure for the truth and power of Heidegger's work of thinking is not the person Heidegger, but experience-based critical thinking. The question is: Does it fit with our understanding of experience and of what needs to be thought, *das Zudenkende*? Thus, whereas in this book the name *Heidegger* sometimes refers to the philosopher himself, it more often and most properly refers to Heidegger's thinking.

b. Different Languages, Different Worlds

Let me mention an interesting fact. Heidegger wrote in German. I am writing in English. How appropriate, this mixture of languages, given how central to our work are the themes of language and translation!

The French artist Louise Bourgeois once wrote:

> People ask me – what do you mean –
> and I answer what do you think of
> when you see the image.[4]

To paraphrase this: If you ask, "What do Heidegger's words in German – and in English translation – mean?," we might answer: "What do you think of when you hear them?" That is, are they a clarion call to *hear* Heidegger's thinking-saying? And above all, do the English words stay true to what is thought and said in Heidegger's German?

c. Not So Useful Ways of Reading Heidegger

There are several dangerous – or not so useful – ways of reading Heidegger. The first one is *chronologically*: Heidegger I and Heidegger II; early, middle, and late Heidegger; earlier "less perfect" works and later "more perfect"; or the earlier "more philosophically rigorous" and the later "more poetic" thinking. This not-useful way includes the idea/goal of putting all of Heidegger into a complete "system" or seeing/taking Heidegger's thought as some kind of complete "whole." This approach amounts to a kind of ambush.

The second not so useful way of reading Heidegger is to focus on *influence*. As if Heidegger's reading of Buddhism and Daoism is more or less important than his reading of the poets. Or reducing Heidegger to his place "over against Husserl." Heidegger took this idea from Schelling … This or that thought by Heidegger is a Daoist thought …

The third – and perhaps least useful? – way is to imagine that this or that thought in Heidegger is similar to some idea found somewhere in some text. Here I would mention *deconstruction* and its dedication to what it calls "a text." Sometimes this way of reading Heidegger forgets about the question of being, which claims us in our thinking and which is surely something more than the text. When Derrida compares a text of Heidegger to *Robinson Crusoe*, the dynamic of the question of being, as well as its power to claim us, gets lost.

This third not so useful way of reading Heidegger includes *comparative analysis* or scholarship, which is limiting if not reductive – Heidegger versus Kant, Heidegger versus Husserl – a reading that is not driven by *das Zudenkende* but rather by scholarship and not thinking.

d. Thinking with and after Heidegger

Here I attempt to think with and after Heidegger. To think "after Heidegger" does not mean post-Heidegger in the usual sense. Our thinking here is not (a) to leave Heidegger behind, but rather (b) to carry his thinking along with us, letting it enrich our questions and (c) to think *das Zudenkende* as it comes to us from in front – from the future – as possibility.

In *Sein und Zeit* Heidegger says that the words and the grammar are lacking to get to the time-space of the other beginning. Thus the impossibility at that time (1927) of writing the second part of *Sein und Zeit*. What happens when we, "after" Heidegger, learn to think non-conceptually (see the Second Moment)?

In *Beiträge zur Philosophie (Vom Ereignis)*, he says:

> The relapses into the hardened/stiff ways and claims of metaphysics will continue to disturb and will block the clarity of the way and the firmness of the saying. Yet, the historical moment of the crossing [from first to other beginning][5] must be enacted from within knowing that all metaphysics ... remains incapable of shifting humans into the basic relations to beings [to what is].[6] (GA 65:12)

We thinkers cannot remain within the metaphysical conceptual and linguistic structures; but rather, as we participate in the saying of beyng, we are called to become open to the opening that beyng's saying provides. This is part of what Heidegger means in *Sein und Zeit* when he says that "the ultimate business of philosophy is to preserve the force of the most elemental words" (GA 2:291).

What happens when we, "after" Heidegger, try to do this preserving? When fresh words and wordings emerge in the crossing from the first to the second beginnings (from the beginning in chronological time to the other beginning, that is, the "timeless" *starting*), and we begin to say the emerging insights? If we pay attention to these in our questioning, we will experience how language arises in its saying/showing. And we will start to *think* "after" Heidegger. The path of thinking is neither bound to nor built on the philosopher. Rather, what comes to us in thinking "after" Heidegger is from what is own to language as saying.

Heidegger's thinking is always underway, going-along-with what is in front of us – as phenomenon, as matter for thinking, as the question of being – until a new emergence is released in language. So too is our thinking, which goes along with Heidegger while being underway in the same way that Heidegger's thinking is underway. Not that we are Heidegger, but that we participate in the way-making of language, with the possibility of a new opening in the saying. For example, in my own work I take steps in reading Greek thinkers that Heidegger himself did not take, even as he showed us the way to these possibilities.[7]

After Heidegger: following after, thinking along with, going along with, following in the footsteps of the thinking/saying that we call "Heidegger." This presents a big responsibility to the joyful work of thinking!

e. The Dynamic That Is No Thing Nowhere and in No Dimension of Time as Specific

To go with Heidegger to a newly unfolding possibility in thinking language and the way things are, that is, in thinking-saying the way things are – which includes beings/things, Da-sein, the being of metaphysics, beyng (*Seyn*) and Ereignis – is to understand the dynamic that grants *Seyn*/beyng and Ereignis/ enowning and to understand how they all say what is no-thing, even as it is at work and does something. Ereignis/enowning is not a being, not a thing, but *es ereignet*. To use the English words: enowning is not a being, not a thing, but *enowns* (or: there is enowning).[8]

It "is" not, but it works and is in play. There is unfolding or enowning, even as there is no thing (nothing) and "it" does not exist in time or place. It "is" nowhere and in no time, even as it "grants" time. Dynamic unfolding, emergent emergence-withdrawal, granting-refusal, unconcealing-sheltering concealing, along with *Sein, Seyn*,

Ereignis – all saying this radiant emptiness or this non-dual dynamic of radiant emptiness.

How can we learn to hear and to say this quality that is beyond our conceptual thought process? The self-revealing and self-sheltering as one? Always hiding within revealing and revealing within hiding?

Let me offer the following comment. These many words – *beyng, Ereignis, Unverborgenheit-aletheia, logos* – say what is no-thing whatsoever but emerges, what is no-thing whatsoever even as it is at work, what is no-thing whatsoever even as we can experience it. The dynamic that is named with these words is in no time, but hands over or proffers time (*Reichen*), grants time (*geben,* as in *es gibt*)[9] or hands out, applies time (*Brauchen*[10] as *ausgeben, verwenden*) – the non-dual one-ing of true time as near-ing nearness.[11] And these words say what is nowhere in space – not "exterior" but permeating beyond predication.

In *Das Ende der Philosophie und die Aufgabe des Denkens* Heidegger writes:

> Only through it [light, clearing, *Helle*] can the shining show itself, i.e., shine. But the lighting-up for its part resides in an open, a free, which here and there, now and then, may light up. The light/clearing plays in the open and therein contends with the dark.
>
> We call this openness, which grants a possible letting-shine and showing: lighting-up [*die Lichtung*, clearing] … To light up something is to set it free and open.
>
> It becomes necessary for thinking to pay special attention to the issue that here is called *Lichtung* [lighting-up, clearing, opening] … The phenomenon itself – here *die Lichtung* – gives us the task, in questioning it, of learning from [within] it, i.e., of letting it say something to us.[12] (GA 14:79–81)

We are not conditioned for seeing-saying-thinking this dynamic of no-thing, no-where, and no-time. But it is where Heidegger's thinking takes us. The road there is rich, necessary, and possibly long.

f. Revolutionizing Western Philosophy

As I said earlier, these five moments in Heidegger's thinking have revolutionized – and will continue to revolutionize – Western thinking, such that there is no turning back. One day the world will again be grateful to Heidegger for his contributions to genuine philosophical thinking.

Here are other examples of revolutionary insights that the world can hardly think: Einstein and the theory of relativity; Heisenberg and the principle of indeterminacy; the ungraspable dynamic of energy as foundational; and, most recently, the discovery of the Higgs boson particle. Technically what was discovered was not the Higgs boson "particle" but what the Higgs boson decays into – pointing to the Higgs field, which points to energy and influence that may well not be merely physical. Heidegger's groundbreaking thinking is equally hard to fathom, and we have scarcely gone beyond the surface.

g. Dynamic Onefold

Everything here is a onefold, a dynamic one. Thus all five topics are interconnected. Whereas the main thread of each moment is named in the specific title and focused on in the specific chapter, threads from all five will be interwoven – we might say "inseparably" – as we travel the road called Heidegger's thinking. This dynamic onefold invites and challenges us to engage and to be engaged. I call this the *richness of possibilities*.

h. The Richness of Possibilities

Regarding Heidegger's groundbreaking thinking, one day it will be easier to envision (a) that the metaphysics of presence, substance metaphysics, and rationalism no longer dominate Western philosophy, and (b) that all is possibility.

Possibility and change offer the richness of freshness. Let us ponder this, not from the personality- and ego-based culture that dominates many parts of the world today, but from the non-dual dimension, from the fullness and richness of affordance (*Geschick*), namely from the dynamic onefold that is said in Heidegger's word *Geschick*. The English word for *schicken* is "to send." But there is another English word that says *schicken* and *Geschick*: to afford, an affordance. *Geschick* affords to us, bestows, grants, offers or makes available, opens up and gives, sustains thinking-saying-beyng. This onefold (a) holds us who receive and respond to what is afforded to us, (b) holds that which is afforded and (c) holds the affording as such. One could name these three aspects of the onefold: (a) we who participate in the affording even as we do not accomplish or control it, we who are claimed by the affording to us and necessarily respond to it (whether non-thinking or not-yet-thinking or even in a thinking response), (b) that which is afforded, even though it is hardly known what "it" is; and (c) the affording as such. All of this together is the dynamic unfolding of this onefold.

How do non-dual thinking the inseparable phenomenon, non-conceptual language as saying, the thinking that is always at play in translating, retrieving the thinking in Greek philosophy, and time-space as ab-ground – how do these five moments promise a breaking away from that which was, such that it is hard to fathom that "it" once was? And how do they open up and say the emerging, enriching possibility from/in/for the future? What do they call for in our thinking? What is this retrieval, this saying anew?

i. Thinking as Always Underway

At the heart of Heidegger's thinking is being-underway. Is it possible that the dynamic unfolding of the way-making of Da-sein and of beyng is about way-making as such? That the saying rather than the said is "it," more than any "thing"?

When Professors F.-W. von Herrmann, Parvis Emad, and I founded the journal *Heidegger Studies*, thirty-five years ago, our intention was to take seriously Heidegger's distinction between mere scholarly research in philosophy and philosophy as thinking that is underway, i.e., is *being accomplished* as we "think." Heidegger called his writings "ways not works" (*Wege, nicht Werke*). Thinking is always going-along-with. On the first page of the first issue of *Heidegger Studies*, in 1985, we read:

> *Heidegger Studies* takes seriously the essential distinction that Heidegger made between mere scholarly research in philosophy and philosophy as thinking that is underway, is being accomplished.
>
> ... philosophy as thinking that is underway refuses to limit philosophy to research and to this latter's fixed scientific mold. Thinking that is underway can be understood precisely in its character as different from objectifying investigation. The underway-character of this thinking gives it its phenomenological character – if phenomenology is seen as the praxis of the self-showing of thinking's subject matter.
>
> ... thinking in this place in the history of thinking, in its historical emergence, still awaits the responsive thinking that thinks-along-with ... and offers an inestimable richness of possibilities yet to be developed ...
>
> ... according to words that Heidegger himself prepared for a preface [to the *Gesamtausgabe*] that was planned but not executed: "The *Complete Edition* is meant to be a showing in different ways: a being-underway within the whole array of ways in which the question of being is transformed in its movement. The *Complete Edition* ought thereby to offer a direction for taking up the questioning more essentially."[13]

Ours is an experiment in this thinking-along-with, in reading Heidegger and thinking possibility. Rather than analysing and comparing, leading to theory – the way of scholarship and intellectual-conceptual work – we *go the way*, go along with. Rather than comparing stages in Heidegger's "development" and looking critically at commentaries on Heidegger (scholarship, identifying the "schools" of Heidegger scholarship)[14] – we read and listen to the original thinker. This may seem revolutionary. Not all see the matter at hand. Time will tell.

What we are doing here is not saying "others are wrong"; rather, we are checking out the possibility in non-conceptual thinking and in poi-etic words. We are not reading for contradictions or who is right or which Heidegger is right ("Heidegger is wrong here" is not useful); rather, we are reading in order to clarify the said and what it involves – what is to be thought in the said – always reading to see what is going on for the sake of thinking that is engaged in the world, within the question of beyng.

The common enemy of this way is objectivism and absolute conceptualizing.

j. Possibility Changes Us

It is obvious and simple but useful to remember that, for Heidegger, thinking is always (a) about exploring possibility, (b) about being engaged in the thinking and saying process, and (c) about how this thinking transforms. It changes us, it changes being. Finally, for Heidegger the question of being/*Sein* and eventually beyng/*Seyn* – which is necessarily not a substance and no-thing – is always dynamic. Whatever being or beyng names, it is dynamic. Starting with *Sein und Zeit*, a way is opened in which all is transformed; and Heidegger is always keen to think more deeply, away from concepts and inherited language – an underway-thinking.

Thinking changes us, we are changed. The change is a change within the non-dual "one" of the dynamic of Dasein-beings or Dasein-world, of the dynamic of Ereignis in the oneness of the enowning throw of being that enowns Dasein and Dasein's responding to this enowning – all named in Ereignis as a dynamic at-oneness.

Heidegger's possibility. His unceasing efforts to think the question of being – which had not been asked since the Greeks – called him to new possibilities, to new words and wordings. And from the start it is about openings. *Open* is a key word throughout Heidegger's life of thinking. Dasein is about openness, names the open expanse of the Da. And in *Parmenides* (GA 54) he calls being *das Freie* and *das Offene*.

k. The First and the Other Beginnings – First Beginning "in Time" and the "Timeless" Start

The first beginning is with us from the past and is the history of metaphysics, while the second beginning is in front of us and is not about chronology at all. German has one word for these two meanings: *der Anfang*. This German word says both the "first" beginning as "then, in history, long ago," and the "second" beginning as "setting into motion, source or well-spring, the start of something." This second meaning of *Anfang/anfangen* has nothing to do with some beginning or other at some time in the past. It says: getting things going/moving (outside of time as measured or as chronology). This *Anfang* is not the beginning "in time," but is fully "in" where we are, where everything "starts." The English word *starting*[15] does a good job of saying this "second or other beginning."

One beginning took place and is now in the past. But the starting! – what starts something – is something else. What sets things in motion, going out from. Not beginning to move "from somewhere," but the ongoing well-spring, which is always in front of us. Setting out, calling up. Not the beginning of an action in time, but setting into motion. Springing forth, birthing. An opening, the begetting. In Old English the word *styrtan* says: to leap up, to get things moving. This is always at work.

The first beginning happened somewhere "in time" as measured chronologically. The starting, on the other hand – the second or other beginning (*der zweite oder andere Anfang*) – is an inexhaustible, dynamic energy or empowering and is nothing derived! For it is a dynamic but no-thing, nothing at all!

We must learn to think and say the "starting" (Heidegger: the other beginning), what gets things going, in its timeless character, that is, the withdrawal of this start in the sheltering-hiding. Heidegger says that this starting is always unique to every start. "There is no law of the start, in the sense that it would reign 'over' the start" (GA 70:13).

I will come back to these "beginnings" as we go along.

l. The Inexhaustible, the Withdrawing, the Hidden, the Sheltered

This dynamic start – starting – cannot happen via concept. (Concept is always second, always comes *after* the starting.) We can dwell in the dynamic but never exhaust or "possess" it. This requires a turn from calculation to wonder. Heidegger says: That which withdraws from us draws us along. Space and time is not where the universe begins, but resides *in* – or emerges *from within* – the starting.[16] From within the "start" Dasein does not see any "opposite over against us" – or separate from us. Da-sein is also the name for the non-dual phenomenon of being bound with that which withdraws, bound with the incalculability of the way things are.

Unverborgenheit and *Verbergung*: unconcealing and sheltering self-hiding. *Enteignis* as part of Ereignis: the hidden in Ereignis. Everything that is endures/undergoes the circle of emerging and disappearing (falling out of appearing, as part of appearing). Max Planck:

> Matter comes from a force that sets into motion [starts] and holds together. Behind this force is an ungraspable dynamic.

The world is not firm, it unfolds, it comes into its own (*ereignet sich*), dynamically. The world and the way things are is more than a concept.

Normally we do not see the world and the way things are, but only our explanations of what the world is. How can we think back to (retrieve) world? By thinking the "start," the springing forth, the ongoing well-spring. This is in front of us, in possibility; and we are called to retrieve it from the "future."

The withdrawal, the hidden-sheltered, is inexhaustible. The rich dynamic is ungraspable in the duality of concepts.

m. Hermeneutics

Husserl's is a reflexive phenomenology. Heidegger's is a hermeneutic phenomenology: the laying out (*Auslegung*) of what shows itself. In *Unterwegs zur Sprache* Heidegger tells us that *hermeneuein* says: to make known, to announce. This dynamic is non-dual and needs a non-conceptual, poi-etic languaging to say it. It brings about or starts off. Something happens, and being or beyng shows through – beyng as non-dual dynamic.

Heidegger was well acquainted with biblical hermeneutics, as interpretation of texts (i.e., with Schleiermacher). But from the beginning, his hermeneutic phenomenology was an interpreting or laying-out of phenomena. Later he thought *hermeneuein* unto its deeper meaning: announcing: the announcing language of being. This way of hermeneutics was utterly hidden until Heidegger saw it as *hidden*. Husserl's "adequate self-givenness" in the phenomenological reduction is not primordial enough, not *anfänglich*, not a "starting" for the way things are. The non-conceptual saying of *logos* is more a start – more primordial – than Hegel's dialectical logic. (More on Heidegger's usage of and misgivings about the word *hermeneutics* in the Second Moment.)

n. The First Beginning in Dualist Metaphysics

Our journey begins "now," in the twenty-first century, with metaphysics, the first beginning (long ago) having reached its culmination and power and dominance in our epoch. Since the five groundbreaking aspects of Heidegger's thinking belong to the second beginning, to the "start," while including the first beginning, let us name the dualism that emerged with the metaphysics from out of which we "start."

Thing: Somewhere in early Greek thinking, the thing was still "there" in its ownness. The thinging of the thing. Things flourished in their "own" richness and "conditions" – the *Be-dingungen* of *Dinge*, also known as gathering of the thing amidst other things, dynamically – without being reduced to something less. In Aristotle, *ousia* still says concrete thing, gathered into its own flourishing. Greek and Latin scholar Joseph Owens – not particularly interested in Heidegger – rejects the notion of *ousia* as beingness, because beingness says something abstract and universal, "while Aristotelian *ousia* means something concrete (a 'this,' a particular thing)."[17] Owens also rejects the Latin *substantia* – English *substance* – as a viable translation of *ousia*.

Aristotle always started with the concrete existing thing, in what he called *empeiria*. Aristotle did not mean what we now call "empirical" in today's scientific sense. The word for Aristotle meant experience, experiential. Thing was a sensible *ousia* as the dynamic of *eidos* and *dynamis*: *this* being with its history (read: conditions/ *Be-dingungen* and the context of things/*Dinge* that surrounds them). Thing here is never completed once and for all, but is always still active in dynamic process – even when "actualized," as we traditionally say in English, for the Greek *energeia* – rather than "completed result," as traditional Aristotelian scholarship calls it. (See the Fourth Moment.)

Things are simply "there" – as perceptible bodies or "there from touch and contact": *pathemata aisthetika* (Timeaus 61d). The gathering of the thing thinging includes the *dynamis* or active force that rings in the thinging of the thing.

For sure, Plato and Aristotle asked *how* contact of the *psyche* with the sensible is achieved. But they never inquired into – because they did not doubt – *that* the concrete thing is always there.

So in the early history of things – flourishing concretely, rich in their thinging – "thinging" was in play and enriching. Along with serving other uses and understandings, a tree was still a tree in its richness and flourishing. A river was fully a river. But then! *Thing* went from being there dynamically, shining and radiant in being what it is in its thinging,

> ... to being reduced to a product or tool of *techne* (things as useful),
> ... to being reduced to a mere entity in Scholastic philosophy, to just something that is, over against *anima* or *intellectus* – as in Aquinas: *Veritas est adaequatio rei et intellectus*, where *intellectus* is the rule of *res*/things,
> ... to being reduced to the object of objectifying subjectivity (cf. Kant),
> ... to being reduced to commodity in exchange of goods in capitalism (cf. Marx),

... to being reduced to a disposable in the epoch of technicity and the regime of disposability.

In that first beginning duality set in; and the concept of what a thing is veered away from direct experience of dynamic thinging, until the "thing" got pretty much obliterated by being reduced to a disposable item for further disposal, thus becoming no longer a thing at all. Thus is the culmination of things in the first beginning, also known as metaphysics.

The story of *psyche* is similar. The Greek word ψυχή[18] got translated into Latin as *anima* and into English as soul/mind/reason – a lightning bolt of missing what the Greeks were saying. Heraclitus's unfathomable *psyche* cannot simply be said in Latin as "anima" or in English as "soul." Aristotle says that *psyche* is the principle of life of any living being and that the human *psyche* is the principle of human life. What belongs to this *psyche* has several names: *nous*/awareness, *sophia*/wisdom, *episteme*/knowledge of things that cannot change, *theorein*/ insight, *logos*/speech-gathering-thinking.

Translating Heraclitean *psyche* as "anima" and then *Seele* and "soul" does not fit. Nor does the German *Geist*.

If all of these are names for what the *psyche* is or does, perhaps we can use the English word *mind* as a way to render *psyche* into English.

But then! *Mind/psyche* went from this rich activity

- ... to being reduced to *anima* or soul, including that soul's being created by a divine power, with soul quite distinct from the body and mostly thought as static,
- ... to being reduced to the *res cogitans* as quite distinct from the body, which now is a machine (Descartes),
- ... to being reduced to the seat of objectifying subjectivity (Kant),
- ... to being reduced to absolute reason (Hegel),
- ... to being reduced to something that computers can do as well as humans (AI)[19] or that emerges from the physiological brain (traditional neuroscience).

From the first beginning, every step of the way – away from the start – mirrors a dualistic thinking that takes phenomena (both things and the mind) as ensconced in duality.

Let me close here with a list of names for dualistic thinking:

- assumptions, prejudices, theories – because they do not emerge from the things themselves and their self-showing
- activities of mastering, x trumping y
- objectifying or reifying
- seeing what is measurable as existing and what is not measurable as not existing
- reducing things to disposables
- conceptualizing, dichotomizing, calculative thinking, the *cogito*, objectifying subjectivity
- information technology
- consciousness as physiologically based
- linear thinking, reflexivity or reflexive thinking, self-based thinking.

How can we say what is "other than" – and encompassing "more than" – what is named dualistically in the above words?

Chapter Four

First Moment: Heidegger and Non-Dual Thinking, Inseparable Phenomenon

a. The Dynamic of the Non-Dual

Heidegger does not often use the word *non-dual* to say the *Sache*/matter for thinking. But he does use a number of words that, when taken from within the crossing from the first to the other beginning – and perhaps when he is thinking-saying from within the other beginning – are words that say "non-dual" dynamic. Let me offer some examples for consideration.

Heraclitus and *logos* as "gathering lay." Read: the gathering that holds everything together. The onefold dynamic. Belonging-together. *Verhältnis*: holding-together or joining. The holding-together is what gathering is. Gathering is *logos* is being. What holds together is itself no-thing, but there is holding-together. The dynamic gathering is the joining or holding together of what we have for so long thought of as separate items. It is moving beyond the duality of "things" as distinctly separate.

Lethe-aletheia, Unverborgenheit-Verbergung: hiding and unhiding (coming out of hiding) as a one. *Sichentbergenlassen*: self-unconcealing. *Lichtend-verbergendes Freigeben von Welt*: shining-clearing-lighting up, while hidden-sheltered, releasing of world. *A-letheia*: both the revealing and self-sheltering/hiding – as dynamic onefold.

Grund that is *Abgrund*: grounding as abground or staying away of ground. Staying-away [*Ausbleiben*] of ground. *Anwesen-Abwesen*: emergent emergence from within the non-emergence, disclosing-hiding/sheltering. Emerging sheltered in hiding. *Anwesen* that is sheltered in *Abwesen* ... deeper than the *Anwesen* of *Anwesendes*. The dynamic of emergence is hidden-sheltered – as a *one* – in the dynamic non-emergence. This gets lit up and manifest in the *Anfang*/starting of language as saying. (More on this when we discuss the Second Moment: the holding-to-itself of the deep sway of language as saying.)

Dynamic togetherness [*Bezug*] of the truth of being to Da-sein and to thinking. Da-sein as *Inständigkeit*: inabiding/standing in the clearing of being, actively.

All of these words say the inseparable.

Given the significance of *Beiträge zur Philosophie (Vom Ereignis)* – which von Herrmann calls Heidegger's second major work, and I agree with him – perhaps the most exciting, enriching (but perhaps also the most difficult) at-oneness to think-say is in the name *Ereignis*. Professor Emad and I translated this word into English as "enowning." The dynamic dimension of what is at work here is as beautiful as it is complex. (More on this later.)

In section 133 of *Beiträge* Heidegger speaks to this beauty and complexity:

> Beyng needs man in order to hold sway; and man belongs to beyng so that he can accomplish his utmost determination as Da-sein.
>
> ... *This oscillating of needing and belonging* makes up beyng as enowning [*Seyn als Ereignis*], and the first thing that behooves us in thinking is to lift the pulsing of this oscillating into the simplicity [literally: onefoldness, just so, purely and simply so, without any fanfare or complexity, *Einfachheit*] of knowing awareness [*Wissen*] and to ground it in its truth.
>
> But with that, we must give up the habit of wanting to secure this deep swaying of beyng as arbitrarily representable for everyone at any time. (GA 65:251)

Heidegger says this dynamic ongoing engagement of Da-sein and being with various words:

- *Zusammengehörigkeit*: belonging-together (active, inseparable, non-dual phenomenon)
- *Bezugsverhältnis*: holding together in relation

- *Wahrheit als Ganzheit*: truth as whole
- *sich gegenschwingend*: oscillating one with the other.

There are four core aspects to this phenomenon or matter for thinking-saying. All four of them point to the non-dual character of this dynamic:

1. The issue here is that all of these names say a dynamic onefold/oneing that we have to *experience* – and not just talk about or try to define or conceptualize.
2. The many different words that are used to say this dynamic is an indication of how non-conceptualizable the dynamic named in *Seyn-Ereignis-Unverborgenheit* is.
3. Whatever is being said here, it is no "existing" thing, it is no-thing – even as the dynamic is at work, doing, holding, releasing.
4. The hiding-sheltering is a core aspect to the onefold of this dynamic.

From within our inherited conceptual-linguistic structures, we think of two poles that come together, but somehow we have a hard time thinking and saying them as dynamic non-dual at-oneness. Although we know there is this joining, we still *think* the poles as two. Somehow we find it hard to think this non-dual dynamic. We also have a hard time thinking the dynamic oneness as no-thing. We stay tethered to the two, and this necessarily holds us and traps us within the language of metaphysics and duality. We know that we do not want this, but how to break from this way?

If we continue to think-say dually, we will continue to objectify and substantiate everything – including ourselves as Da-sein, beings, the being over against beings of the ontological difference, being as *aletheia, physis, Unverborgenheit, anwesendes Anwesen*. (I playfully offer a "simple" rendering of these Greek and German words into English, in order: un-hiding, emergence, unconcealing, emergent emerging.) These are names for the dynamic onefold of that which is no-thing, no being, but which shows and sustains all unfolding and emergence. We dare not objectify what these names say or make them into things or beings – or worse yet, continue to think them in that way. Remember that dual thinking is woven into our language (the traditional language of dualistic metaphysics, including the grammar of subject/predicate) and our inherited being (substance/accidents). After Heidegger, we are called to "leap" out of this confinement.

Letting go of dualism in thinking and language – and in taking in the phenomenon – calls us

- to register, see, realize how pervasive dualism is,
- to become clear as to how it has operated for centuries, and
- to comprehend what it has closed off.

The dual subject-object in the history of metaphysics – for example, humans are rational animals in a separable world of substances and/or objects and/or disposables within the regime of disposability in the mindset of technicity – has been there for a long time and is quite entrenched. But we now see the rich possibility of thinking through it such that we can "get over it" (*verwinden*). And: This very dualism belongs within the inseparable one-ing dynamic that we are called to think. Paradoxically, the dualism of metaphysics and objectifying subjectivity belongs within the at-oneness of the dynamic of radiant emptiness – non-dually. How to become aware of this, to "feel" it? Let me repeat my suggestion from early in this book:

> Go deep – all the way – into the thoughts and duality. Dwell there awarely, and the seed of radiant emptiness will show itself. Within the full flourishing of the dual/conceptual is the emerging non-dual and non-conceptual. Heed the full blossoming of the non-dual dynamic of radiant emptiness.

If we can think-say the radiant emptiness of beyng – the dynamic that it shows and the no-thing that is opening – this transforms our understanding and experience of beyng and leads to a transforming of language, now as "saying."

This is not easy! In *Beiträge* Heidegger says:

> Beyng, who is concerned with [pays attention to, minds] beyng? Everything chases after beings. (GA 65:443)

And why do we not shake up these presuppositions – that a being is something objective or substance, that thinking being is about what is most general and about categories? Heidegger's response to his own question:

> Because we hardly recognize what is needed for that to happen: namely, shaking up this "we" of modern man, who as *"subjectum"* has become *the* refuge of those presuppositions, to such an extent that the subject-character of man itself has its origin and *the* hold of its unbroken power in the accepted [and not questioned] predominance of those presuppositions (of the understanding of being that is consolidated in Western, modern thinking). (GA 65:444)

This is our challenge. Non-dual thinking inseparable phenomenon requires our thinking-saying to *think* non-dually. Thinking "with and after" Heidegger requires this. Can we do it? Let us try!

b. Thinking-Saying in the Non-Dual Crossing

The crossing: I suggest that Heidegger's thinking is "all"[1] – explicitly or implicitly – thinking *in* the crossing, not *from* the first beginning *to* the other beginning as two items. And right away we have to clarify what this says: staying, lingering, dwelling, abiding, tarrying … in the dynamic of the crossing from the first beginning in chronological time to the other, "timeless" "beginning," not as two events – the from and the to – but as the *starting* getting things going. And this is where we are, in possibility.

Thus it is not a crossing "from–to" at all. Thinking in the crossing is transformation of thinking in the leap into the interweaving interplay of the first and the other beginnings (the beginning somewhen in time and the core dynamic of the "timeless" starting, setting things in motion). I stress the at-oneness of this interweaving interplay.

In *Anfang* as the "start," the first beginning is an inherent part of the dynamic. The first beginning is in play in the other beginning, which we hear as "timeless" starting, the getting things going. It is this interplay that we focus on in Heidegger's non-dual thinking. This "starting" – Heidegger calls it the second or other beginning – will eventually bring thinking to the one-ing, inseparable/non-dual dynamic that we mention here and will delve into later.

This other way – the way of the starting – is not about concepts or scientific knowledge. And the first step is to transform our relationship to language. What does language do in the other way? Here, language itself is way-making. (More on this when we discuss the Second Moment.)

For now I want to present briefly two stories that tell of Heidegger's underway thinking, on the way to a fuller and richer saying of the thing or phenomenon in this non-dual inseparable dynamic of the intertwining within the crossing. The first example is from the Memorial Address that Heidegger gave on 30 October 1955 in his hometown of Messkirch, on the occasion of the hundredth anniversary of the death of another Messkirch native, the composer Conradin Kreutzer. This story is relatively simple. (The second, from *Beiträge*, is much more complex, as we will see.)

Gelassenheit or the Memorial Address

In the Memorial Address – called *Gelassenheit* in the German text[2] – Heidegger speaks of the domination of calculating thinking (*das rechnende Denken*) and what is today virtually absent, namely the counter-dynamic: mindful or minding thinking (*das besinnliche Nachdenken* and then *das besinnliche Denken*). The latter is an "anticipatory"[3] look – in 1955 – into another way of saying, into the question of "the other beginning, i.e., starting." This mindful thinking hints at the thinking that belongs to the "start" or other beginning. Here Heidegger uses a language that hints at this start.

We today – as in 1955 – are confronted with the domination of calculating thinking in the extreme form that it takes in the world of technicity that dominates today. Note that this is not about technology, but about the mindset of technicity.[4] Calculating thinking is trapped in the "jaws of planning and computation, of organization and automatic operations" (GA 16:522). And "the world now appears as an object that calculating thinking attacks, which nothing should be able to resist any longer" (GA 16:523).

Calculating thinking is planning, investigating, researching, setting up a business or industry. Calculating thinking rushes from one opportunity to the next. It never stays still, never comes to mindfulness.

In the form of modern technicity, calculating thinking has a hidden power to determine how humans are connected to the way things are (to what is). This form of calculating thinking controls/rules/commands the whole planet. It subdues, controls, and steers. Its powers bind/chain/trammel, transmigrate/press forth, and beset/besiege.

All the words in the last two paragraphs are Heidegger's words here, to describe the *"flight from thinking"* (GA 16:519). But there is another way to think:

Mindful thinking. When we come to know what is own to us as humans, namely that we are thinking beings, we become minding beings. We are oriented to think. Minding thinking

> is careful, minding thinking [*nachdenken*] of the sense of things, which is at work in everything that is. (GA 16:520)

This minding thinking (*das besinnliche Denken*) requires

> a greater effort ... a longer preparation ... a more subtle care/diligence ... And it must also be able to wait, just as the farmer [has to wait] to see whether the seed sprouts and grows to maturity [becomes ripe]. (GA 16:520)

Minding thinking or careful minding dwells with what is near to our awareness. It asks: What way of being lies behind scientific technicity? What is own to what is, to the way things are? It "demands from us that we do not remain one-sidedly stuck in an idea/conception and that we do not keep rushing on a single track in a conceptual direction" (GA 16:526). It asks: Is there something else besides calculating thinking and the mindset of technicity that is own to humans? Can mindful thinking open out onto "thing" as inseparable phenomenon within the no-thing, non-dual dynamic of radiant emptiness? And then: What *is* this dynamic emptiness? And if it *is* not, how do we learn to think-say it?

We can allow ourselves to be slaves to the dominant way of thinking that is rationalism or technicity. Or we can do something else. Heidegger:

> We can use technical objects as they were meant to be used. But we can at the same time let these [technical] objects just be and not intrude on us in our inner and ownmost being. We can say "yes" to the unavoidable usage of technical objects, and at the same time we can say "no," insofar as we bar them from claiming us totally and thus bending out of shape, confusing/unhinging, and finally demolishing what is ownmost to us. (GA 16:527)

Heidegger calls for two ways:

1. *die Gelassenheit zu den Dingen*: releasement to the things. This lets us see things as more than technical. Not denouncing or wanting to destroy what is technical in things, but to see the "more than," to experience things in the richness of things in their flourishing as such, as what is own to things – as phenomena inseparable from beyng as Ereignis as radiant emptiness.
2. *die Offenheit für das Geheimnis*: openness for the mystery. When we become aware that in the technical world (i.e., the world of technicity) there still dwells a hidden sense, this lets both of these strategies show the connection to the hidden, to what comes forth to us, in things. What shows itself, emerges … and simultaneously withdraws.

About these two ways:

> Releasement to the things and openness to the mystery belong together. They preserve for us the possibility to stay in the world in a totally other

way. They promise us a new ground and soil on which we can stand within the world of technicity and, unthreatened by it, can endure. (GA 16:528)

Gathering the saying within these words, we see some of the aspects of the second beginning, aka the dynamic of the "start," over against – or "beyond" the extreme form of the dualism of the first beginning. And we have a first inkling how the non-dual, inseparable dynamic of being/beyng gets thought in Heidegger: Nothing is thrown out or removed. The question becomes: How can we think the "start" of the other beginning, as it introduces another, transforming way of thinking – from within the first beginning, to which technicity belongs – and as it opens our seeing and hearing to things beyond their being technical objects?

This address is an example of how Heidegger explores the whole of thinking, always pushing thinking and language to the edges of what is possible, and brings thinking around to the broadest and deepest dynamic of what is own to humans, own to things, and own to being – inseparably. And there is still some way to go. I propose that looking at and thinking through the non-dual thinking of inseparable phenomena and non-conceptual language offers enriching possibilities in our quest.

Section 5 of *Beiträge*: For the Few – for the Rare

Taken together, sections 5 and 6 of *Beiträge* might be called "The Core Attuning of Thinking in the Other Beginning" – as Heidegger himself says in the text here: *Die Grundstimmung des Denkens im anderen Anfang*. Here is the site of the second story or way of saying what is required for the crossing and what is more detailed and complex. The aims here include (a) overcoming the duality of metaphysics and (b) learning to dwell within the non-dual dynamic of the crossing. Here Heidegger says: *"What grounds and attunes thinking in the other beginning* resonates in attunings that can only be named obscurely [I add: because the issue is too unclear or too un-unfolded for 'now']" (GA 65:14).

das Erschrecken: startled dismay
die Verhaltenheit: reservedness
} *die Ahnung:* intimating

die Scheu: awe

Startled dismay is the aspect – of the crossing from first to other beginning – that is moving *from* the traditional comportment to what we know – for example, in the how of epistemological certainty or objectifying subjectivity or the straightforwardness of the being of metaphysics – *to* the echo of self-hiding/sheltering. In this opening, what has seemed familiar becomes strange and confining. What is most familiar and unknown is the abandonment of and by being. This is our first real awareness of abandonment of and by being. Being turns out to be nothing like what we have thought it was, namely the being of metaphysics. This is startling or shocking. We are startled into engaging with what can be barely known, with the being of beings now said (in *Beiträge*) as beyng, beyng as Ereignis. (The name *beyng/Seyn* is Heidegger's attempt to think this "nothing like." Eventually we will delve into the thinking-saying of beyng.)

Whereas the startled dismay attunes thinking to how being has been abandoned in metaphysics (the first beginning) and hints at how this abandonment in turn is held within being, **awe** attunes thinking to the nearing of what is the most distant in the starting (the second beginning), that is, that which "gathers in itself all relations of beyng" (GA 16:520). Far from shyness (the usual meaning of *Scheu*), this awe sees the power of beyng and Ereignis, *including* its reservedness.

Thus **reservedness** is the midpoint holding together the startled dismay at the abandonment of and by being and **awe** in the face of Ereignis – we might say: holding non-dually.

Reservedness names the holding-back of the deep swaying of beyng. Here belong the words: hiddenness, not-granting, immeasurability, reticence, sheltering-concealing, All of these words say: We do not yet know how to travel in the other beginning. And when we *do* travel there, the self-withholding named in these words will not go away! For this withdrawal/hiding-sheltering belongs inseparably to the beyng/Er-eignis of the crossing.

Intimating opens up the breadth of what is hidden in abandonment of and by being and of what is not-granted – the sheltering-concealing as well as the reticence. Heidegger says:

> Intimating in itself holds open the attuning power and grounds it back into itself. Towering far above all uncertainty of mere opinion [common sense], intimating is the hesitating *sheltering* of the unconcealing of the hidden as such, of the refusal. (GA 65:22)

Now we can say: Intimating is the move *from within* our forgetfulness of being and from the abandonment of and by being (the **startled dismay** from before), and heeding this, "beyond" *to* **awe** in the face of the possibility in the other beginning.

All word-images, taken together, determine the style of thinking that gets started in the other beginning (the starting). What grounds and attunes the other beginning "can hardly ever be known merely by one name, especially in the crossing to that beginning" (GA 65:21).

Here Heidegger says something crucial about words to think-say the other beginning:

> Every naming of the grounding-attunement with a single word is based on a false notion. Every word is taken from tradition. The fact that grounding-attunement of another beginning has to have many names does not argue against its at-oneness [its non-dual, inseparable character] but rather confirms its richness and strangeness. (GA 65:22)

It is, all of it, an at-oneness – rich and strange. And it is this "having many names" that gives me the gumption to pursue naming beyng-Ereignis as non-dual dynamic of radiant emptiness.

Given that conceptual language dominates today within metaphysics, we thinkers in the crossing need to go a stretch of the way with this language of concepts, because only by our dismay and intimation and awe – along with the reservedness or reticence of beyng – can thinking and language overflow this container (conceptual language) and emerge to say beyng in the other beginning.

Again I remind the reader what I said very early in this text:

> Think within duality (subject–object, subject–predicate, body–mind, I–world), conceptually. Go deep – all the way – into the thoughts and duality. Dwell there awarely, and the seed of radiant emptiness will show itself. Within the full flourishing of the dual/conceptual is the emerging non-dual and non-conceptual. Heed the full blossoming of the non-dual dynamic of radiant emptiness.

When we heed our relationship to language and enter into it, then the words of a transforming language emerge, from within beyng, of which we thinkers are a part. We need to *experience* the startled dismay (*das Erschrecken*).

Let us return to the German word *Anfang*. What does "Anfang" say? In *Über den Anfang* (GA 70) Heidegger emphasizes the German word *Anfang/anfangen* in its deep sense, what I am calling in English: the starting, starting things, getting things going. He says: The word *Anfang* usually and at first means "beginning" as in a sequence or progression. But, he says:

> If here the word *Anfang* is meant to name the deep sway of beyng and the deep sway of that holding sway, if at the same time beyng does not get derived from beings, and if beyng is anyhow not the absolute and unconditioned – which can be said only of beings – then *Anfang* has to name what holds sway in itself and what from within this deep swaying prohibits taking what holds sway as an unconditioned thing. Beyng and its deep sway as starting [*Anfang*] (Er-eignis) holds sway (gets things going, en-owns, brings things into their "own" [*fängt an, er-eignet*]), outside the circles of absolute-relative and their distinction … *Anfang* is the en-owning of this oneness. (GA 70:10)

Note that the absolute and non-conditional, as well as the "circles of absolute-relative and their distinction," belong to metaphysics, for these words by definition name a duality:

> The starting-off is always unique in every start. There is no rule and no law of the start, in the sense that this rule or law would reign "over" the start. (GA 70:13)

c. Experiencing the Inseparable Onefold, Non-Dual and No-Thing

For Heidegger *die Sache* means, first, phenomenon as what shows itself from out of itself – *phainomenon*. Then, Heidegger heeds the *appearing* as such – *apophainesthai* – to see what it shows. It shows that the human being is always already in the world, Dasein. Then it shows that Da-sein is the open expanse in which beings emerged. This undid the dualism of subject–object – I would suggest: forever.

In *Sein und Zeit*, *logos-Rede* (*sagen*) says: say, reveal, show, let be seen. *Logos* is syn-thesis, putting things together, *beisammen*. Truth/*Wahrheit* as *Unverborgenheit* is uncovering, emerging out of hiding – or hiding-not-hiding simultaneously. *Aisthesis* is taking in the phenomenon directly, without mediation. *Logos* is directly letting something be seen/shown, gathering the dynamic one into its own, without mediation. This, then, leads eventually to the dynamic that is Er-eignis.

From *Sein und Zeit*:

> Phenomenology then says: *apophainesthai ta phainomena:* Letting that which shows itself, as it shows itself from within itself, be seen from itself. (GA 2:46)

> What is in its ownmost *necessarily* the theme of an *explicit* presentation? Clearly that which first and foremost *does not show itself*, what – over against what shows itself – first and foremost does not show itself, is *hidden/sheltered*, but is simultaneously something that belongs essentially to that which first and foremost shows itself, so much so that it [the hidden] is what makes up its [what shows itself] sense and ground.*
> *Marginal note: Truth of being. (GA 2:47)

Again from *Sein und Zeit*:

> Philosophy is universal phenomenological ontology, proceeding from the hermeneutic of Dasein, which as analytic of *Existenz** has affixed the end of the guiding thread of every philosophical questioning there from where it *arises* and to where it *returns*.

*Marginal note: *Existenz* fundamental-ontological, i.e., directed to the truth of being itself, and only this! (GA 2:51)⁵

Where is this "there"? And what does it do? Proceeding from the analytic of Dasein to understand the being of intentional connections – the understanding of being as *Existenz* – this "there" is about the beings to which Dasein is connected ... but is also always already the question of the "truth of being," which remained mostly hidden and unthematized in *Sein und Zeit*. But it was the beginning of truth as non-concealment, revealing/self-hiding. Already in *Sein und Zeit* the "there" "from where it arises" and the "to where it returns" – this non-dual dynamic inseparable at-oneness – names the question of being, which, within the dynamic unfolding of Heidegger's pathway, will become explicitly the question of the truth of beyng and beyng-as-Ereignis.

So Da-sein is always already being-in-the-world. This expression already shows that what is said is "*one* phenomenon [*einheitliches Phänomen*]." This phenomenon is not two or dual, but of one piece, an at-oneness. Heidegger says: "This primary finding [discovery, *Befund*] must be seen in the whole." Da-sein names the expanse of the Da.

Heidegger takes the "*in-sein*" one step further. It is not as if Da-sein is "in" some ontic place or container. No, *in-sein* has its origins in the word *innan*: to dwell, inhabit, stay, "be one with." Not "first" Da-sein, who "then" is "in." Rather this very dwelling-staying of Da-sein is inseparably the non-dual way of being of Da-sein. Not being "in" something or some place, but always already dwelling non-dually.⁶

The next step: Da-sein as the open expanse in which the open of being participates. This shows the question of being as central. The being of beings.⁷ And it is not a thing. No-thing.

How to think anew this dynamic? This led Heidegger to think the ontological difference, the difference between beings and being that can be thought "as such."

But then Heidegger saw the limitations of the ontological difference, because it got measured and said "in terms of beings," that is, whatever we say about being in its ontological difference from beings, the words and the thoughts are framed "over against" beings, that is, in contrast to them. Beings provide the framework, the vocabulary, and the container in which to say what is "not-beings."

So in the next step Heidegger said: No more putting the ontological difference in the forefront of *das Zudenkende*, the matter for thinking. For the ontological difference is "derived" from how it differs from beings. There, beings become the measure for getting to being. Now it becomes question of thinking-saying "being as such," on its own turf, as it were. Here emerge the words *aletheia, physis, Unverborgenheit* – and then *Ereignis, beyng as Ereignis*.[8]

The big step and the big question, then, is: How to think being "unto itself" or as such? This opens the door to thinking/saying being in the interwoven dynamic of *lethe/aletheia*, of *Verborgenheit-Unverborgenheit* (to become *Verbergung-Unverbergen*, now as verbal), *physis* as emerging but also hiding, and then Ereignis: the non-dual togetherness of the enowning throw of being and Da-sein's responding to the throw of being that Da-sein encounters. And then timing-spacing as ab-ground, where Da-sein is the flash-point[9] (*Augenblicksstätte*) for experiencing beyng as Er-eignis in the non-dual dynamic of radiant emptiness and where Da-sein "ina-bides" (*innestehen*) in the open expanse, the inseparable, non-dual dynamic of beyng as radiant emptiness. Note that this last sentence is a lot! I am aware of that. Hopefully it will make more sense toward the end of the book.

Not two, but emerging as the one and self-same dynamic. Part of that dynamic is that Da-sein can be *distinguished from* beyng as Ereignis, but it cannot be *separated out* in any way. Thus the "not-one" of what can be distinguished is held within the "one and not two" of beyng as Ereignis.

Finally, this "one, not two" of Ereignis needs the hiding-sheltering dynamic of *Verbergen* in order to show itself for what it is. (In *Beiträge* this is called "hesitating self-withholding," *das zögernde Sichversagen*. See the Fifth Moment.) Thus sheltering-hiding is at the core of the non-dual dynamic of the inseparableness of subject–object in Da-sein and its always already being-in-the-world *and* of the inseparableness of Da-sein and beyng.

In order to say this, Heidegger in *Beiträge* introduces the spelling of being as: beyng (*Sein* as *Seyn*). *Seyn* says the radiant emptiness that is beyng, the one-not-two of the whole dynamic, and how that which is no-thing and empty "plays forth."

Sein/being ... *Seyn*/beyng ... *Sein-Seyn* as Er-eignis

Heidegger says that this dimension or dynamic is *"kaum bekannt"*: barely or hardly known. This "hardly known" or obscure/hidden belongs at the core of the non-dual dynamic of beyng/*Seyn* – that which holds the full and rich dynamic of Da-sein and being together.

Non-dual is shown in the phenomenon of *appearing*. Not just what appears (traditionally called the object) and then the one to whom it appears, the perceiving one (traditionally called the subject) – as two. The dynamic of appearing as such – as opposed to the appearance or to what appears, the phenomenon – is non-dual, beyond the separation of subject and object and a dynamic that is all in one. What is experienced, who experiences, and the experience itself – all three non-separably in the non-dual dynamic of radiant emptiness.

(Merleau-Ponty tried to name the onefold, non-dual dimension of "primary" perception – to look outside and "before" any reflection, which he called secondary perception. He could not find a "one" word to say this onefold, non-dual dimension. He said body-consciousness or perceptual consciousness – words that taken in themselves say duality. And as his thinking unfolded – and after he had seriously thought through Heidegger – he named the issue: *flesh*. Does this word lean one way or the other ... toward the "consciousness" side or toward the "body," sensual side? Does this word "say" the non-dual dimension that Merleau-Ponty was looking to? I think that Merleau-Ponty "heard" Heidegger's call of beyng and was struggling with this and how to name it when he died prematurely.)

Da-sein undermines the duality of subject–object, the duality of what appears, to whom it appears, and the appearing itself. Heidegger looks to the dynamic of appearing "as such." No separation among Da-sein (to whom it appears, who perceives), what appears, and the appearing itself.[10] How to name this?

Ongoing mutual unfolding. The mind that distinguishes, the distinguishing, and what is distinguished are a dynamic "one." What about this "mutual"? Does mutual necessarily imply a two that is "mutually connected"? Perhaps we could say: the "one" of "not one" and "not two." Wherein lies the non-dual in this wording?

It is true that Heidegger's quest was always the question of being. But it is also true that, along the way, his thinking "had not yet entered the word that would accomplish" the explicit saying of the non-dual dynamic of beyng … and then did … as he "understood 'better,'" that is, other than what the immediately meant wording said.[11]

Gathering up the moments on the way, we might say that Heidegger goes from

1. the being of Dasein as ontological – hinted at in *Sein und Zeit* but not pursued beyond the ontological dimension of Dasein – to
2. the ontological difference, which opens up the question of being as "not a being." Thus in the name "ontological difference" beings still have a hold – as a starting point – keeping the word from being freed from metaphysics. From within this awareness Heidegger's thinking no longer starts from ontological difference, but rather opens onto
3. the dynamic unfolding in hiding–non-hiding (*lethe/a-letheia*), then truth-truthing, *physis*, *Unverborgenheit*, or better: *Unverbergen*, the verbal dynamic name. Another name for this is *Anwesen*/emergence: *anwesend anwesen*/emergent emerging. All of this includes the dynamic onefold of that which is emerging, what emerges as appearance or phenomenon, and the one to whom emergence emerges (human being as Da-sein). Finally the moment of
4. Er-eignis/en-owning. It is here that the new spelling of *Sein* as *Seyn* fits. One might say that being/*Sein* belongs to metaphysics and beyng/*Seyn* names the dynamic that opens up in the second beginning, or the start.

I am a little nervous enumerating these moments, one after the other and delineated. For they are all inseparably intertwined. One could say that staying with the issue for thinking (*das Zudenkende*) allowed Heidegger to hear and say this deeper dynamic – to enter the word that earlier did not allow that hearing and saying – and along the way to understand "other than" what was meant. But these four moments are not "in time," that is, separable and in chronological order. Being non-dual and inseparable – and taking into account *Anfang* as start – thinking/saying shows, in a kind of mirroring, various petals of the same flower blooming, "timelessly."

Already in 1976, Heidegger scholar and translator Albert Hofstadter suggested saying *Ereignis* as "enownment."[12] That was pre-deconstruction, and most serious Heidegger scholars at the time took Hofstadter's word seriously, as he was perhaps the translator *par excellence* of Heidegger into English. He grounded this decision in the knowledge that Heidegger wanted *ereignen* to say its connection to *eigen*: own: to make one's own, to be own to, the owning work as such.

Hofstadter quotes Heidegger, saying how we must simply experience this *eignen*, must experience how humans and being are "en-owned" (*ge-eignet*) to one another. Ereignis/enowning is the letting-belong-together, the one befitting the other, of being and time, humans and being. To explain this, Hofstadter states:

> At the center of *das Ereignis* is "own," [and] the most literal possible translation of *das Ereignis* ... en-, -own, and -ment: enownment ... the letting-be-own-to-one-another ... the letting be married of any two or more ... Enownment is not their belonging, but what lets their belonging be.[13]

This "own" has nothing to do with "self-centred" possession but everything to do with the work or dynamic by which the different dynamics are brought into belonging to and with one another and are helped to realize themselves and each other in realizing this non-dual belonging.[14]

We could perhaps say what is happening in Ereignis as "the dynamic of owning." Here we are reminded again that in 1972–73

Heidegger wrote that *Eignen* and *Eignis*: own, owning, are more useful than *Ereignis*, because it is hard to think Ereignis as other than event or happening (GA 81:47). Enowning is the gathering of each into its own. In *Beiträge*, Ereignis says beyng's enowning call to Da-sein (the enowning throw of beyng) and enowned Da-sein's throwing open this dynamic. In section 133 of *Beiträge* Heidegger writes:

> Beyng needs man in order to hold sway; and man belongs to beyng, so that he can accomplish his utmost destiny as Da-sein. (GA 65:251)

As I wrote in my book *Heidegger's Possibility*, "The thinking that thinks enowning (the enowning throw of being to Da-sein and, thus enowned, Da-sein's throwing open the enowning throw, all of that together making up 'enowning as such,' 'the midpoint that is enowning') manifests the way things are in this dynamic."[15] I would now say: one inseparable, non-dual dynamic.

Beyng as Ereignis is the joining together of humans and being in a belonging-together that befits humans and being for each other in their deep sway of beyng, in what is own to each and own to the befitting. Ereignis is the region, self-oscillating, through which humans and beyng attain to each other in each one's "own" owning dynamic, as well as in the "enowning" of their countering sway. Ereignis is the withdrawing-preserving region that grants being. Ereignis is both the impetus for being to emerge and the withdrawal that keeps hidden. Ereignis, finally, is the deep sway of unfolding that is beyng as emergence.

Each dynamic enjoins the one, non-dual dynamic of enowning/Er-eignis.

Reminder: The dynamic enowning/Ereignis is no-thing whatsoever even as it appears, is no-thing whatsoever even as it is dynamically at work, is no-thing whatsoever even as we can experience "it."

The non-dual dynamic of Dasein-being is implicitly said in *Sein und Zeit*. But, as Heidegger says there, the words (language) and the grammar were not yet available to pursue it. Not available until *Beiträge*, written between 1936 and 1938? But in *Beiträge* he makes clear that these words and this thinking are preparatory[16] ... waiting until beyng grants to us to think/say it. Is that what gets said then in the retrieval of the Greeks (Anaximander, Heraclitus, Parmenides)? With a kind of reticence, is Heidegger trying there to say it? (Here we see how important the Fourth Moment – retrieval of thinking in Greek philosophy – is for the fullness of my project.)

How to follow that? With a dynamic in anticipation? By heeding experience itself, outside reflection and conceptualization? Rather than seeing experience as fallible – within the framework and domination of epistemology and the urge for certainty – look to experience as "what sustains"? In an experience-based critical thinking?

Already in *Sein und Zeit* the "sense" (*Sinn*) of being goes beyond sense for humans. Sense is not something accomplished or performed by humans. Humans and human thinking become strong enough to abide the domain of beyng and to actively respond. We take part in being's disclosure – or beyng *as* disclosure. Heidegger's word for this sense of being gets transformed later into "truth of beyng."

Perhaps we can say something like this: What beyng "is" changes because of Da-sein's being claimed – or as Da-sein is claimed – by beyng. And what Da-sein "is" changes as it is claimed and responds to beyng. Thus there is no such thing as "beyng" or Da-sein as independent of emergence/*aletheia*. It is for this reason that in *Beiträge* the thinking and saying is focused on *er-eignen*, which names this owning, being owned, and becoming own to itself in this owning–enowning dynamic.

Perhaps we can say it in both ways:

1. What beyng is changes what Dasein is, and what Dasein is changes what beyng is.
2. There is no beyng outside Dasein and no Dasein outside beyng.

In either case it is the same non-dual dynamic of radiant emptiness that shines through. Dasein is beyng, beyng is Dasein, beyng and Dasein inseparable.

Da-sein beyng Da-sein

We keep looking for a "thing" or a "place" or even a kind of dynamic where we can rest our mind – as if we have reached some where (not "somewhere" but "some where"). But there is no-thing there and no where. The emptiness of beyng and the oneness of the dynamic – which shows itself and hides itself at the same time – are of one piece. Even though it is no thing, it is in play.

Own-owning-enowning-owning over to: naming a dynamic, a movement that is ongoing, flowing from one to the other. "Other" as in one aspect of a non-dual phenomenon. That is, there is nothing other. Our minds can distinguish, and this critical thinking helps us understand. But in the deep swaying (*Wesung*) of beyng as Ereignis, what is at stake is not separable, either as dynamic or in thinking.

The non-dual dynamic of Dasein-being is said in *Sein und Zeit*. As Heidegger says at the end of the Introduction to *Sein und Zeit*, the "vocabulary" of *Sein und Zeit* is "awkward" and "ill-suited." And then he tells us why:

> ... it is one thing to report on *beings* by explaining what they are; it is another thing to grasp beings in their *being*. For this latter task, not only are most of the words lacking, but above all the "grammar" is missing ... and as we open up the area of being, way more difficult than what was afforded the Greeks to think, the complicatedness [enigma, intricacy, incomprehensibility – muddy, unfathomable, indecipherability, *Umständlichkeit*] of concept formation grows and the expression gets tougher. (GA 2:52)

Again we think of "translating" Kant "after" Kant – to bring to word what was not understood then – being able to enter the word that would accomplish it.

Later Heidegger will turn away from conceptualization altogether, will distinguish words from "the word," speaking from saying. *Die Sage* (*das Wort in der Sage*) and not *die Wörter*. *Sage* and not *Sprache*. (I will go into this issue in the next chapter, on the Second Moment, and again in the Fifth Moment.)

Heidegger calls the dynamic holding together of the enowning throw of beyng and the enowned throwing open by Da-sein – a *Gegenschwung* (GA 65:251) of beyng's needing Da-sein and Da-sein's belonging to beyng, swinging back and forth in this dynamic of enowning throw of beyng and the enowned throwing open by Da-sein – Heidegger calls this: *eine Ganzheit*, an unbrokenness. It is a one-ing dynamic.

This *Bezug*/relation of Da-sein and beyng is dynamic and calls for us to experience it. Just as we need to experience, for example, the startled dismay (*das Erschrecken*) and the intimating (*die Ahnung*).

Heidegger gives us four directives with which we must prepare ourselves, in order to get a first taste of the strangeness, over against the assumed self-evidence of beyng:

1. *Die Einzigkeit des Seyns (als Ereignis)*:
   The *uniqueness* of beyng (as enowning).
2. *Die Unvorstellbarkeit (kein Gegenstand)*:
   The *unrepresentability* (no object).
   [The non-dual and the non-conceptual in it itself.]
3. *Die höchste Befremdlichkeit*:
   The utmost *strangeness*.
4. *Das wesentliche Sichverbergen*:
   The deep/core *hiding/self-sheltering*.
   (GA 65:252)

This is a far cry from definition, concept, or theory.

d. Some Examples from Heidegger That Say-Show the Non-Dual Dynamic

> *Das Dinghafte des Gefäßes beruht keineswegs im Stoff, daraus es besteht, sondern in der Leere, die faßt.* (GA 7:171)
> The thinghood of the vessel in no way resides in the material of which it is made, but in the emptiness that holds.

Die Leere ist dann dasselbe wie das Nichts. (GA 12:103)
The empty is then the same as the nothing.

Dieses Nichts ... ist nichts Nichtiges. Es gehört zum Anwesen. Sein und Nichts gibt es nicht nebeneinander. Eines verwendet sich für das Andere in einer Verwandtschaft, deren Wesensfülle wir noch kaum bedacht haben. (GA 9:419)
This nothing ... is nothing nihilistic. It belongs to emergence. Being and nothing do not exist side by side. One is brought into play for the other in a relationship whose ownmost fullness [the fullness that is own to it] we have up to now barely thought.

Nichts ist die Kennzeichnung des Seins. Sein: Nichts: Selbes. (GA 15:363)
Nothing is the mark of being. Being: nothing: same.

... ***jenes*** *Nichts denken, das gleichursprünglich das Selbe ist mit dem Sein.* (GA 9:421)
... to think *that* nothing which is co-originarily the same as being.

Das Sein "ist" so wenig wie das Nichts. Aber **Es gibt** *beides.* (GA 9:419)
Being "is" as little as the nothing "is." But both *are granted*.

Inmitten des Seienden im Ganzen west eine offene Stelle. Eine Lichtung ist. Sie ist, vom Seienden her gedacht, seiender als das Seiende. Diese offene Mitte ist daher nicht vom Seienden umschlossen, sondern die lichtende Mitte selbst umkreist wie das Nichts, daß wir kaum kennen, alles Seiende. (GA 5:40)
Amid beings in the whole there sways an open place. A lighting-up is [there]. Thought from the perspective of beings, it is more of being than beings. This open middle is thus not encompassed by beings, but rather the lighting-up middle itself encircles all beings, just like the nothing, which we barely know.

In his book on Heidegger's thinking, Walter Biemel proposes that up until today there has appeared no appropriate dialogue with Heidegger, "because the partner for that [dialogue] is missing and we have actually remained estranged from this thinking."[17]

e. Heraclitus, Fragment 16

In my opinion a most stupendous example of non-dual thinking the inseparable phenomenon occurs in Heidegger's reading of Heraclitus, Fragment 16 (GA 55).*

He considers this fragment the "first" fragment. Before he takes up the fragment, he says:

> The more originary the thinking [what starts thinking, gets it going] is, the more intimately its thought is one with the word. (35)

> τὸ μὴ δῦνόν ποτε πῶς ἄν τις λάθοι;
> Literally: To that which never goes under, how can anyone hide from that? (44)

Heidegger's translation:

> *Dem niemals Untergehenden kann keiner verborgen bleiben.*
> No one can stay hidden from that which never goes under. (46)

That which never goes under is the mystery of the whole fragment. (48) And what is that? It has to reside in the never going under by which every human being, human as human (the human in what is own to him/her), stands in the un-hidden, "such that he is the unhidden with relation to that which never goes under – and is such through this [the never going under]" (49).

This going-under is "disappearing from presence." It says: "*Going into the hidden/hiding*" (49). What is that "which as the never going-under remains suspended from that happening" (52)?

Da-sein is who Da-sein is by virtue of its dwelling in – and cannot evade – the un-folding of the non-dual going-under-never-going under, always emerging. Or: the hiding-sheltering and the emergence is a onefold dynamic, never other than both-and in

---

* Numbers in parentheses in this section refer to this volume.

one. Then add Da-sein, who – as what is own to it – is also one with the at-oneness of emergence and hiding-sheltering. But this is just another way to say Ereignis: The enowning throw of beyng to Dasein and Da-sein's – being enowned by beyng – throwing open precisely this undivided onefold.

f. A Way of Gathering

I conclude this chapter by presenting words from Heidegger's lecture *"Was heißt Denken?"*:

> There is no bridge from the sciences to thinking, but only a leap. There where it brings us is not only the other side, but a wholly other place. (GA 7:133)

> For what announces itself only by appearing in self-hiding – we also meet/comply with this only by turning toward it and, with that, giving ourselves the task of letting what shows itself come forth into the unconcealment [coming out of hiding] that is own to it. (GA 7:134)

> What withdraws does not make it to arrival, But – the self-withdrawing is not nothing. Withdrawal here is keeping-back [withholding] and is as such – enowning. (GA 7:134)

> What withdraws holds sway, namely in the manner of drawing us on [attracting us], whether we immediately or ever notice it, or not at all. What attracts us has already preserved the arrival. When we enter the draw of the withdrawal, we are in the draw to what draws us along by withdrawing itself. (GA 7:135)

> For example, we do not learn what swimming means via a treatise or paper about swimming. What tells us what swimming means is the leap into the stream. In this way we first learn the element in which swimming must move. But what is the element in which thinking moves? (GA 7:138)

Chapter Five

Second Moment: Heidegger and Non-Conceptual Language as Saying[1]

For a hint of how language works non-conconceptually, hear this:

> *Denken ist das Nahe-Wohnen*   Thinking is dwelling near
> *ist der stille Dank.*   is the hushful thanks.
> *Denken ist ...* (GA 97:69)   Thinking is ...

If nothing else, the ellipsis at the end of this poi-etic saying shows a dynamic that is open-ended and for sure not a conceptual language.

Heidegger says that beyng as enowning (Ereignis) must be "correspondingly thought and that means *said*."[2] All thinking involves saying – involves language in an essential sense, in the sense that is own to language. In his lecture *"Was ist das – die Philosophie?,"* Heidegger says that in Greek thinking what is own to language manifested as *logos* and that we need to have a dialogue with this Greek experience of language:

> Why? Because without an adequate mindfulness on language we will never truly know what philosophy is as re-sponding [speaking in return, *Ent-sprechen*] what philosophy is as an eminent way of saying [*Sagen*]. (GA 11:25)

Language becomes central to the work of philosophy presented here: the rich possibility for thinking the deep sway of beyng. But what kind of language? What does "language" say here? Linguistics? Grammar and syntax? Dictionary language? Or what is *own* to language, in such a way that something of what language does is at the heart of the rich possibility of philosophy when it thinks and says the deep sway of beyng?

a. Traditional Understanding of Language

Without thinking much about it, we carry with us an inherited, traditional notion of language: Words have meanings. We speak a language, with sounds. The sound (*phone*) is what is given and received by the senses. These words carry meaning. Without much thought, we think that meaning is "produced" in the intellect and then communicated through words.

Our usual conception of language fits this pattern. Language is a means of expression and communication. It consists of the sound in sensation and the meaning in the mind/intellect. A rough definition of language goes something like this: a system of communication using sounds, words, and grammar as symbols ... combined in various ways ... with a set of rules ... to communicate thoughts, feelings, or instructions ... arbitrary sounds ... words in a structured and conventional way.

But what happens when we attentively observe what is taking place? It seems at first that, in our everyday speaking and use of language, we seem to be as close as possible to language and what is own to it. And without much mindful reflection we assume that how we are with language is evident and well-defined.

However, when we allow our awareness to open out to this dimension, we become aware that we do not really know definitively or with total clarity what is going on in language. Heidegger says that our awareness brings us to the insight that our relationship with language is still "undefined, dark" (GA 12:150).

Philosophies of language and linguistics usually do not open us up to this awareness. The usual theories about language focus on language as a human activity, something that human beings do. Some say that language consists in the above-mentioned sounds and the non-physical, spiritual meaning. The meaning is about inner experiences that are other than the external world, to things "out there." Some understand language as a formal, symbolic system – whether interpreted within semiotics or linguistics, including neurolinguistics.

But what if these "definitions" or paradigms are themselves interpretations, which cover over other and perhaps more essential possibilities for language? Possibilities that are perhaps closer to what is "own" to language, to what language has as its own? In discussing these issues of language – and in reiterating Heidegger's distinction between knowing "about" language and having an experience "with" language (GA 12:150) – von Herrmann asks: "The question that is up for decision is whether, in these fundamental representations of language and of the human relation to it [e.g., see above], what is own to language has been fixed once and for all – or whether in these fundamental representations an essential interpretation of language and humans gets manifest that is not the only one." And if there is another way – aside from these inherited ways, which rely on specific interpretations with their own preconceptions – then our knowing awareness might begin to see and to think an "other, perhaps more originary way of language and of the essential relationship of humans to language."[3]

b. Experiencing "from" Language

If our thinking moves beyond what we know *about* language and words – to having an experience *with or from* language – then we open up to the possibility that language is more than these parts (sounds and meanings and symbols, given in dictionaries). "The word might even belong to the truth of beyng."[4] Then what the word *says* is said from within the originary thinking of beyng.

Usually words mean things, beings. Every "something" that is spoken about is a being. But the "is" just spoken is not a being. This word names beyng. Herein lies the self-showing that belongs to beyng as emerging, as unconcealment, and as Ereignis. Saying beyng, in the "is," points to something that is other than beings.

Beyng is what grants to beings their "sense." Beyng enowns beings, and this is what is done when thinking says beyng.

> Only because language [*Sprache*] arises from the saying [*Sage*] of beyng can language become language. But the saying of beyng can never be thought and experienced from out of language as usually understood or from out of the metaphysical explanation of language.[5]

With these words – *being, is* – humans already have the protection of knowing that beyng is said and sayable *before* beings take their place in presence – or in concepts. To think this saying is to think the starting (*Anfang*) of language, what is own to language. And this "own" to language is not what is spoken in sounds.

> Humans have language [*Sprache*] because language emerges in the word [*das Wort*]; but as the saying [*Sage*] of beyng, the word has humans, i.e., determines them in their determination [attunes them in their attunement]. The attuning [*das Be-stimmende*] is the voice [*Stimme*] of beyng, which does not sound but is silent in the stillness of the winding of beyng into its truth.[6]

In the earliest shaping of word/saying and being in Greek thinking, the one word *logos* is the name for both word/saying and being (Heraclitus). *Logos*: gathering, being as gathering, emerging, word and saying. What is own to language – *das Wesen der Sprache* – is saying – *die Sage*.

> As way-making [*das Be-wëgende*], saying gathers everything into the nearness of the over-against-one-another [i.e., the encounter] – and does this soundlessly ... [which is named] the ringing of stillness. (GA 12:215)

This calls for a different understanding of "word," one that is neither linguistic nor literal but poi-etic: word that says and in saying brings forth. (*Poiesis*: creating, bringing about.) Poetry and thinking are sheltered-hidden in beyng and its granting/enowning. The poi-etic word is the originary saying that gives both poetry and thinking what they have as their own.

These are the matters that we need to take up as we think and say what is own to language, that is, what is gifted to language: the saying power of the word.

One of the texts in which Heidegger opens up this matter for thinking is the dialogue with the Japanese philosopher, published under the title *"Aus einem Gespräch von der Sprache"* in Unterwegs zur Sprache.*

This text is most useful, in that the very way of language and saying that happens within this dialogue enacts precisely the matter that is questioned and presented. As we handle this text mindingly, we find that our *enacting* the very question presented – thus letting emerge in action (deed, enaction, *poiesis*) precisely what the issue (*Sache*) is – is a far cry from a theory or a definition "about" language.

If phenomenology is engaged in attentive awareness of what shows itself (the "phenomenon"), in laying out that phenomenon (unto the issue becoming manifest), and in putting into words what has shown itself and has been laid out – then two things are of paramount importance:

1. Along with everything that is disclosed or unconcealed, the very dynamic of disclosing or emergence is manifest – *along with*.
2. The laying-out and the saying (putting into words) are of one piece.

That dynamic is an undivided action of thinking. It is poi-etic. That is why thinking is always saying. This notion is a bit foreign to our traditional ears.

With this interweaving of emerging and interpretation (what I just named as "laying-out"– and the further core interweaving of interpretation and saying ("language"), which is even more enigmatic to our philosophical ear – we need to think through the connection of interpretation, hermeneutics, and laying out (*Auslegung*) to language, saying, and the word. This is precisely how the dialogue unfolds. Whereas we could try to distinguish the issues of hermeneutics and of language as they unfold in the dialogue,

---

* The dialogue was translated into English as "A Dialogue on Language" and published in Heidegger, *On the Way to Language*, trans. P. Hertz (San Francisco: Harper and Row, 1971). Unless there is a clear reference to *Beiträge*, numbers in parentheses in this chapter refer to these published texts. The first number refers to the original German of GA 12. The second number refers to the *Einzelausgabe* (separate edition) (Pfullingen: Neske Verlag, 1959). The third number refers to the English translation, for orientation purposes.

the enactive thinking therein shows that the issues of language, hermeneutics, and saying are all essentially and irretrievably intertwined throughout the dialogue.

c. From within a Dialogue from Language

The German title of this dialogue is "*Aus einem Gespräch von der Sprache.*" Quite literally, this says, "From within a Dialogue from Language." This is the same *from* (*von*) that is in the title of *Beiträge zur Philosophie* (**Vom Ereignis**) – *Contributions to Philosophy* (**From Enowning**). This word *von/from* becomes central for saying the enactive thinking of *Beiträge*. In *Beiträge* it is a matter of "from" enowning:

> It is no longer a matter of talking "about" something and presenting [posing] something as objective, but rather of being owned-over to enowning – which is the same as a core/deep transformation of human being from "thinking animal" (*animal rationale*) to Da-sein. The fitting title [essential title, contrary to the public title *Beiträge zur Philosophie*] is *Vom Ereignis*. And that does not say that something will be reported on or about, but wants to say: Enowned from enowning, a thinking-saying that belongs to beyng and in the word "of" beyng. (GA 65:3)

Here it is a matter of "from" language, in the sense that language itself has something to do with how the dialogue unfolds. Language "plays" with *us*, we could say. Rather than being a dialogue "about" language and hermeneutics, what is happening is that language itself is having its say with us, with our thinking. We think *from within* that place/dynamic. Phenomenologically speaking, it is the saying/showing that language and the word itself do that we are heeding and actively engaged in. So it is not "about" language at all. Rather it is *from* language: we in our thinking are called on to undergo an experience with language, from within language. But what does "language" say here?

Referring in the dialogue to a lecture course from 1921[7] and to his attempt to think the relationship of language and being, Heidegger tells how in that lecture course "there was quickening in it the attempt to walk a path of which I did not know where it would lead" (87/92/6). An attempt was emerging, arose, came to the fore. Grappling with the issue, thinking could not say precisely what the outcome would be. This is the "nature" of this kind of thinking. "Only its immediate openings were known to me, as they never let up in drawing me in – even as the range [horizon, scope, orbit of vision, purview] often shifted and clouded over" (87/92/6). Can we today allow (dare we not allow) such a thinking, a beckoning-call, including the hidden and withdrawing aspect?

Heidegger dealt with the same question in his *Habilitationsschrift* titled *"Die Kategorien- und Bedeutungslehre des Duns Scotus"* (GA 1:92). "Theory of Categories" is the usual name for explaining the being of beings; "Theory of Meanings" means the *grammatica speculativa*, the metaphysical reflection on language in its relation to being. Here, too, "all of these relationships were still unclear to me at that time" (87/92/6).

Then Heidegger refers to his lecture course in the summer semester of 1934,[8] where – he reminds his Japanese visitor – the theme was *logos*, "wherein I sought what is own to language."

Still, he says,

> It took almost another ten years before I was able to say what I was thinking – the suitable word is still missing today [1953–54]. The horizon for the thinking that struggles to respond to what is own to language is still veiled, in all its vastness. (89/93/8)

The dialogue then turns to *Sein und Zeit* and its discussion of hermeneutics. Phenomenological description is *Auslegung*: laying-out, interpreting. It is *hermeneuein*, by which the own sense of being and its basic structures are announced (get laid out, not defined or proven) to the understanding of being that belongs to Da-sein. Heidegger writes in *Sein und Zeit*:

> Philosophy is universal phenomenological ontology, proceeding from the hermeneutic of Dasein, which ... makes fast the end of the path of all philosophical questioning *there, from where it arises and to where it returns*. (GA 2:51)

Hermeneutics was initially (historically, with Schleiermacher, for example) about the interpretation of literary works. But for Heidegger it is not that:

> In *Sein und Zeit* hermeneutics means neither the theory nor the art of interpretation ... but rather the attempt to determine first and foremost what is own to interpreting [*Auslegen*, laying-out] from within the hermeneutical [i.e., from within what hermeneutics does]. (93/97/11)

Still, what the word *hermeneutics* says is enigmatic. Is it in *any* way suitable? Or was it once and no more? Heidegger points out that in his later writings he no longer uses the word. The question then becomes this: Why is it that Heidegger in his later writings no longer uses this word?

This use of and then use no longer of the word *hermeneutics* has something to do with how the "way" belongs to thinking. Ways of thinking have this mysterious dimension whereby they take us into what is nearest at hand, which in its turn would bring us "back" to the beginning as start or starting (*Anfang*), to what gets thinking going. What gets thinking going reveals and holds back simultaneously.

Gathering both (a) how Heidegger's thinking did not say this matter in a full-blown way (because it did not show itself clearly at first, and even as it did reveal itself more and more, it remained veiled); and (b) how within the matter itself there is a withdrawal, a hiddenness, a vibrant stillness – gathering all of this up in a pregnant exchange, the Japanese offers this comment:

> We Japanese do not think it strange when a dialogue leaves what it really means [intends] undetermined [in the realm of the undetermined] or even shelters it back into the indeterminable.

And Heidegger responds:

> This [trait] belongs to every dialogue among thinkers that turns out well [that works]. This [thinking dialogue] can, as if of its own accord, take care, not only that what is indeterminable does not slip away, but

that its gathering force [its power to gather] unfolds ever more brilliantly in the course of the dialogue. (95/100/13)

Notice how language and the word play their *own* role in the unfolding of the dialogue, how the dialogue "works" from within the *saying* of language and the word.

So what is this indeterminable, this gathering? It shows itself, says the Japanese visitor, in "a beholding that is itself invisible, a beholding that in its gatheredness bears itself over against the empty." And Heidegger adds, "The empty then is the same as the no-thing, that deep swaying [*jenes Wesende*] that we try to think as the other to all that is present and absent." And the Japanese responds: "To us, 'empty' is the best name for what you want to say with the word *being* ..." Then Heidegger: "in an attempt at thinking whose first steps are still today necessary. This attempt led to much confusion, which originated in the question and is connected with the use of the word *being*. For the word *being* belongs to the language of metaphysics, as its 'property'" (103/108/19).

By contrast, Heidegger is using the word in an effort to bring forth *what is own* (*das Wesen*) to metaphysics and thereby to gather metaphysics into the constraints of its limits. Asked if that is what he meant by the "overcoming of metaphysics," Heidegger says: "Precisely and only that; neither a destruction nor simply a denial of metaphysics."[9]

Given the myriad ways of its historical unfolding, the limits to what the word says in metaphysics, and the rich possibility that inheres in the words *being* and *is*, the word *being* itself draws thinking unto reticence and reservedness. Holding back the word (for *being* or for the indeterminable or for the gathering or for the *owning-to*) is called for, "not in order for the thinker to keep it to him/herself, but rather in order to carry the word out over against [toward and back from] what is worthy of thinking (what calls for thinking's response)"[10] (111/117/26).

In section 276 of Beiträge (GA 65:500–1) Heidegger asks:

- How does what is own to language arise in the deep sway of beyng?

- How does language hold sway in the deep swaying of beyng?
- How so ... does language become experiencable in its relation to beyng?

In *"Der Weg zur Sprache"* in *Unterwegs zur Sprache* Heidegger provides clues toward what these questions say:

> The saying [*Sage*], which resides in enowning, is – as showing [*Zeigen*] – the most own way of enowning [said here in its even more enactive form, as a verb, *er-eignen*] ... Saying is the way in which enowning speaks ... For enowning saying brings forth what emerges [things, beings, *das Anwesende*] from its ownhood – from that where it belongs as an emerging – and lauds it, i.e., allows it into its own way of being [allows it into what is its own, its *Wesen*] ... Saying [is] the way/manner of enowning.[11] (GA 12:255)

The emerging named here is what beyng, *aletheia*, *logos*, Ereignis, "does." It is the dynamic of the empty as opening, carrying within it an active surging possibility. It is the non-dual dynamic of radiant emptiness.

If the above ruminations and their resonatings open out to what is "own to language/*Sprache*" in its ownmost way of being as saying/*Sage*, then the dialogue "From within a Dialogue from Language" is the pathway that enacts that thinking/saying whereby *saying* says what is own to language – not "about" language, linguistics, or the usual philosophies of language, but enacting saying/showing.

So we mindingly listen – and co-enact in thinking – the opening of this pathway from within a dialogue *from* or *from within* language.

Heidegger says that the word *hermeneutic* modifies phenomenology, but not as a "methodology of interpretation." This leads the dialogue to move in and out of the issue of words; this is, for example, why, whereas Heidegger no longer uses the word *hermeneutics*, it still says something useful in the discussion that opens up "saying": saying what is own to language and from where the dialogue "from" language emerges. Language as saying.

These words point to the "site" or "point" in language where the dichotomy between the spoken and written word and its meaning (signifier and signified) yields to the issue for thinking, which the distinction "word-to-meaning" covers over. Rather the discussion is "from" what is own to language. The deep sway of language – what is own/owning to language – (*das Wesen der Sprache*), whether spoken or written, is something else besides what we are accustomed to think. The matter for thinking is the saying of beyng. Thus language in its owning reveals the "directing" or "pointing" to this site.[12]

Heidegger thinks the word *hermeneutics* (115/121/29) as follows:

> The expression "hermeneutical" comes from the Greek verb *hermeneuein*. The verb refers to the noun *hermeneus*, which we can connect to the name of the god *Hermes*, in a play of thinking that is more binding than the rigor of science. Hermes is the messenger of the gods. He brings the message of the sending/shaping [*Schick*]; *hermeneuein* is that laying open [*darlegen*, revealing] that brings tidings, insofar as it is capable of hearing a message. Such laying open becomes the laying-out of what was said earlier by the poets, who themselves (according to Socrates's word in Plato's dialogue *Ion* (534e) … [are] "messengers of the gods."

Hermeneutics here is other than interpreting texts. It must be heard phenomenologically (116/123/30):

> Because it was this originary sense that moved and helped me to characterize the phenomenological thinking that opened the way for me to *Sein und Zeit*. What mattered then – and still matters – is to bring forth the being of beings; of course, no longer in the manner of metaphysics, but rather such that being itself comes to the fore. Being itself – this says: emerging of what emerges [*Anwesen des Anwesenden*, unfolding of what unfolds, active presenc*ing* – and not presence – of what presences], i.e., the twofold of the two from within their at-oneness. This is what speaks to humans and calls them to what is their own.

What matters is to bring forth in language – as saying – emergence and what emerges. Being as emergence includes what emerges. However, what emerges does not encompass the emerging. Thus being as emerging is the issue here. One could say: the emerging of emergence. And again, being as emergent emergence is no-thing, not a being, but the non-dual dynamic of emptiness.

This twofold of emergence and what emerges speaks to humans, and humans respond to its enowning. What holds in this dynamic – in something like a threefold: humans-emerging-the emergent thing – is language/saying. (Notice the non-dual onefold of this threefold.) This is what is own to the hermeneutical.

Let us pause for a moment. Interpreting the dialogue, perhaps we are enacting the thinking *from* what is own to language in its owning. Language and hermeneutics are of one piece. They are in action as humans think/say the one-ing of emerging and of what emerges (beings as the emerged within beyng as emergence).

The dialoguing partners[13] continue (121/127/34):

> JAPANESE (J): Thus your minding language ...
> INQUIRER (I): language in its relationship to the deep sway of being, i.e., to the holding sway of the twofold. [This "holding sway" holds the non-dual onefold/at-oneness of the twofold.]
> J: But if language is the basic trait in the hermeneutically determined needfulness, then from the beginning you experience what is own to language very differently from what happens in the metaphysical way of thinking. This is actually what I wanted to refer to earlier.
> I: But what for?
> J: Not for the sake of contrasting something new over against what has been up to now, but rather to remind us that – precisely in the attempted mindfulness of what is own to language – the dialogue speaks as an historical [*geschichtlich*, historically unfolding] dialogue.
> I: From within the thinking recognition of what has been.

Later in the dialogue, returning to the question of language and hermeneutics, the partners in dialogue say the following (130/138/42):

> J: ... But I believe that I now see more clearly the full import of the belonging-together of the hermeneutical and of language.

I: Full import in what direction?

J: Toward a transformation of thinking – a transformation, however, that cannot be brought about as readily as a ship can change course – and even less as the consequence of an accumulation of the results of philosophical research.

I: The transformation takes place as a wandering …

J: … in which one site is left behind in favor of another …

I: … which requires a dialogue that opens up.

J: The one place is metaphysics.

I: And the other? We leave it without a name.

Now the dialoguing partners return to their earlier question, How to say "language/*Sprache*" in Japanese? With some hesitation the Japanese dialoguing partner finally gives the Japanese word for language: *koto ba*.[14] The word *koto* says a graceful attraction, the coming to radiance in fullness, what gives delight, something like the bringing of a message, the "enowning of the clearing-opening message of the graceful attracting, the swaying enowning." The word *ba* says "leaves," including and especially the leaves of the blossom, the petals.

Koto ba is the Japanese word for language: Language, then, could be said to be the unfolding/opening/letting emerge (which is what enowning/Ereignis is, the beyng-historical sway that is the deep sway of beyng) that attracts gracefully, like the opening of the leaves and the petals of a flower. This notion of language allows for much reticence, for the saying power of language says/ shows without pouncing on the phenomenon (on what emerges in emergence) with definitions. This way of language does not define, delimit, reduce – but rather opens up and says and points to what is own to language in the context of *koto ba* (136/144/47):

I: That [*koto ba*, the petals that emerge from *koto*, i.e., "language" in Japanese] is a wondrous word and thus not able to be thought through all the way. It names something different from what the metaphysically understood words like *Sprache, glossa, lingua, langue* and *language* represent to us. For a long time now I am hesitant to use the word *language/ Sprache* when I ponder what is language's ownmost [*ihr Wesen*].

J: But can you find a more appropriate word?

I: I think that I might have found it – but I want to protect it from being used as a common [i.e., faddish, current, too familiar] label and from being corrupted [falsified] to signify a concept.

J: What word do you use?

I: The word *Sage*. It means: saying and its said and the to-be-said [read as the saying itself, the "what" of the said, and what calls for saying – what calls unto us, what turns its gaze to us, what calls for gathering in the saying].[15]

This is a very important interlocking web for understanding what it is that language does to us and what it is that grounds as well as opens up in saying/*Sage*. Humans say things in words. I write to say thank you. But we also say things in gestures – your glance tells me a lot, it says it all. The way you looked says that you already knew. And we say that things that are not human also "say": The clock says midnight. The receipt says that you paid ten dollars for that. Nature has a lot to say to us. Say = show:

J: What does saying mean? [*Was heißt sagen?* What does saying "say"? What calls for saying?]

I: Apparently the same as showing [*zeigen*] in the sense of letting appear, letting shine [forth] – but all of this in the manner of hinting.

J: In accord with that, saying is not the name for a human speaking [*Sprechen*] …

I: … but for that deep swaying that your Japanese word *koto ba* hints at: shaped and sent in saying [*das Sagenhafte*, deeply connected to saying, coming from saying itself – not coming from merely human saying] …

J: … in whose hinting I am, only now through our dialogue, at home – so that I also now see more clearly how well-guided Count Kuki was when, under your guidance, he tried to think and be mindful of the hermeneutical.

I: But you also see how meager and inadequate my guidance was bound to be; for, with the look into what is own to saying, thinking only *begins* that pathway which takes us back, from a merely metaphysical representing, into heeding the hints of that message, whose message-bearers we would really want to become.

J: The pathway thereunto is long.

The dialogue is moving around within the question of language, saying, and hermeneutics. It has become clear that it is not the usual sense of language that is at stake and that Heidegger prefers to use the word *saying/sagen* rather than *language/Sprache* or *speaking/sprechen*, to name this matter for thinking. So that thinking needs to wander "into the site/point where the own/owning of saying is [*Wanderung in die Ortschaft des Wesens der Sage*]."

Whereas this somehow distinguishes between language/speaking and saying – and all that that entails – not enough is won with that distinction. What is called for is this: Within a certain and essential reservedness, thinking must be attentive to the "mystery" of saying, to the withdrawal that is said in the saying. So that mystery becomes mystery and shines forth as mystery. Only when the matter (showing, self-showing, emergence) of mystery's holding sway within saying itself does not come transparently to the fore!

The danger is (a) to talk too loudly about mystery and then (b) to miss and misread its sway. We need to shelter the mystery's wellspring – and that is perhaps the most difficult thing to do. It seems as if we must speak "about" language, but when we pay this close attention to language/speaking, the question emerges: Given that Heidegger attends to what announces itself in the word *saying*, there is at this point no such thing as speaking/languaging "about" language.

The dialogue now moves to this crucial matter: thinking "from" language rather than "about" language, clarifying all the interweaving dimensions of the saying and enactive thinking *from* (141/150/50):

> I: A speaking *about* language [*ein Sprechen über die Sprache*] almost inevitably turns language into an object.
>
> J: Then what is its own [i.e., what belongs to it in its deep sway] disappears.
>
> I: We have positioned ourselves above [*über*] language, instead of hearing from it.
>
> J: Then there would only be a speaking/languaging *from* language …
>
> I: … in such a manner that languaging would be called *out from* and guided *to* what is its own.
>
> J: How can we do that?

I: A speaking *from* language could only be a dialogue.
J: Without a doubt, we are moving in a dialogue.
I: But is it a dialogue *out from* the owning of language?
J: It seems to me that we are now moving in a circle. A dialogue from language must be called from its own. How is the dialogue capable of such without first letting itself into a hearing that, as it were, reaches into language's own/owning?
I: I used to call this estranging relationship the hermeneutic circle.
J: It prevails everywhere in the hermeneutical, that is to say – according to your explanation today – where the relation/connection between message and message-bearer holds sway.
I: The message-bearer must already come from [well up from] the message. But she/he must also have already gone to it.
J: Didn't you say earlier that this circle is inevitable – and that, instead of trying to avoid it as a seemingly logical contradiction, we must walk it [go on it, practise it]?
I: Yes. But this necessary recognition of the hermeneutic circle does not yet signify that, in the representing of the recognized circling, the hermeneutic circle has been experienced.
J: You would thus abandon your earlier position.
I: Of course – and especially insofar as the talk of a circle always remains in the foreground.
J: How would you now portray the hermeneutical relation?
I: I would like to avoid such a portrayal as decisively as I would avoid a speaking *about* language.
J: So everything would depend on achieving a co-responding saying from language.
I: Any such saying co-responding could only be a dialogue.
J: But obviously a dialogue of a very special kind.
I: Such a one that would remain originarily joined and enowned to what is own to saying.
J: But then we dare not any longer call every talking-together a dialogue …
I: … in case from now on we hear this name as naming the gathering unto what is own to language [as it gathers in its owning].

In this sense dialogue works when what is own to language – that is, saying – owns humans, unto their ownhood, and in human responding, to language's own/owning – a one-ing, inseparable human-saying ownhood. This cannot happen in speaking *about* language, but only in saying *from* language, from the deep sway of what is its own.

This dynamic obviates the question of either "written" or "spoken." Rather it involves the question of whether or not the dialogue is poi-etic, that is, a saying that brings forth – and this can happen in either written or spoken dialogue. Indeed, this poi-etic dynamic in the own of saying undermines any priority given to the written or the spoken.

The dialoguing partners, embraced as they are by the dynamic owning that language as saying is and does, are very much aware of how difficult – well-nigh impossible – this venture in thinking/saying is. Indeed the Japanese dialogue partner says as much (144/152/53):

> J: Are we not attempting the impossible?
> I: Indeed, so long as that message-bearing has not been sheerly guaranteed for humans who need the message, which speaks-to humans the disclosing of the twofold.
> J: To call forth this message-bearing – and still more to go on it – seems to me incomparably more difficult than to discuss openly what is own to Iki.[16]
> I: Surely. For something would have to take place by which that vast distance, in which what is own to saying comes to the fore, is opened and illuminated to message-bearing.
> J: Something like a stilling would have to take place, a stilling that would let the wafting of vastness settle lightly into the conjoining of the calling saying.
> I: The hidden relationship of message and message-bearing *plays* everywhere [i.e., is dynamic].
> J: In our ancient Japanese poetry an unknown poet sings the intermingling scent of cherry blossom and plum blossom, on the same branch.
> I: That is how I think the owning sway unto each other of the vastness and the stillness in the same enowning of the message of the disclosing of the twofold.
> J: But who today could hear therein an echo [resonating] of what is own to language that our word *koto ba* names, flower petals that

> flourish from within the clearing message of the graceful attracting that brings forth?
>
> I: Who can find in all of this a useful clarifying of what is own to language [in its owning]?
>
> J: We will never find that, so long as we demand information in the form of theses [*Leitsätzen*, theorems] and catchwords.
>
> I: But any number of us could be drawn into the preliminary play of a message-bearing, as soon as we get ourselves ready for a dialogue from language.
>
> J: It seems to me as if we ourselves, right now – instead of speaking about language – might have attempted some steps on the way entrusted to what is the owning of saying.
>
> I: [The way] that, in saying, folds in [*zusagt*] with it [this owning]. Let us rejoice if it not only seems so but is so.

In drawing the dialogue to a close, the dialogue partners let be said/shown how this "folding-in-with the owning of saying" takes leave of the "is," not as a loss but as the arrival of deep swaying as such – in the language that I am using here: arrival at the no-thing of beyng, the non-dual dynamic of radiant emptiness.

Turning now to other texts in *Unterwegs zur Sprache* (GA 12), we ask: What is own to language (*Sprache*) as saying (*Sage*)?

> Saying [*Sagen*], *sagan* means to show: to let appear, to set free in lighting-up-concealing as to reach out and offer what we call world. The lighting-up-concealing and veiling offering of world is what sways in saying.[17]

And so, finally,

> *Das Regende im Zeigen der Sage ist das Eignen.* (GA 12:246)
> The quickening in showing of saying is owning.

> *Die im Ereignis beruhende Sage ist als das Zeigen die eigenste Weise des Ereignens ... Die Sage ist die Weise, in der das Ereignis spricht ...* (GA 12:255)
> The saying that resides in enowning, is, as showing, the most own way of enowning ... Saying is the way in which enowning speaks.

d. Gatherings

Now that we have tried to think along with Heidegger "from language," checking out our own experience, let me ask the question: What about Heidegger's non-conceptual language? What does that look like? How is his language non-conceptual? I will try to show how, as Heidegger continues to explore the terrain of the question of beyng, his sentences often become less convoluted and more simple in grammar, even as they plumb the depths of the "riddle" that is sheltered in the saying of the enowning of beyng. This fits with a thinking that is underway and with a non-conceptual language, working to say the non-dual dynamic.

First, let me simply put into words some of the salient, key things that belong to this issue.

1. Language as saying carries and carries out this thinking.
2. We experience a transformation of language and a transformed experience of language.
3. The path taken here is to a kind of hiddenness, what Heidegger calls a path to "namelessness." Why did Heidegger drop the words *hermeneutics* and *phenomenology* for a while? He says: "That did not happen – as many think – to disown [or repudiate] the significance of phenomenology, but in order to let my pathway of thinking in the nameless" (GA 12:114).

    Ownmost to language as saying is its ability to show, to conceal (to disclose and to hide), and to transform us in thinking. Above all, in naming what is own to language as saying/*sagen*, this non-conceptual thinking holds the question in the indeterminate – and then, in saying it, non-conceptually.
4. Language as saying becomes a way-making (*Be-wëgen*). It is how showing and self-showing take place: Saying makes ways, "creates" pathways for thinking, brings forth these pathways, poi-etically. What is being thought-said is thought-said through the pathway itself. Heidegger:

    > When speaking, as hearing language, lets saying be said, then this letting can only emerge [*sich er-geben*], insofar as and in so near as

[*insonah*] what is ownmost to us is let [actively] into saying. We hear it [saying] only because we belong to it. (GA 12:244)

5. Words and names have usual, ordinary meanings, stemming from our habits of language. We need to encounter these usual meanings within certain boundaries, and we need to go along with these boundaries and this usual meaning, until thinking-saying breaks out of this usual way, until there is a flow beyond these boundaries and the unthought breaks through. Heidegger:

We must first encounter what is usually meant within certain boundaries and we *must go some stretch of the way with this usual meaning* [italics mine], in order at the right moment to claim the turning-around [*Umschlag*] of thinking ... (GA 65:83)

He goes on:

This turning around (*umkehren*) is not just a "formal" trick of switching meanings [*Bedeutungsumschlag*] in mere words, but the *transformation of man himself* [*die Verwandlung des Menschen selbst*] [italics by Heidegger]. (GA 65:84)

6. Since this thinking-saying is outside the usual boundaries of our inherited language, grammar, and syntax, we experience a bit of dismay, unrest, edginess, even a haunting unease – along with a certain gentle reverence. This happens, not only because we ourselves are a bit uneasy and restless, but also because the issue itself – Ereignis, the reticence of beyng, the unease as well as the reverence – emerges for thinking.
7. This kind of hinting in what is to be thought and to be said draws us along in its withdrawal and reticence – as non-conceptual thinking the non-dual dynamic.
8. And that which is hidden and withdraws is not something. It *is* not, but it holds sway. The dynamic of enowning is no-thing, the radiant emptiness in the dynamic of beyng as enowning.

9. "What stirs in the showing of saying is owning [*Das Regende im Zeigen der Sage ist Eignen*]" (GA 12:246). Saying is showing, manifesting. The moving force in saying, what stirs up and starts, is owning, that is, the gathering unto the own of beyng. This is enowning's saying, the saying of/in/from enowning. This "is" can also be said as *logos*/gathering (*Versammmlung*): gathering together, gathering into their belonging-together – of things, of Da-sein and world, of beings and being – in the truth of beyng as enowning. Another name for this "in" is the non-dual dynamic of radiant emptiness.
10. Saying-showing lets many names emerge for saying the same, as is called forth in non-conceptual language, where words say-show but do not prove anything and do not fit into a conceptual-linguistic framework. Rather, they open up the manifold possibilities. These words do not say the deep sway of beyng as properties, but in each case say-show the fullness of the deep sway "itself" – nothing more and nothing less. Words of saying are not definable. They say/show what is interwoven in the interwoven dynamic of the radiance of beyng-enowning. We in thinking-saying stay open to the "strangeness that lies in the issue itself" (GA 8:15).
11. Gathering all of this: The saying-showing of enowning stays within the dynamic one-ing at-oneness or emptiness of disclosing-hiddenness, with what is not shown. Beyng as emergence as unfolding as arising is said within the non-dual and non-conceptualizable dynamic at-oneness of emergence-withdrawal or disclosing and hiding. Emergence shows itself only in the hintings of this withdrawing. The non-dual dynamic of radiant emptiness.

Now let me indicate ways in which Heidegger breaks down the subject–predicate duality of our languages and thus engages in non-conceptual saying.

Ereignis ereignet.
Enowning enowns. Or: enowning.

Die Stille stillt.
Stillness stills. Or: Stilling.

Die Gegend gegnet.
The region regions. Or: regioning.

Die Nähe näht.
Nearing nears. Or: Nearing.

Be-wëgung bewegt.
Moving moves. Way-making makes ways. Or: Moving. Way-making.

Die Welt weltet.
World worlds. Or: Worlding.

Die Zeit zeitigt.
Timing times. Or: Timing.

Der Raum räumt.
Space spaces. Or: Spacing.

Das Ding dingt.
The thing things. Or: Thinging.

Das Nichts nichtet.
Nothing nothings. Or: No-thinging.

Die Wahrheit des Seyns ist das Seyn der Wahrheit.
Truth of beyng is the beyng of truth.

Das Wesen der Sprache: Die Sprache des Wesens.
The deep sway of language. The language of deep sway.

Das Wesen der Wahrheit ist die Wahrheit des Wesens.
The deep sway of truth is the truth of deep sway.

Eon emmenai: Anwesend anwesen.
Emergent emerging. Or: Emerging.

Das Wesen des Seyns ist die Wesung. Wesen als Wesung.
What is own to beyng is deep swaying. Deep sway as deep swaying.

In so many ways, these are sentences that we cannot think conceptually at all! Here is an example: When Heidegger is speaking of the fourfold, earth and sky, gods and mortals – especially of the over-against-one-another (*Gegen-einander-über*) – he says that this over-against-one-another comes from far away, namely from that open expanse in which each of the four "reaches" the others. And then he says:

> In the reigning over-against-one-another every one [of the four] is open, one for the other – open in its self-hiding.* In this way one crosses over to the other, one gives itself over to the other, while each one stays itself; one is over-to the other as what watches over, protects – thus as covering-protecting "over."
> *Marginal note: the distancing that is entrusted to one another. (GA 12:198)

Finally, there are the many words that say the same, while being words with differing ways of saying (what we might call "different meanings," except for the fact that they are saying the same).

Das Schweigen entspricht dem lautlosen Geläut der Stille der ereignend-zeigenden Sage. (GA 12:251)
Staying silent accords with the soundless ringing of the stillness of the enowning-showing saying.

Das Wesen der Sprache ist die Sage als die Zeige. (GA 12:242)
The deep sway of language is saying as showing.

Das Regende im Zeigen der Sage ist das Eignen. (GA 12:246)
The moving in the showing of saying is owning.

Das Ereignis, im Zeigen der Sage erblickt, läßt sich weder als ein Vorkommnis noch als ein Geschehen vorstellen, sondern nur im Zeigen der Sage als das Gewährende erfahren. Es gibt nichts anderes, worauf das Ereignis noch zurückführt, woraus es gar erklärt werden könnte ... Das Ereignis ist das

Unscheinbarste des Unscheinbaren, das Einfachste des Einfachen, das Nächste des Nahen und das Fernste des Fernen, darin wir Sterblichen uns zeitlebens aufhalten … Das in der Sage Waltende, das Ereignis, können wir nur so nennen, daß wir sagen: Es – das Ereignis – eignet. (GA 12:247)
Enowning, glimpsed in the showing of saying, can be presented [proposed] neither as an occurrence [incident] nor as an event. Rather it can only be experienced in the showing of saying as what does the granting [affording]. [This thinking-saying is non-conceptual.] There is nothing else to which enowning leads back, from out of [from within] which it could be explained at all [in any way] … Enowning is the most hidden of the hidden, the simplest of the simple [the most onefold of the onefold], the nearest of the near and the farthest of the far, in which we mortals stay [dwell] all of our life … We can only name what holds sway in saying, enowning, by saying: It – enowning – owns.

*Vielleicht verbirgt sich im Wort **Weg**, Tao, das Geheimnis aller Geheimnisse des denkenden Sagens, falls wir diese Namen in ihr Ungesprochenes zurückkehren lassen und dieses Lassen vermögen … Alles ist Weg.* (GA 12:187)
Perhaps the secret of all secrets of thinking-saying is sheltered-hidden in the word *way* or *dao*, if we can let these names return into their unsaid and if we are capable of this letting … All is way.

Wege, nicht Werke.
Ways, not works.

Chapter Six

Third Moment: Heidegger and the Symbiosis of Translation and Thinking, from Saying

We philosophers have not paid enough attention to the intertwining of translation, interpretation, and thinking. It is not easy even to name this configuration of important aspects of a Heidegger-text in translation. I offer four alternative ways to title this chapter:

1. Thinking and Doing Translation, from Saying
2. Thinking Woven within the Task of Translation
3. Thinking as Integral Part of Translation
4. Translation as Always Doing Philosophy and Always Underway

Why is the work of translating such a necessary and impossible task? From one language to another, for example, from German to English? Or within the one language, for example, from one way of German to another, from one way of English to another?

The issues of translation, interpretation, and thinking are deeply intertwined, all three having a significant bearing. Certain issues in this regard stand without contention. Let me begin with a list of these.[1]

1. *There is translation*. Regardless of how much certain sceptical voices name the difficulties in translation – going all the way to the "impossibility" of translation – still translations exist and people do translate texts.
2. *All translation is interpretation*. Since the language of the original text and the language of the text in translation

cannot ever fully coincide, what the text in translation says cannot possibly be identical with what the original text says. There is a dimension of non-transferability in the original language and its saying, something that remains hidden and inexpressible. Thus the translator must needs interpret.

3. *There is no perfect translation.* It is impossible to duplicate the original text "in translation." No translation is equal to the original language.
4. *Translation, then, is a kind of pledge or promise.* The translator ponders the words in both languages, trying to find the word that fits best. Especially for Heidegger, very often this is not the word that appears in the lexicon of either language or in the typical two-language dictionary. And when the translator has found the word that the original text "wants to say," this calls for a kind of pledge, namely that the translation opted for is a viable way to say what is being said in the original text. Again, the lexical dictionary cannot be the arbiter of this pledge. Rather the measure must be the *Sache*/issue itself, its *being said*, and the way that is own to language's saying, in its vitality and in the engagement therein. And all critiques of translations must be measured from this "saying."
5. *Translations, then, retain an honest questionableness.* Since there can never be an "objective," one-to-one translation or an "absolutely accurate" translation, there is always room for thoughtful dialogue. Thus no one can claim that his or her translation is the "only one possible." I would say that a translation that is true to the original text and to the text in translation – taking into account the inexpressible, the gap that necessarily exists between the original and the translation, and the inherent difficulties of translating from one language to another – is in all cases *viable*.
6. *Never forget the original*, which the translation can never match. How can translating be true to the original text, with its hiddenness and inexpressibility, and to the text in translation, with its necessary impossibility of saying everything that the original says?

a. From Saying to Translation

Beyng speaks or says. Beyng as emergence says. Beyng as *a-letheia* says. Beyng as enowning says. With acute hearing and listening, humans can hear the word of beyng-emergence. The saying of beyng, this hearing, and how human Da-sein says beyng/emergence in response – all make up the non-dual dynamic of enowning – or radiant emptiness.

Whereas beyng/emergence/enowning says and "rings" with poi-etic saying, it is easy for us to not-hear this saying/ringing of beyng. Hearing the saying/gathering of the word can undo this deafness.

Any "true"[2] translation emerges from and is sustained by this saying, the telling word – the word of beyng and human Da-sein's word in response, the saying of beyng as emergence and human saying-after or active saying in response. Both sayings are bundled together in the ongoing dynamic of the inseparable "one not two" – not a static unity but a dynamic one-ing.

Translation rests in and is sustained by deep saying. Residing in this deep saying is poi-etic dwelling: Poi-esis as saying, poi-esis as bringing to the fore, showing.

What is the word *saying*? And how do we translate it?

Perhaps a translation of instructions for installing a new washing machine can be a simple, one-to-one translation from one language to another. A translation of a legal document is a bit more complex, calling for more caution with words and their nuances – for example, a business contract for international trade – but still more straightforward than not. Third, translation of works of literature and above all poetry require more attention to the nuances of words and phrases, since *what* the words reveal and express carries more nuance. In this context – and beyond that – translations of Heidegger-texts are examples *par excellence* that much more is at stake in carrying the "message" from one language to another. Here we encounter the necessity of utmost care and attention in translating. We are no longer translating a text about installing washing machines!

Words convey more than their literal meanings. How do we translate this "more than"? As we indeed and necessarily translate this "more than," how do we stay "true" to the text in the original language? Heidegger's German is not normal – neither "normal German" nor "normal German philosophy." How are we carried over (*trans*-lated) into this domain, *within the German language*? Then, how do we carry what the German says over into English – translate it into English?

In a sense, translation is being suspended between two languages and two worlds of thinking/saying – or even two languages in the original text itself and then the text in translation. Not just one text, but not two separate texts either. Translations move in the "between" of this not-one-not-two.

Texts in translation can be literal or "free." And here the measure for knowing is often called "readability." I call it "the devil of readability." The umbrella of readability covers several sins. Does translation craft words in the translated text, in order for it to be readable? Does translation create words in the text in translation? What if the author, working with the translator, offers an insight into the original text – sometimes then changing the text of the translation in ways that the original does not "say"? If the author of the original becomes involved in the translation, does the text in translation become in some sense, at least in part, a new original?

If words in translation are not simply lexical, then the translation cannot be simply literal. This is obvious. But what to do with the way of saying that manifests this when one is translating? How does translation *stay in the between* of the two texts and two languages, even as it necessarily "creates" a new text, the one in translation? Where do we find the words, if not in the dictionary?

In learning a new language, it is recommended that at one point we use a monolingual lexicon or dictionary (German–German, English–English) rather than a bilingual dictionary (German–English), because the bilingual dictionary invariably missteps. Within poi-etic saying, from within the saying-showing of the word, it is not possible to have a one-to-one correspondence of all words; and when the dictionary tries, it often misrepresents a word. This is especially true when translating Heidegger.

All of these considerations lead to our awareness that **translation is itself a work of thinking**. This involves especially the "originary translation" that one must make "from" the original text "into" another text, still in the original language. In Heidegger's case this means translating the language of his work of thinking (German) into words of that same language (German) that "say" beyng as emergence in the way things are (the enactment of intralingual translation). And then the way-making and showing power of "essential translation," as interlingual translation, forms words in the language different from the original. Here language in translation tries its best to say what is own to beyng as emergence as well as what is own to language as saying.

Following Heidegger, Parvis Emad, in an essay from 1993, makes the distinction between intralingual and interlingual translation. First, translation *within* the original language and then the translation *between* languages. At the end of that essay he writes: "Gathering all of this, we can say: the unresolvable foreignness that always remains in interlingual translation is the occasion for experiencing the *Wesen* [deep sway] of [that which is own to] language as a soundless saying/showing within the horizon of being."[3]

Heidegger shows this distinction by using two German words, whose infinitives look alike: *übersetzen*. But there are actually two verbs. In German the meaning of each verb is distinguishable, depending on whether it is separable or inseparable. *Über**setzen*** = to translate from one language to another. ***Über***-*setzen* = to carry oneself or one's thinking from one way of thinking to another *within the same language*. In German the distinction is made by the context or by using the hyphen: *über-setzen*. Heidegger adds a third way, which is, by italicizing the one or the other part of the word. *Trans*lating happens within the original language. Trans*lating* is from one language to another.

Here is Heidegger:

> The change in the choice of words is already the consequence of the fact that what one has to say has been *trans*-lated into another truth and clarity or even questionableness. This *trans*-lating can take place without a change in language's expression … The so-called trans-*lating* and rewriting always comes after we have *trans*-lated our whole being into the region of a transformed truth. Only when we have been owned over to this *trans*-lating are we in the care of the word. (GA 54:18)

Every translation of Heidegger's texts takes its measure from the saying word – the saying of beyng, that which is own to language and saying – a way-making that overcomes the obstinacy of imagining that we always already understand the words because we understand how they are used "normally." Translating "from saying" requires that thinking deal with "more than" normal words and their seemingly automatic meanings.[4] The opening that happens when translation moves from one language to the other, *from saying*, makes way for the emergence of what is own to language as saying, what is own to translation as a work of thinking, and what is own to the saying-showing.

The mystery of translation is that it is, that it *works*, and that it *plays with us* – while all the while what is deeply own to language and translation remains impenetrable.

b. Hearing Heidegger's Words

1. For both languages the translator is "bound ownmostly to the language and the experience of the deep sway [the ownmost, *das Wesen*]" (GA 5:328).
2. "Perhaps we will learn to think what can happen in translating. The actual affording encounter [*geschickliche Begegnung*, encounter offered to us] of the dynamic-historical language is a still enowning [*ein stilles Ereignis*]" (GA 5:371).
3. "Neither the translation nor the elucidation carries any weight as long the word of Parmenides's thought does not speak [*ansprechen*] to us." All of this is blocked by "epistemological mastery ... overtrumping ... outstripping ... objectification ... technical assault" (GA 54:4).
4. "One thinks that 'translation' is converting one language into another, converting the foreign language into one's native language, and vice versa. But we misjudge the fact that we are also always already translating our own language, our mother tongue, into its own word. Speaking/saying is in itself a translating. Its ownmost deep sway [*Wesen*] can in no way emerge from the fact that the translating and translated

words belong to different languages. An originary translating reigns in every dialogue and monologue …

"The change in the choice of words is already the consequence of the fact that what one has to say has been *trans*-lated into another truth and clarity or even questionableness. This *trans*-lating can take place without a change in language's expression … The so-called trans*lating* and rewriting always comes after we have *trans*-lated our whole being into the region of a transformed truth. Only when we have been owned over to this *trans*-lating are we in the care of the word. Only when the regard for the language has been thus established can we take on the mostly easier and more confined task of translating the foreign word into one's own word.

"On the other hand translating one's own language into its ownmost word is always more difficult" (GA 54:17–18).

c. Who Are We, the Translators?

I am a translator of Heidegger's German into English.[5] I have the good fortune to know English well (which I learned from my Latin teacher), to have learned German from native speakers and to have learned it thoroughly, to have lived in Germany and Austria for ten years – having there the opportunity to offer lectures and philosophy courses in German – and, finally, to have had several excellent mentors in learning Heidegger's philosophy. Good education in English and German and in the thrust of Heidegger's thinking – a useful combination, for which I am grateful.

We translators need to be lucidly loyal to the original, as well as integrally loyal to the reader of the text in translation. How can we do this? How dare we try? How dare we not?

The translator seeks out what is own to the original text and lets emerge what is his/her own that the translator brings to the text. In seeking what is own to the original and in letting the translation's own word/saying emerge, the translator is a kind of "double agent" – eliciting from the rest of us a certain envy (how exciting to be in this creative possibility, with myriad possibilities in front of one) as well as a certain misgiving (how challenging it is to say the original text in translation, to capture as fully as possible the author's intention, and still produce a "true" translation).

The translator, then, is "trans-lating" in several ways:

1. trans-lating (*über-setzen* or *über**setzen***) or being oneself carried over (*übergesetzt*) into the text of the original and its saying,
2. trans-lating (*über-setzen* or *über**setzen***) or dwelling in and saying from the saying of emergence,
3. translating (*über**setzen***) or rendering words from the original language into one's own language,
4. while trans-lating and then translating – reaching from the original text and its saying to the deep and poi-etic source of words with their nuances in one's own language – suspended, as it were, in the between.

Note that in German, for the inseparable verb *übersetzen*, you hear the stress on the *setzen*. So that when Heidegger puts part of the word in bold, he is doing philosophy!

In all of this, the text in translation must mirror the translator's own work, even as it remains *always* the work of the original writer. That is, the text in translation is *both* that of the author of the original *and* that of the translator. Whereas this requirement may be hard to achieve, it is impossible to avoid.

The translator has to stay as close as possible to the *Sache*/issue and to the *Sage*/saying of the words that he or she is translating. And she or he is interpreting and transforming this *Sache*/matter in the work of translating. Intimacy is called for, with the language of the original text and author, with the *Sache*/matter therein, with the words *from* the saying of the original, and finally with the rich possibilities of the translator's own language.

The translator acts creatively to let the original author's saying of the said emerge in the translation. Heidegger says things in words – and in a certain way of wording/saying – that mirror what is own to his thinking. The translator does this as well, in his or her "own" way, by responding to what is own to saying "itself" as well as what is own to the saying of beyng. Finally, all of this is directed to the possibility that is own to us the readers. I remind the reader of what the artist Louise Bourgeois says, from the first part of this book:

> People ask me – what do you mean –
> and I answer what do you think of
> when you see the image.

For us: What thinking/saying opens up when you hear the word-images in translation? And how does this opening in translation mirror the opening in the original text?

Being true to the saying and the said in the original text includes co-mingling (a) what is own to the original saying, (b) what is own to the translator – who lets the own of the original emerge in translation – and (c) what is own to the reader of the translation and original, in terms of the thinkable and the sayable. This is new territory for thinking to explore. (Have we translators of Heidegger paid enough attention to this territory?)

Heidegger, the author of the original text, and the translator share several two core things:

- that which is own to the text and
- that which is own to thinking in the text,
- aiming at and responding to the core thrust in the thinking ...

in each case letting the *word* resonate well, unto and from the saying of beyng as emergence.

At the same time there are differences. Unlike the author of the original, the translator has a text to work from. The opening of the original is already there, the opening onto what emerges as new, as possibility, a thinking that emerges as the original thinking pursues and responds to the word of beyng. Thus the translator's opening is "after the fact," that is, after the first opening that is the original – even as it is a first in terms of the text in translation.

(An interesting phenomenon occurs here, when the translator refers to another translation of the same original. For example, when translating *Beiträge*, we referred to the French translation of key words. And word has it that the Japanese translators of *Beiträge* used the English translation in order to clarify what the original text was trying to say, that is, to help them find the appropriate words in Japanese. What does this mutual mirroring of translations mean?)

Translators try things, let words roll around in the mouth or on their tongue or in the mind or at the tip of their finger – trying, rejecting, considering the possibility, until something says: That's it! You got it! This process involves bringing the original text to life, enlivening it: choosing a word-inflection that is own to the saying, that is, enactively responding to the original and interweaving what is own to the original with what is own to the translation.

In a certain sense the "true" translator simply engages in the taxing and exciting work, rather than discussing its impossibility. The translator of Heidegger ventures into challenging territory, on the margins of what is possible – and necessarily so.

d. In the Translator's Workshop

It has been fifty years since I translated my first Heidegger text: *"Die Kehre."* Since then, my thinking has matured and I have learned a lot about translating. What would happen if I were to translate that first piece again, fifty years later? How would that manifest the hands-on experience of translating, that is, the work that is done in the translator's workshop? Let me meander back (i.e., re-flect).

Heidegger's essay *"Die Kehre"* was one of four lectures given in Bremen in 1949. It was first published in 1962 in a little volume titled *Die Technik und die Kehre*.[6] Early in the lecture/essay Heidegger says/writes:

> *Wenn das Wesen der Technik, das Ge-Stell als die Gefahr im Seyn, das Seyn selbst ist, dann läßt sich die Technik niemals durch ein bloß auf sich gestelltes menschliches Tun meistern, weder positiv noch negativ. Die Technik, deren Wesen das Sein selbst ist, läßt sich durch den Menschen niemals überwinden. Das hieße doch, der Mensch sei der Herr des Seins.* (GA 79:69)

Because *"Ge-Stell [ist] ein Wesensgeschick des Seyns selbst"* (GA 79:68).

My translation of this essay appeared as "The Turning" in volume 1 of *Research in Phenomenology* (1971). That translation of these passages reads:

> If the way to be of technology – Gestell as the danger within Being – is Being itself, then technology can never be mastered, either positively or negatively, by means of a human activity that is simply dependent upon itself. Technology, whose way to be is Being itself, can never be overcome by man. That would mean, after all, that man is the master of Being.[7]
>
> Because "Gestell is an essential mittence of Being itself."[8]

William Lovitt's translation of this essay appeared as "The Turning" in the book *The Question concerning Technology* (1977). His translation of these passages reads:

> If the essence, the coming to presence, of technology, Enframing as the danger within Being, is Being itself, then technology will never allow itself to be mastered, either positively or negatively, by a human doing founded merely on itself. Technology, whose essence is Being itself, will never allow itself to be overcome by man. That would mean, after all, that man was the master of Being.[9]
>
> Because "Enframing is a destining of the coming to presence of Being itself."[10]

From today's perspective – after sixty years of English translations of Heidegger texts and after the publication of nearly a hundred volumes of the *Gesamtausgabe* – we translators have learned much more about Heidegger's thinking and have much more to go on, as we parse the sentences in German and render them into English. Furnished with the experience of years and the gaining of some wisdom, let me revisit this text from "The Turning," look again at the key words – and then retranslate them.

*Capitalizing the word **being**.* In 1971 the word *being*, translation of the German word *Sein*, was almost universally capitalized in English. This decision or action was partly motivated by the wish to distinguish *das Seiende* from *das Sein*: "beings" from "Being." Today the word is sometimes capitalized, sometimes not. When Professors von Herrmann, Emad, and I started *Heidegger Studies* in 1985, we made the decision not to capitalize the word in English. This decision was based on English usage and on our conviction that capitalizing the word runs the risk of reifying what is said with the word *Sein/being*. When capitalized, the English word gave the misleading impression that, whatever the word *being* meant, said or referred to, it felt to many like a substance, a thing, a *res* – often interpreted to mean a "highest being." This is exactly the opposite of what Heidegger means by *das Sein*, let alone *das Seyn*. Today perhaps this is obvious, but then it was not so obvious.

*Distinguishing **das Sein** from **das Seyn** in English translation.* Already in 1971 we had evidence that Heidegger sometimes used this unusual spelling of the German word, for example in these Bremen-lectures from 1949, published in 1962. But what the distinction really meant was somewhat difficult to decipher, until the publication of *Beiträge zur Philosophie (Vom Ereignis)* in 1989, where he makes this distinction thematic. In *Beiträge* Heidegger uses the word *das Sein* to refer to the being of metaphysics, that is, being as other than beings but somehow still thought *in terms of* beings (the ontological difference). On the other hand *das Seyn* names a dynamic that no longer thinks in terms of beings. To think *das Seyn* is to think beyng not in terms of beings, to think without reference to or holding on to beings. Beyng is not thought from beings, but rather from within the deep sway of beyng as disclosing, as emergence, as clearing-opening.[11] One might say that the word *being* was "mediated" through or in its relationship to *beings* – and the word *beyng* is, as it were, unmediated. Note that mediation here implies a duality, whereas the non-mediated implies "it itself" or an at-oneness.

Neither Lovitt nor I took into account any difference between *Seyn* and *Sein*. For myself, I do not think that I knew at the time how to make the distinction. In translating this text today, I would be compelled to make this distinction. I would do this by using the English words *being* (for *das Sein*) and *beyng* (for *das Seyn*). (In our translation of *Beiträge* Professor Emad and I used the spelling "being." Today I prefer "beyng.")

*Saying in English what the word **die Technik** wants to say ... other than "technology."*[12] Already in 1971 I knew that Heidegger's word *Technik* in this essay did not mean the usual technical apparatus, technical means, or even technique as in "strategy." But the idea of translating the word as "technicity" did not occur to me. So, whereas I knew that Heidegger's word did not simply mean "technology," I somewhat innocently translated the word with "technology." Lovitt translated it in the same way.

In ordinary German, *Technik* means both "technology" and "technique" – even though the word *Technologie* fits here as well. The English words *technique* and *technology* carry a similar ambiguity. Or better said: Neither the German nor the English word in its normal usage indicates anything like what *die Technik* means for Heidegger here. As used in this essay, *Technik* does not mean the machinery or instrument of technology (as in: "We do not have the right technology for that job."). Nor does it mean strategy (as in: "If I knew the right technique, I would do it.").

Rather, for Heidegger the discussion of *Technik* and *das Wesen der Technik* has to do with a way of revealing, that is, the way in which being shows itself in a particular epoch. The issue of *die Technik* manifests a certain efficiency at the core of this revealing – efficiency above all else, at the expense of things emerging as the things that they are, that is, gathering world (what some might call "what is natural").[13] (One way in which Heidegger says what is meant by *Technik* is when he contrasts it with "releasement to the things" and "openness for the mystery" – as we discussed in the First Moment.)

Today I would translate *die Technik* as "technicity" and would say it in conjunction with *das Wesen der Technik*: what is own to technicity. What is own to technicity Heidegger calls: *das Ge-Stell*.

*Saying **das Ge-Stell** in English.* In 1971 I left the word untranslated. Lovitt translated it as "Enframing" – note that he also capitalizes the word, most likely in an attempt to keep the reader from assuming that she or he somehow "already knows" what the word means.

The prefix *Ge-* is used in German to suggest something of the totality or "whole range" of something – as in *Ge-birge*, the whole range of mountains. *Ge-Stell* comes from *stellen*, to place, put, pose, *posit*, in the meaning of *establish* and *make firm*. Heidegger uses the word *Ge-Stell* to say the whole range of posing-positing-establishing of the calculative thinking of "technicity." *Ge-Stell* means the whole range of positing and disposing that characterizes the way in which *Technik* unfolds. In *Ge-stell* things are pre-established (posited in advance), for the sake of their disposability, without letting them appear or emerge in all their disclosing possibilities. Thus in this regime of disposability "things" get reduced to disposables – and no longer appear or work as "things."[14] In *Ge-stell* there is the provoking that forces things to be merely calculable for the sake of disposing – and ultimately for further disposal – and, in that very disposal of *Ge-Stell*, losing their whole, deep sway as things, their thinghood – or better yet, their dynamic thinging.

No single English word can render all of what the word *Ge-Stell* mirrors and says. It is often translated as "enframing." While this English term somehow reflects the gathering and collectedness of the German prefix *Ge-*, the word *enframing* hides the dimension of *stellen* in *Ge-Stell*: positing, putting, placing, disposing. Today I translate *Ge-Stell* as "regime of disposability," using the word *regime* to say the whole range or "system" or "guiding paradigm" of disposability, positing, setting up in advance while not letting things be things. The regime of disposability is other than emergence of what is "natural," that is, other than gathering the world or emerging of "things" in what is own to them as things.

This regime of disposability (*das Ge-Stell*) is nothing thing-like. It is the way of disclosing that happens in modern technicity, even as it is itself nothing technical, but rather a way of beyng. And this regime of disposability is not simply in the hands of human actors in the world. It is a way of revealing/disclosing that belongs to beyng. It is something that is sent to or shaped for or afforded to humans. Thus it is connected to *das Geschick* ...

Learning what the word **das Geschick** *wants to say. Das Geschick* in normal usage means "fate" or "destiny." This is clearly not what

Heidegger wants to say. *Das Geschick* is "of and by beyng." It is something that beyng itself does or grants. It has been translated as "sending," as "shaping," as "handing-over," as "historical unfolding," as "mittence" – this last one an attempt to stay close to the notion of "sending" in the verb *schicken*. (Trying to say *Geschick*, I used this word *mittence* in my doctoral dissertation – even putting it in the title.)

Today I would use the word *affordance* to say this dynamic. To afford is to supply, to give over to, to bestow or yield. Affordance of beyng is the dynamic whereby beyng grants, supplies, hands over – affords. The regime of disposability is what is own to the affordance of beyng in what is own to technicity (its *Wesen*).

*Understanding and saying the myriad turns in the word **das Wesen***. It may well be that this is the German word in Heidegger that is most difficult to translate. When I reminisce about the biggest challenges in translating Heidegger, a number of words come to mind: *Da-sein, Ereignis, Ab-grund, Seynsgeschichte* ... *Das Wesen* surely belongs in this list.

In my first attempt to translate this word, in "The Turning," I chose to render it into English as "way to be" or "way of being." First of all, this preserved somewhat the verbal sense or the dynamic character. It avoided the static sense of the word in its usual meanings of "essence" or "quiddity." Thus, second, "way to be" reaches for the fresh and rich meaning that *das Wesen* has in Heidegger's thinking of possibility. It says or shows the emergent dynamic that *das Wesen* says, more so than does the word *essence*. (It is true that Heidegger uses the word *das Wesen* at times to name what belongs to the static "essence" that inheres within metaphysics. But not here! I will come back to this in a moment.)

Sometime later, I decided to use the words *root unfolding* to render *das Wesen* into English. When I introduced "root unfolding," I was aware that it carried a certain risk. In the meantime I am convinced that it is not an appropriate way to translate *Wesen*. It is simply not a good translation. Having said this, I am convinced that these early attempts at translating the German word *das Wesen* were useful steps in the transition from the usual, traditional, metaphysical language of "essence." During many turns in Heidegger's thinking, he lets language break thinking free from its encrustations and obscurations within the tradition of metaphysics. What was a "wrong" translation was motivated at the time by this same call to let language help thinking and saying to break free from this limitation. (For sure the word *essence* hampers our thinking *das Wesen*.)

To render the German *das Wesen* into English as "root unfolding" is misleading when it says "root," as if there is some place "from out of which" or "in which" something is "rooted." Clearly the word in Heidegger says nothing of "root." In hindsight I see this translation of mine as an honest though failed attempt to get at the emergent dynamic that Heidegger wants to say.

For Heidegger *das Wesen* points to a dynamic that is much more and much deeper than the usual, static "essence" or "nature." It needs to be heard in its verbal sense of emerging, unfolding, deep swaying. Thus in *Beiträge zur Philosophie (Vom Ereignis)*, *Wesen* includes and points to *Wesung*, a participial – dynamic – way of unfolding, emerging, or deep swaying. In this sense *das Wesen der Technik* is the deep sway of technicity, that whole range of relationship whereby positing and disposing and commoditization is the primary way that "things" get dealt with – and thus cancelled as things. In other words, what is own to things in the deep sway of technicity is that they lose what is own to them as things (the thing, gathering) and get reduced to disposables and commodities. In this sense what is own to (*Wesen*) is also what enowns in this dynamic (*ereignet*).

In the Translators' Foreword to our translation of *Beiträge zur Philosophie (Vom Ereignis)* (*Contributions to Philosophy* [*From Enowning*]), Professor Emad and I distinguished four English renderings of the word *das Wesen*, depending on the context:

1. *essence*. In certain specific cases the English word *essence* is the correct translation of *das Wesen*. In the context of the first beginning, that of metaphysics, Heidegger uses *Wesen* as *essentia*. But even here the *Wesen* is not simply a rendition of *essential*. The word *Wesen* is not simply ensconced within

metaphysics, but is always in a broader context, one that the word *essence* cannot say.
2. *deep sway, swaying, in-depth-sway, enduring-abiding*.¹⁵ Central to Heidegger's intentions when he thinks *Ereignis* – and, here in *"Die Kehre,"* *Seyn* – is this notion of the "in-depth-sway" that is the core dynamic of *Seyn* – here, the dynamic of *Ge-Stell*, which is own to beyng as *Geschick*.
3. *what is own to … (Sprache, Technik, Ereignis, Seyn)*. What belongs to a thing, an issue or a dynamic in its ownmost, what is own to it. What something is in its ownhood.
4. *way of being*. A somewhat neutral way to say what determines what it is, dynamically – not necessarily what is own to it, not an in-depth-sway, and certainly not the limiting *essence* of metaphysics.

With these better understandings of Heidegger's thinking and of the words he uses to express it, I will now attempt an "improved" translation of the passages quoted at the beginning of this section (from 1971). Translating these passages is still not easy, but I enjoy making the effort.

I repeat Heidegger's words:

Wenn das Wesen der Technik, das Ge-stell als die Gefahr im Seyn, das Seyn selbst ist, dann läßt sich die Technik niemals durch ein bloß auf sich gestelltes menschliches Tun meistern, weder positiv noch negativ. Die Technik, deren Wesen das Sein selbst ist, läßt sich durch den Menschen niemals überwinden. Das hieße doch, der Mensch sei der Herr des Seins. (GA 79:69)

Because *"Ge-Stell [ist] ein Wesensgeschick des Seyns selbst"* (GA 79:68).

And here is my revised translation (as of 2020):

If what is own to technicity, namely the regime of disposability as the danger in beyng, is beyng itself, then technicity can never be conquered by a human doing that is founded merely on itself – neither positively nor negatively. Technicity, whose deep sway [owning or ownhood] is being [beyng] itself, can never be conquered by humans. That would mean, after all, that humans are the masters of being.

Because "the regime of disposability is an owning affordance of beyng itself [is an affordance of beyng that is own to beyng itself]."

Having done this work of translation, I am reminded that the work is never done, as in "never reaches an end."

e. Markings, in Closing

Heidegger is reported to have said to a colleague, near the end of his life, that the word *Dasein* should in every instance be read with a hyphen: Da-sein. I have always imagined that he wanted the word to say the ongoing dynamic of what Da-sein as word says. This is in line with what is obvious to me, namely that Heidegger's question of being was always going after a *Sache*/matter that is dynamic, ongoing, emerging, never static, never a unity in concept or in the world (neither epistemologically nor ontologically) – so that his thinking always stressed the *-ing* in disclosing or unconcealing, the emergent dimension of *anwesen*, or the enactive originary turning that is and is *in* Ereignis/enowning. And Da-sein is a key dimension of this inseparable dynamic.

Also, with the word *Da-sein*, or *Dasein* in *Sein und Zeit*, Heidegger was already thinking beyond the dichotomy or duality of subject and object. The hyphen helps to stress this fact.

Whereas I do not doubt that Heidegger said this to a colleague, I have always "translated" the word *Dasein* in accord with Heidegger's own text, that is, with or without a hyphen. For two reasons. First, the word *Dasein* or *Da-sein* is well-established now as an English word. Second, whereas the hyphen elucidates and emphasizes the dynamic aspect of what the word says, one can easily think that dynamic without seeing the hyphen.

When I translate, I am confident that in the midst of the myriad players in any work of translation – the author of the original text, the translator, the reader, and the given discourse/context of both languages – there is the possibility of rendering the original in the language of translation in such a way that the saying and what is being said in the original get said in the text in translation.

Then there is the "world," the totality of meanings in which dwell the saying and the said and the to-be-said, leading to a certain recontextualizing of the original within the text in translation. But the translation must always afford the saying of the original, unto the sayable.

There is translation. All translation is interpretation. There is no perfect translation. Translation is a kind of pledge, to a measure held and hidden within the unsayable of the sayable. Translation retains an honest questionableness. Finally, translation is about viability, not perfection.

My experience as a translator of Heidegger texts is that this work is most exciting, provides a benefit to others who can hear and think along-with, and calls for extremely subtle awarenesses and critical thinking as well as a deep humility. I relish the moments when, after much consultation and careful attentiveness to words and their possible nuances, there comes the moment of: That's it! I got it!

> *Stammt der Mut des Denkens aus der*
> *Zumutung des Seyns, dann gedeiht*
> *die Sprache des Geschicks.* (GA 13:77)

> When the courage to think stems from
> the summons of beyng, then
> the language of affordance flourishes.

Chapter Seven

Fourth Moment: Heidegger and Engaging in the Retrieval of Greek Thinking-Saying

Following on the pathway that Heidegger's work with Greek thinking has taken us, we note that it involves all of the first three moments: non-dual thinking the inseparable phenomenon; non-conceptual language; and the symbiosis of thinking and doing translation, from saying. But then! Also the Fourth Moment.

We also note that this Fourth Moment is vast and profound, for it calls into question (a) the traditional way of reading Greek philosophers, (b) the long-standing missteps in translating the Greek texts, and (c) the dominant way in which epistemology and dualistic metaphysics have encroached on the traditional way of translating and interpreting the Greeks. For these reasons, limiting the treatment of these issues to one chapter in this work of thinking is simply inadequate for dealing with this question.[1] At the same time, since this Fourth Moment is intertwined with all the other moments, it is important to at least situate the question within the thinking of this book.

Another way to say this vastness is that such an attempt as I am making here is only the tip of the iceberg – albeit an important tip. For this reason I ask the questions that are important and call for thinking, granting here at the start that this attempt is only a beginning. So here are the questions that need to be addressed, in order to get at the complex and often hidden dimensions of retrieving Greek thinking:

- Why is it necessary and useful to return to the Greeks?
- How can thinking accomplish this going-back in experience?

- How are we to understand the difference between "back to what is merely the past" in Greek philosophy and "forward to what is to be thought in a fresh way" in Greek thinking?
- How do we do this?
- How can we learn to transport ourselves (*uns über-setzen*) to what is there in "ancient" philosophy, in order to think it anew?
- How are we called to trans-late ourselves there – in order to appreciate Heidegger's translations of the Greek into German, to bring Heidegger's translations into English, and ultimately to translate the Greek into English with a meaningful freshness?
- What is it that gets re-trieved and re-enacted (*wiederholen*: to retrieve, take up again) in the fresh way that the original Greek texts call for?
- How do we understand Heidegger's central question of the truth of being – and then of beyng and beyng as enowning – in taking up the thinking-saying in the Greek texts in a fresh way?
- How can we understand/think/say the movement or dynamic that belongs to this engagement of retrieval?
- Wherein lies the difference between the traditional, inherited interpretation/translation of Greek philosophy and the fresh and accomplishing thinking from within Greek thinking?
- Finally, how can we think and say beyng when the "is" is not a thing, not a being, and still shines forth dynamically and is at work, accompanying us at every moment and emerging beyond time and space as we recognize and comprehend it?

In order to open up as much as we can to the tip of the iceberg of retrieving Greek thinking in a fresh way, I will take this pathway:

1. Listening in on Heidegger as he says the task of translating Greek thinking, using his words as signposts or guidelines.
2. Reminding us of what thinking does when it is not "about" something.

3. Applying this to the richness of possibility in retrieving Greek thinking, not from the past or some historical moment, but from what is in front of us, what beckons to us, now. This is a retrieval of what calls on us to think, *das Zudenkende*. I do this by working with the words λόγος and φύσις.
4. Translating early Greek fragments and wordings in a fresh way, revealing how traditional translations hide and cover over what these fragments say, and intimating how this fresh translation opens up a whole new way to read and think "the said" in these fragments – a revolution that emerges when hearing (a) what these early Greek thinkers did *not* say along with (b) a new possibility to hear what they *did* say. I do this in a brief look at Heidegger's own work with Anaximander and Parmenides.
5. Offering a first glimpse into this revolution when it applies to the thinking of Aristotle, a major player in how Western philosophy unfolded – revealing another if not a truer Aristotle.

A brief autobiographical note: When I was younger, it was my privilege to learn German very well and Greek somewhat less well. Then I encountered Heidegger's thinking and found it exciting and groundbreaking. And eventually I learned through reading Heidegger that the Greek philosophers were sometimes badly translated, such that it covered up the real, true, bonafide, legitimate (i.e., not fake) *Sache* (question, matter) for thinking. This idea inspired me.

From Heidegger I learned how to hear the words of thinking for what they "said" beyond the confines of the dictionary. For me this happened in a big way for English, German, Greek, and Latin – and in smaller ways with Spanish and French. Everywhere I saw how certain nuances in the original needed great care when they were translated into English, in order not to sacrifice any more than was necessary of the richness of the original – a richness that dictionaries necessarily do not recognize. Above all, I learned about what was hidden behind the Latin through which, for a long time, the Greek came into English. My passion for words and translating them only grew through hearing how Heidegger rethought and retranslated the Greek.

So when I taught Greek philosophy at the university – roughly thirty times – I demanded that the students learn the Greek alphabet. And then I did not translate – or write in Roman letters – the key words in Anaximander, Heraclitus, Parmenides, Plato, and Aristotle, so that we always stayed aware of how dangerous each translation is. Λόγος, μύθος, ἔργον, ἐνέργεια, πόλις, ἀλήθεια, ἐὸν, φύσις, ψυχή – all words whose deeper meanings have been so often covered over in the usual translations into English.[2]

Given what I just shared, in this chapter I will put all the Greek words into Greek script. This is an invitation to you, the reader, to let go of the traditional and accepted English words for the Greek words – especially for the crucial Greek words that I listed in the last paragraph. Seeing these words written in Greek script will help us not to fall so quickly into the traditional and mostly accepted translations: λόγος = logic, ψυχή = soul, and so on. Rather, it will help us be more open to what Heidegger wants to show, more open to what is *not thought* in many of the traditional words and translations. This dynamic is at the core of refreshing, rethinking retrieval of Greek philosophy.

a. Thinking When It Is Not "About"

Repeating what I said earlier – now in reference to Greek thinking – I am reminded of how thinking proceeds when it opens up the question of beyng in Greek thinking and how retrieving Greek thinking looks from within the way of thinking called for in the opening that beyng reveals.

When thinking is not "about" something, what does thinking do? Heidegger offers us a different way of thinking: Rather than thinking "about," thinking is expanding into and having a genuine experience of connection to what calls on us to think, the unthought. It says to us what is worthy of thought (*denkwürdig*) and what calls for or draws forth thinking.

A first deep hint relates to the seemingly unavoidable and not yet unresolvable tension or ἀπορία when it is beyng that calls on us. In *Grundbegriffe* Heidegger writes:

> In every attempt to think being, being always gets turned the wrong way and changed into a being – and thus what is own to being is destroyed. And yet: Being in its otherness to beings [being other than beings] cannot be denied.[3] (GA 51:82)

Beiträge opens up this field, asking this question: How can we think-say beyng/ἀλήθεια/Ereignis without stumbling over and being waylaid by this ἀπορία? Rather than letting duality sneak in here, let us think the question here – named as beyng/ἀλήθεια/ Ereignis – as an opening. An expanding. Thinking-saying the interweaving and nuance of the dynamic at-oneness of beyng as radiant emptiness.

The unresolvability of thinking-saying being is the gift that turns us toward the one-ing of beyng, of Ereignis, of ἀλήθεια. To genuinely hear this is to be gathered into beyng and how it works, even as it is no-thing.

What is called for is a thinking that does not go back and forth between differences, but one that expands into and opens out onto the clearing-opening of the onefold of beyng/ἀλήθεια/Ereignis in its own unique dynamic emptiness.

b. The Step Back ... Re-trieving Greek Thinking

In the essay "*Die onto-theo-logische Verfassung der Metaphysik*" Heidegger writes:

> For us the requirement for the dialogue with the historical tradition is ... to enter the power of the earlier thinking. But we do not look for the power in what has already been thought, but rather in an unthought dimension, from which the thought receives the space that is own to it ... The requirement of the unthought does not lead to incorporating what was formerly thought into a higher development and systematization

that outpaces what was thought. Rather it demands that traditional thinking be released into what was still preserved [unthought] being afforded from the past [*sein noch aufgespartes Gewährnis*]. This pervades the tradition originarily [*anfänglich*], always holds sway upfront without, however, having been thought expressly and as the starting [*das An-fangende*].*

*Marginal note: *Starting*: Ereignis, [*An-fang*: Ereignis]. (GA 11:58)

Here the holding sway of what was is not "in the past and perhaps dissolved" and irrevocable. Everything that belongs to beyng is without an existence or a presence that can disappear and thus can never be simply over with, in the past. Therefore, what here holds sway (what is swaying as such, no-thing), is always already and always still outstanding (is still pending). For Heidegger the holding sway is "the still swaying from afar, different from what is merely past and gone away [*im Unterschied zum nur Vergangenen das fernher noch Wesende*]."[4]

In "*Die Herkunft der Kunst und die Bestimmung des Denkens*" Heidegger says:

> The step back is necessary. But back to where? Back into the starting [*Anfang*] ... But this step back does not mean that the old Greek world has to be restored in some way and that thinking should seek refuge in the presocratic philosophers.
>
> The step back means: Pulling thinking back from the world civilization – distancing itself from this civilization without denying it – and getting involved in what at the start of Western thinking had to remain yet unthought, while at the same time it was already named there and thus set in motion for our thinking.[5]

Retrieving Greek thinking is about this pulling back from the cultural overlays, what Heidegger here calls "world civilization." Not to repeat, but to retrieve the originary possibilities in Greek thinking.

Back to the start ... Thinking's return ... and getting involved in what at the start (not the beginning in time, but the "timeless" and always current starting) of Western thinking remained unthought

… but at the same time was named and thus intimated or hinted at for our thinking.

In *Gedachtes* (GA 81, 59) Heidegger says:

> ***wieder**-holen – sagt: das ursprüngliche*
> *hin zu – in ihm her aus*
> *"holen" – als **Ver-sammeln***
> $\qquad\qquad\qquad$ Λόγος

> *Re*-trieving [getting it *back*] – says:
> "fetching" the originary –
> in moving out from it –
> [fetching] as *gathering*
> $\qquad\qquad\qquad$ Λόγος

How are we to understand this? We return to the start – do it again – retrieving the originary, from within the start, and moving out from it, to think what calls for thinking (*das Zu-denkende*). Retrieving afresh. Retrieving what the Greek words have to say, in our experience of thinking-saying. This means to think and to say beyng, to let it get said in its freshness.

As we will see soon, this means to uncover the veils that the traditional translations and interpretations have laid on these words. And the proof, as well as the way, is to let the Greek words be read and said for what they themselves reveal-say.

In *Aristoteles, Metaphysik* Θ, *1–3* (GA 33:192–3) Heidegger says:

> It is about the How of the starting, which is the key here, and about the origins of the How from within the empowering of possibility [*aus dem Vermögen*, verbal and active].
>
> We must always bring these phenomena to mind in a new [fresh] way and let the whole wonder that lies in them be compelling. If in doing this we go beyond what is said in Aristotle, that happens, not in order to improve on what is said there or anything like that, but rather for the time being in order simply to understand it in the first place … The very understanding … depends entirely on the degree of

understanding penetration of the whole context [*Zusammenhang*] of the phenomena in question.

For Heidegger it is a matter of the origins of the start (*Anfang*) precisely from within the power, the potential – from what in the starting (also named as the second beginning) did not come to light in the thinking (or got lost in metaphysics). What is more originarily prevailing is what still needs to be thought and what makes the whole wonder that lies in it compelling: beyng.

If we understand that translation is doing philosophy and always involves interpretation, how does this work of retrieving Greek thinking unto what is to be thought (*das Zu-Denkende*) and unto the sayable (*das Zu-Sagende*) play out in "translating"?

First, Heidegger has taught us how many of the translations of Greek thinkers "read into" what the Greeks said, without carefully thinking through what the Greeks thought.

Second, the question for us is to see to it that our thinking is true to what calls for thinking. It is not to establish whether the Greek thinker actually thought this or that, but rather to heed that which calls on us to think.

Third, we test the fittingness of Heidegger's translations of Greek words in accord with our experience of the phenomenon, of the no-thing dynamic, and our critical thinking. Every critical thinker is called to come to terms with Heidegger's translations of the Greek. The most important question is not whether Heidegger is "perfect" or "correct" in every one of his attempts. First of all, there is no "perfect" translation. And when some people call Heidegger's translations "doing violence," where is the measure for that assessment? It is important to know what is required, and that follows from our experience of the question and the dynamic and from our critical thinking. The question then is: Does our translation of the Greek words fit this measure? With that background we test what works "entirely on the degree of understanding penetration of the whole context [*Zusammenhang*] of the phenomena in question" (GA 33: 193). This "whole context" includes the experience of what shows itself, the showing, and our thinking involvement – altogether as a non-dual dynamic.

Fourth, more important than Heidegger's translation of specific Greek words is his challenge to us (a) to recognize how the traditional translations are inadequate or unfit and (b) to make an honest attempt to re-trieve Greek thinking and saying, with the caution that we must pay heed to the words and to what is to be thought as the measure for a "genuine" retrieval.

There are at least three levels to consider when learning how to "retrieve" Greek thinking. First, we need to remember the vastness of the context of their saying language. For example, the style at the time was epic stories. We see this in the setting in Parmenides Fragment 1: The goddess Aletheia meets a young inquirer on the road. And in Fragment 2 it is the goddess Peithous who is invoked. So we see that the philosophical discourse is not a *tractatus*/treatise à la Wittgenstein, nor is it a methodical unfolding of the thought à la Kant. We can say about Parmenides: Here too thinking takes place. And for sure, within this style of narrative, philosophy does take place.

Second, the more nuances there are to words and the more words used to say the nuanced, the richer the language and the thinking. This goes both ways: one Greek word has many meanings, and what is to be thought can be said in many words. (This will be elucidated later under the subsection "Heidegger's Words on Translating the Greeks.")

Third, retrieving Greek thinking is not repeating the Greeks. Heidegger tells us that we think the issue from where we are. He is reading Greek saying-thinking from within the saying and the said, thus not trying to repeat the Greeks in what they said "literally" – if indeed they even ever said "literally"! As he goes about this task of retrieving from the future, sometimes his fresh translations into German seem so obvious, while at other times they raise questions for us (to have that Greek word be expressed in this German word). Heidegger often grants that at first sight this may seem to be the case.

Heidegger has taught us to appreciate how many of the translations from the Greek – into Latin, German, English – have "read into" what the Greeks were saying, without thinking through carefully what the Greeks thought. The issue for us is to bring *das*

Zudenkende to bear on our thinking: What in the words calls on us to think? Not to establish whether or not Aristotle has actually thought this or how he might have thought it, but rather what calls on us to think.

In his lecture course on *Aristotle's Metaphysics* Θ, *1–3*, Heidegger writes that "it is a matter of the ownmost 'how' of the beginning/start [*Anfang*] and of its background/origin [*Herkunft*]" (GA 33:192). Then he says:

> We must always bring these phenomena to mind anew and let the whole wonder that lies in them come into play. If by doing that we go beyond what Aristotle has said, this takes place, not to improve on what is said there and such, but first simply to understand what it is all about. Thus it does not matter in what manner and form of expression Aristotle for his part may have carried out the observations necessary here. Indeed, the understanding ... depends on the degree of comprehending penetration of the whole context of the phenomena being talked about. (GA 33:192–3)

Gathering these matters up, we can say: (a) We test the appropriateness of Heidegger's translations of Greek words according to our experience of the matter for thinking and to our critical thinking. Heidegger does not have to be perfect and correct in every one of his attempts in order to show what is called for. (b) We test what works by "the degree of comprehending penetration of the whole context of the phenomena being talked about." (c) More important than Heidegger's translations of specific Greek words is his call for us to recognize our traditional translations as misguided and to confidently try our hand at retrieving Greek thinking and saying – with the caveat that we too must heed the matter to be thought (*das Zudenkende*) as the measure for a "true" retrieval.

In my own assessment, Heidegger's readings of Anaximander, Parmenides, Heraclitus, and Aristotle show the most radical break with the traditional interpretations of Greek thinkers. I will try to show this (a) by listening to Heidegger's own words on translating the Greeks, (b) by taking a brief look at two core words in Greek philosophy, λόγος and φύσις, (c) by taking a brief look at the saying of Anaximander, (d) by working through a small text on sayings of Parmenides that Heidegger worked through and read at the end of the Seminar in Zähringen in 1973, and (e) by working through Heidegger's own thinking on Aristotle and δύναμις and ἐνέργεια, from *Aristotle's Metaphysics* Θ 1–3. All together these are attempts to show how Heidegger's opening up a new path for translating Greek philosophy renewed and reinvigorated English translations of the Greeks.

c. Heidegger's Words on Translating the Greeks

First, from *Parmenides* (GA 54:16–17):

> The Greeks call what we like to "translate" with the word *truth*: ἀλήθεια.[6] But if we translate the Greek word "literally," then it says "*Unverborgenheit*" [disclosure, non-concealment, coming out of hiddenness]. It looks as if "literally translating" consists merely in recreating for the Greek word the corresponding German word. With that the literal translation already ends. But translating is not exhausted in such recreating of "words" – which then appear in one's own language as artificial and uncomely. If we simply replace the Greek word ἀλήθεια with the German *Unverborgenheit*, we are not yet translating. We come to that [translating] only when the word to be translated, *Unverborgenheit*, translates us [carries us over] into the region and kind of experience from within which the Greek world – and in this case the originary thinker Parmenides – says the word ἀλήθεια. Thus it remains a conceited game with words if we – as has recently become the fashion – simply render ἀλήθεια with *Unverborgenheit*, but then simultaneously give this word *Unverborgenheit* (which now replaces the word *Wahrheit*) just any meaning that comes to us at any given moment from the later usage of the word *Wahrheit* ...[7]
>
> With that, what is meant by *Unverborgenheit* ... what we have to think with the name ἀλήθεια is not yet experienced, let alone held fast in a rigorous thinking.

Then, from *Heraklit* (GA 55:45):

> In the case of translating the words of Heraclitus, the need is great. Here trans*lating* becomes *trans*lating [crossing over] to another shore, one that is hardly known and lies on the other side of a wide stream … Translations in the realm of the exceptional word of poi-etic saying and of thinking are always in need of interpretation [*auslegungsbedürftig*], because they are themselves an interpretation. Such translations can then introduce interpretation or complete them. But it is precisely the completing translation of Heraclitus' words that must necessarily remain as obscure as the original word.

Earlier I mentioned that there are nuances to words and that words say these nuances in ways that make language and thinking richer. As I said there, one Greek word can have many meanings and what is to-be-thought can be said in many words.

d. Retrieving the Words Λόγος and Φύσις

Let us take two significant examples. First λόγος. In many translations of Aristotle the word λόγος is reduced to – by being named as – "account" and "rational account."

But wait! There are so many meanings for the one Greek word λόγος. Looking through several Greek dictionaries, I find the following words/definitions for λόγος: the word by which the inner thought is expressed as well as the inner thought itself; a saying, speaking, that which is said or spoken; word, language, name; mere utterance (no action); sentence, statement; dialogue, conversation, discussion; talking about a person; a saying, report, narrative; prose writing; oratory; the right to speak (as in "giving someone the word"); that which is laid out in reason or logic (proposition, principle; articulation).

There are many texts where Heidegger (a) has questioned the traditional translation and interpretation of the Greek λόγος and (b) offers an opening for us to think λόγος in its rich possibility, one that has become hidden in our inherited translations and interpretations of Greek philosophy. The question raised here is so encompassing

Fourth Moment 111

that it needs its own book. So what I now present are only hintings of the way that needs to be opened up in/for thinking.

The text *"Logos (Heraklit, Fragment 50)"* in *Vorträge und Aufsätze* (GA 7)* offers us a lot to think through in this question. Along with the other two essays in this third part of *Vorträge und Aufsätze* (*"Moira [Parmenides, Fragment VIII:34–41]"* and *"Heraklit, Fragment 16"*) the *Logos* text tackles the move from the first beginning of Greek philosophy to the "other beginning," namely there where the "starting" is still open to our thinking, being not just past and gone but in front of us for vibrant and fresh considerations. What I present here is meant to indicate these questions. To "answer" them – if one can even really "answer" them – belongs to another project.

> We take what λόγος is from λέγειν. What does λέγειν say? Everyone who knows the language knows that λέγειν means: saying and speaking; λέγειν as saying/revealing [*aussagen*] and λεγόμενον as what is said [*das Ausgesagte*]. (214)

This takes us beyond the simplistic notion that λόγος is about reason or logic. Then Heidegger moves beyond λόγος as saying to λόγος as gathering:

> Ὁ λόγος, the laying: the sheer letting-lie-there-together of that which, in its lying, lies there as it is, out of itself. Thus λόγος emerges [*west*, holds sway] as the sheer drawing-together, gathering laying. (221)

Having opened λόγος to the saying and then gathering aspects of what the word says in Greek, we find ourselves in unfamiliar territory. Here Heidegger says:

> The translation of λέγειν as letting-gathered-lying-there and λόγος as gathering-lay may seem strange. But it is healthier for thinking to wander into the strange instead of setting-up in what is familiar and known. Apparently Heraclitus alienated his contemporaries in a wholly

---

* Numbers in parentheses in this section refer to this volume.

other way by interweaving the words λέγειν and λόγος – words that they were familiar with – into such a saying [λέγειν as letting-gathered-lying-there and λόγος as gathering-lay] and by making λόγος the leading word for his thinking. (231)

Here Heidegger shows not only how estranging this might be for us today, but also how estranging it may have been for Heraclitus's contemporaries. In any case it calls for a renewed and fresh look at how to translate the Greek word into our language and then how to think and say it.

Second, φύσις. This Greek word usually gets translated as "nature" (Latin *natura*). And the concept of physics stems from this Greek word. The traditional, inherited meaning of this Greek word is: physical nature or material. Going back to the so-called Presocratics, tradition calls them "physiologoi" and maintains that Greek philosophy (all the way from the early Greek thinkers through Aristotle) focuses on the physical/material elements (Thales, Anaximenes, Democritus), referring to objects of nature or atoms – above all physical. The tradition says that some early Greek thinkers focused on the four material elements – fire, water, air, earth – which, in the later periods, got reduced to the physical. (Above all, it is important to recognize how this limiting view was carried over in the very translations from the Greek.) And when Anaximander holds that all of these elements originally arose from the ἄπειρον, the "boundless" or "the infinite," this is taken to be something like a primal mass – and is traditionally and usually still considered physical. And we tend to interpret all of this as a very primitive philosophical speculation, as if they were not able to think beyond these "simple" concepts.

Thinking *beyond* this limitation means going beyond the traditional "reducing to the physical" and retrieving another saying and another translation of what these elemental words of Greek thinking "say." If φύσις names a dynamic that is not reduced to the physical, then it points to the no-form and no-thing of the deep swaying of beyng – or to the non-dual dynamic of radiant emptiness.

When I check dictionaries for the meaning of the Greek word φύσις, I get, first of all, "nature," then "natural order." Over time the knowledge of "nature" or φύσις changed into a natural science about matter and its motion in or through physical space and time. Even Einstein, who discovered the curvature of space, thus space as dynamic – and then space as the fourth dimenstion of "space-time" – never abandoned the idea that this space is still physical. As we have inherited it, the discipline of physics is about the basic principles of the physical world in which we live.

For sure Aristotle thought beyond this simplistic world view of φύσις. But the dominant paradigm that came after him has carried this reduction forward, in such a way that it still dominates our understanding of "nature" as about the physical.

My observation is that some of today's theoretical or quantum physicists understand that this limitation leaves much out of the picture and that these physicists in their honesty begin to think how the way things are in the universe involves something that is not limited to substances in the world that are merely physical. (This theme will come up in the Fifth Moment, to stress that which is not physical – the objectively existing world does not exist; not elementary particles but elemental symmetries; what we call real cannot be regarded as real; matter comes from force, behind this force is an ungraspable dynamic that is beyond the physical. With this move within quantum physics, the cutting-edge thinking by some physicists moves outside the limiting realm of seeing the Greek φύσις as "merely" nature as physical nature.[8] But, even as they move beyond the limitations of a dualistic physical world, they are often hampered by the language that they as physicists have at their disposal, to think/say this "beyond." Is it possible that we thinkers can help the physicists to name the physics that goes beyond the merely physical? Help them to see how already in Greek thinking there is this opening, which today's physicists are seeing for the first time? Help them in their retrieval?)

But what if Aristotle and the Greeks in general were on to something "beyond" the physical and more like the no-thing dynamic of emptiness? What if theirs was a thinking that was not limited to or defined by what is static/inert or the dualistic (over against mind or ψυχή)? What if philosophers and scholars who came after the Greek thinkers "read into" and thus reduced the Greek words to something like a thing as merely physical? To say it another way, what if, while saying that everything is water or fire or air, we retrieve the possibility that these word-images in early Greek thinking come from a thinking not limited to the physical and the dualistic?

In *Einführung in die Metaphysik* Heidegger says that φύσις

> has nothing at all to do with a naturalistic construal. Beings as such in the whole is φύσις – i.e, has as own to it the character of an emerging-abiding prevailing [*aufgehend-verweilende Walten*]. This is then experienced first and foremost as that which in a way comes up and intrudes [*sich aufdrängt*] in the most immediate fashion and which later signifies φύσις in a narrower sense. (GA 40:19)

Φύσις is not simply something like nature as substance or thing or being; it is an emerging-abiding prevailing or holding sway. It is *Wesung*, that deep swaying that is the dynamic emptiness, no-thing whatsoever, which contains and sustains all appearances or phenomena: all things in the way that they are, namely phenomena in their being bound non-dually in the non-dual dynamic of radiant emptiness.

For these reasons, then, Heidegger's thinking calls on us to pursue this path of refreshing our reading and translating and interpreting and thinking the possibilities hidden in the Greek texts. It is in this sense that Heidegger writes, "*Aristotle's* **Physics** *is the hidden – and therefore never fully thought through – fundamental book of Western philosophy*" (GA 9:242, Heidegger's italics).

e. Taking a Brief Look into the Saying of Anaximander

If we go beyond the traditional translation and interpretation of the Greeks – beyond seeing Greek philosophy as something that began in the past and is only in the past (the first beginning) – then we move into the possibility of thinking "anew" what is held in the

Greek words as "starting" thinking, getting this "other" thinking underway (the second beginning).

To see how this "retrieval" can happen, I will look at Anaximander, Parmenides, and Aristotle. In a sense this is a small look at how the retrieval works. Glimpses, if you will.

First we look at the traditional reading of Anaximander, which has dominated the reading and interpretation of Anaximander for many years of Western philosophy. Specifically, we look at Anaximander's key word τὸ ἄπειρον in the fragment ἀρχή τῶν ὄντων τὸ ἄπειρον, as it is presented in Kirk and Raven's *The Presocratic Philosophers*. They present three versions of Theophrastus's account of what Anaximander meant by τὸ ἄπειρον, which they call "originative substance."[9]

Anaximander: ἀρχή τῶν ὄντων τὸ ἄπειρον.

1. Simplicius and Hippolytus:

    Anaximander ... said that the principle [ἀρχή] ... of existing things was the ἄπειρον, being the first to introduce/use this name of the material principle.

2. Hippolytus:

    ... Anaximander ... said that the material principle [ἀρχή] of existing things was ... the ἄπειρον, being the first to use this name of the material principle.

3. Plutarch:

    ... Anaximander ... said that the ἄπειρον contained the whole cause of the coming-to-be and destruction of the world ...

Further interpretations of Anaximander's fragment, as presented by Kirk and Raven:

Burnet on Theophrastus:

... the material principle [ἀρχή] ...] [is named] ἄπειρον ... [Anaximander] is the "first to name the substratum of the opposites as the material cause."[10]

Kirk and Raven:

> Aristotle ... took ἄπειρον ... to mean "spatially infinite." ... Theophrastus seems to have felt that Anaximander had given his primary substance a name which described its spatial property ...[11]

Reading from Karl Borman's entry "Anaximander of Miletus" in *Handwörterbuch der Philosophie*, ed. W.D. Rehfus:

> [Anaximander] was the first one to use the name ἄπειρον (unbounded, indefinite [*Unbegrenztes, Unbestimmtes*]) for primal matter [*Urstoff*], because this primal material is inconceivable and with regard to its quality or nature [*Beschaffenheit*] is indeterminate. That is, the ἄπειρον is not identical with any elementary particle or any mixture of elementary particles. Bound with this thought is that it is nonperishable/immortal. As such the apeiron is divine – and encompasses and "steers" [*steuert, lenkt*] everything.[12]

Conclusion for all of this: ἄπειρον is primal matter, *materia* (even it it is "divine" and "immortal"!), spatially infinite substance. It is primal, unformed substance, According to the tradition we could say that Anaximander understood ἄπειρον to be an infinite material source, such that the genesis of everything in the world would never suffer from a lack of matter. Note the paradox here: ἄπειρον is both primal matter, material, substance *and* infinite, indeterminate, unformed – and even divine! Putting both of those descriptions together – something material but also unbounded – it is difficult to comprehend what ἄπειρον "really is"! How is it that for centuries we have not been concerned about this contradiction?

We will now try to *retrieve* what Anaximander wanted to say. For sure he wanted to say more than primal matter and substance. We will show that it is other than a thing/being and thus names what Heidegger calls beyng and what I am calling in this work radiant emptiness, a non-dual dynamic that is no-thing.

Let us now turn back to Heidegger's reading of this Anaximander fragment (*Grundbegriffe*, GA 51:107–13).*

---

* Numbers in parentheses in this section refer to these pages.

First, the Greek word ἀρχή is not yet used in the sense of principle. On the other hand, the Greek word is an old word with many senses. It does mean "that from which something proceeds." But here it does not say the beginning that, once it has been left, is no longer – that is, nothing is left behind. (This would be one way to say what Heidegger means by the first beginning.)

Here Heidegger reads the word ἀρχή to say: that from which something proceeds, but

> in the proceeding out and its emergence it holds/retains precisely the provision of the going ... The ἀρχή is the priming of the manner and region of the emerging. The priming of the going leads out but still remains as the start and stays itself by itself. (108)

Ἀρχή is not the beginning that is left behind in the movement forward. The ἀρχή releases the movement forward and what moves forward (gets it going, the start), "but in such a way that what is released remains held in the ἀρχή as setting-things-out [*Verfügung*]" (108). This names the "other beginning," the start, what gets it going, what starts it. And that dynamic is no-thing.

Heidegger then turns to the word ἄπειρον – and uses the same German word to say this: *Verfügung*: Setting-things-out. *Verfügen*: dispose, release, issue forth, set things properly, bestow. With emergent things (that which emerges) we have to think what setting-things-out (*Verfügung*) is for what emerges (things, beings), insofar as it emerges and how ... As with ἀρχή, ἄπειρον refers to the threefold way of egressing, staying, and opening-up the realm ... ἀρχή has to do with being. Therefore ἄπειρον cannot be thought as a being (110).

It is not about some generic material. Rather, with setting-things-out (*Verfügung*) it is a question of beyng, namely ἄπειρον "is" not – is no-thing – but it sways or holds sway. Heidegger: "Τὸ ἄπειρον is the ἀρχή of being. Τὸ ἄπειρον is the refusing of boundary and refers only to being, and that means in Greek to emerging" (110).

> *Die Verfügung ist dem Anwesenden das der Grenze Wehrende.* (112)
> For what emerges, setting-things-out is that which protects from any boundary.

The difference and distance between Heidegger's reading of Anaximander and the traditional interpretations could not be more stark. And the question becomes: If one hears the to-be-thought in the Greek words, which reading mirrors the Greek word and its saying? Most importantly, how can one justify limiting the saying of ἀρχή and ἄπειρον to the physical? To substance, which is by definition unmoving, without any dynamic?

f. Working through a Small Text by Heidegger on Ἀλήθεια in Parmenides

Traditionally, when studying the "Presocratics," it is an established "fact" that Heraclitus is the philosopher of becoming and Parmenides the philosopher of unchangeable being. In this interpretation Parmenides's contribution goes something like this: Being is unchangeable, indivisible, independent ... and in accord with that: logical. Along with this interpretation goes the thought that Parmenides had to discover a new vocabulary for logic and logical thinking.

Nietzsche holds this view of the utter distinction between the static being of Parmenides and the dynamic becoming of Heraclitus. Nietzsche describes Parmenides thus:

> A prophet of truth but, as it were [over against Heraclitus], formed not from fire but from ice ... Parmenides had ... at one time a moment of the purest abstraction, unadulterated by any reality and totally bloodless ... [and] with logical rigidity he transformed nature into a completely petrified – almost into a thinking machine.
>
> From this method emerges a defiant capability for abstract-logical procedure, one that is closed off from the whisperings of the senses.
>
> All of that medley and colorfulness of the world known by experience – the change in its qualities, the order of its ups and downs – is mercilessly tossed to the side as mere appearance [false, pseudo] and delusion. And there is nothing to learn there, thus every effort to get through to the artifice of the world, thoroughly void [inane] and swindled, as it were, through the senses.[13]

In the context of the two beginnings, this traditional reading of Parmenides belongs to the first beginning, where the Greeks are interpreted as having made "primitive" efforts to understand the world. This way of "going back" to the Greeks takes their words and thinking as an effort – successful or not – that remains in the past as past, thus left behind and moved beyond.

Heidegger's reading of Parmenides, on the other hand, is the way of the second, other beginning, *Anfang*, which I have translated as a starting, a getting things going. As such, the thinking in the Greek texts still carries the fresh possibility that we, in our going back, take up anew the words and thinking, for what they still offer to us to think. Thus the starting of the second beginning is about this vibrant renewal or refreshing of what calls us to think, itself outside chronological time and the past as past. And this renewal shows itself in the Greek words themselves, in their possibility – *which the words themselves manifest*.

In order to show what Heidegger does with Parmenides, I turn to the protocol of the Seminar in Zähringen in 1973 (*Seminare*, GA 15), especially to the brief text that Heidegger read to the participants of the seminar at the end of the last session (394–407).*

Before reading the small text on Parmenides, Heidegger explains the difference between "returning" to Parmenides and "turning" to his thinking. He tells the seminar participants:

> As I see it, entering the realm of what is ownmost to Da-sein [entering what is Da-sein's ownmost, *Wesensbereich*] – the entry that would make possible the experience of inabiding in the clearing-opening of being[14] – can take place only with a detour of returning to the start [*Anfang*].
>
> But this return is not a "return to Parmenides." It is not about going back to Parmenides. Nothing more is needed than to turn to Parmenides. (394)
>
> It is a matter of getting into the right way of hearing Parmenides. (395)

Let us go step by step, reading Parmenides. The title of Heidegger's short piece is "Ἀληθείης εὐκυκλέος ἀτρεμὲς ἦτορ"

---

* Numbers in parentheses in this part are from this text.

(Fragment I, line 29). Burnet's translation in English: Unshaken heart of well-rounded truth.[15] The traditional German translation that Heidegger gives (without naming his source) is *Der Wahrheit, der wohlgerundeten, unerschütterliches Herz*: The unshakeable heart of truth, well-rounded truth (403).

First we look at the word ἀλήθεια – or ἀ-λήθεια: *Un-verborgenheit*: dis-closure, un-concealment. For sure not truth understood as validity of statements of propositions. But what does unconcealment say?

> In order to better understand the revealing that reigns in the unconcealment, we focus on the epithet εὐκυκλέος. Well-rounded is something that we take as property of things. But ἀλήθεια/*Unverborgenheit*/disclosing is not a thing or a being. We get closer to its bearing [*Walten*] if we translate εὐκυκλέος as "affordingly encircling [*schicklich umkreisend*]." (404)

Again, focusing on the word εὐκυκλέος, Heidegger writes:

> Εὐκυκλέος is usually understood as "well-rounded" and then is meant as property of things. But since here the word signifies ἀλήθεια and disclosing [*Entbergen*] is nothing thinglike, it cannot be translated in this way. It must be understood differently. Therefore we think εὐκυκλέος as "the well-enfolding, affordingly encircling." (396)

Next, what does ἀτρεμὲς ἦτορ say? The "never trembling heart" – "that which pulses throughout and attunes the revealing, but itself stays, lasts and sways" (404).

What is this? This staying-in-itself and lasting heart, which pulses through and attunes the unconcealing, gets it going, "activates" it? Heidegger turns to Fragment VI, 1: ἔστι γαρ εἶναι: "It is, namely, being." But that makes it sound as if εἶναι /sein/being is "a being."

Here we have to pay attention to what the Greek says. Do we "think the Greek saying of the words ἔστι and εἶναι"? Even more: "Using the words *ist* and *sein* [English: *is* and *being*], do we even sufficiently think what was intended?" (404–5).

The whole line reads: Χρὴ τὸ λέγειν τ' ἔμμεναι· ἔστι γαρ εἶναι. We might offer an initial translation like this: It needs be that what can be thought and spoken of is; for it is possible for it to be. Heidegger notes that, without thinking, the usual translations take ἐόν to be a being, something that is (ἔστι). But is that thinking the Greek words in Greek fashion? What if these words are words of being (or even beyng) and thus no-thing but rather empty and a dynamic?

We will soon focus on the words ἐὸν ἔμμεναι. But one sees how the English translation hardly takes any of these two words into account.[16] They are translated by the single word: *is*. And ἔστι γαρ εἶναι is translated as "for it is possible for it to be"!

> Thought in its Greek way, the word εἶναι says: *anwesen/emerge*. This verb speaks more precisely. It brings us into a greater revealing and nearer to the issue to be thought. In accord with this, we must render ἔστι γαρ εἶναι as: "emerges, that is to say emerging" [*anwest nämlich anwesen*]. (405)

The name for the issue for thinking in Parmenides is τὸ ἐόν.

> This fundamental word names neither beings nor bare being. We must think τὸ ἐόν as participle, as verbal. Then the saying says: "*anwesend anwesen selbst*" emergent emerging itself. (405)
>
> The question is: Where and how does emerging emerge [*Wo und wie west anwesen an*]? Answer: "to ..." into *Unverborgenheit* [revealing-non-hiding-disclosure]. If this is how it is, then ἐόν is the "heart" of *Unverborgenheit*. (405)
>
> In accord with this, we cannot envision ἀλήθεια as empty, rigid openness. Rather we must think it as the τὸ ἐόν, the "emergent itself emerging" suitably encircling non-concealing. (406)

The first thing that none of these words of Parmenides says is rigidity or unchanging static being. These words do not say "beings/things" and do not say "static." Rather, when heard in the way that the words themselves afford to us, they are all saying something dynamic, a dynamic emptiness, and beyng that is no-thing. Second, what is the way or access to this thinking, if it is not the "logical" way that scholars of Greek philosophy have assumed until now? Parmenides gives us a hint, and Heidegger points it out to us, thinkingly:

> In Fragment I, 28, the goddess says: Χρεὼ δε σε πάντα πυθέσθαι: "but it is necessary for you to experience everything [*nötig aber ist Dir, alles zu erfahren*]." (406)

For Heidegger this speaks to the way that originary thinking needs to go: an unusual path is called for, one that takes care for the unusual saying that is called for. What is called for is an experience/*erfahren*, literally going-all-the-way-into – not a simple sense perception, but "the pure (non-sensuous) beholding [seeing]" (406).

What is to be purely beholden – purely, as in: not mixed with perceptions, opinions, judgments?[17]

Heidegger ends the short text with this remark:

> *Das anwesend: anwesen selbst durchstimmt die schicklich entbergend es umkreisende Unverborgenheit.*
> The emergent: emerging itself attunes through and through the suitably revealing disclosing that encircles it [emergent emergence]. (407)

In thinking (as pure beholding) beyng (as emergent emerging), the question of being (the place of its opening) is expanded beyond beings (as beings, *Seiendes*, ὄν, *ens*) and beyond being (as *Sein, im Sinne des Seins*) to ἐόν: the no-thing non-dual dynamic of emergent emerging (*Seyn*, beyng, enowning).

Now we can add this wording to the list of names for the unfolding of the question of being in Heidegger: Seyn/Ereignis/ἀλήθεια/ἐόν as emergent emerging – all names to say the dynamic at-oneness that holds being and beings, the one-ing of enowning throw of beyng to Da-sein and enowned Da-sein's throwing open the enowning throw, the non-dual disclosing/sheltering hiding and ἐόν: emergence in its emerging. The thinking of Parmenides is definitely not static being!

g. Reading Aristotle on Δύναμις and Ενέργεια, Inspired by Heidegger

Aristotle is both complicated and exciting. As we know, he discusses the same questions in various texts. We also know that his texts are uneven and also inconsistent in their elaboration. We know that some of what we have as Aristotle's texts was written by him, whereas some seems to be notes provided by his hearers. If it were simply a question of a text-based argument, then the received/inherited and traditional interpretation of Aristotle could be maintained. But this is possible only if one ignores (a) other texts and also (b) that which is so important for Heidegger: how the things are and that which goes beyond logic and thrives in the direction of experience.

Here I invite the reader to join me in looking at several places in the 8th Book of Aristotle's *Metaphysics*, to study how the English translations affect the reading and interpretation of Aristotle. The big question here is the dynamic between potentiality and actuality (also named possibility and actuality) or *from* potentiality to actuality.

The question in this section is the τέλος/goal of things or of movement. The central question here is movement/κίνησις. When observing a phenomenon or a thing, where and how does it begin (δύναμις)? Of what does the "actuality" of a phenomenon or thing consist (ἐνέργεια)? How can we understand the movement (κίνησις) of the transition from potentiality to actuality? And finally: When the whole process comes to an end – when the movement has reached its goal (τέλος), what is reached and what is this reaching? Is the end or goal an end station – an end where there is no longer anything in movement, in action, in process? Or is there always a dynamic, a movement, in this "end"? And what can we know of the phenomenon or thing at this "end"? This is the question of the Greek word ἐντελέχεια. "Literally" ἐντελέχεια says being-in-the-end: ἐν-τέλος-ἐχεῖν or ἐχεῖν in τέλος, being in the end.

The traditional interpretation, handed down to us through the Scholastics and into the modern period of philosophy, is roughly this: κίνησις takes place only in the transition or crossing from δύναμις to ἐνέργεια or ἐντελέχεια. Movement takes place only in the crossing from potentiality to actuality or completedness. It is rather simple. If movement is only in the transition, then the "from where" (δύναμις) and the "to where" (ἐνέργεια) are not in movement – in the one case a static "not yet" and in the other a static "no longer."

When the same thing cannot be in actuality as result and in the crossing, then it is evident that the movement takes place in the crossing or transition and not in the actuality – in the κίνησις or μεταβολή (change) and not in ἐνέργεια or ἐντελέχεια. This we have inherited, both in translation and in interpretation.

What we have inherited from the traditional reading/interpretation of these things seems simple. For Aristotle, in this interpretation, whatever has reached its aim or end (τέλος) – and now is a "static" reality or actuality – has as one of its conditions a "passive, inert potentiality," which is then transformed into an actuality (ἐνέργεια) through movement (κίνησις) – this end Aristotle then calls ἐντελέχεια, something completed.

This is a brief summary of the received traditional interpretation of Aristotle on these matters. But a more precise reading of Aristotle calls for a new translation and a new rendering of these components, which will then show that all three are dynamic and active – not only κίνησις but δύναμις as well as ἐνέργεια/ἐντελέχεια. Heidegger's reading and translating of these key points in Aristotle's metaphysics move in this direction. And it is based on going back to the Greek texts, to see what *they* said and thought, that is, not determined by how these texts have been translated into English in the seventeenth and eighteenth centuries.

What Heidegger's reading of Aristotle opens up is the "but." But, if/when Aristotle calls ἐντελέχεια a movement, then what? The inherited reading of Aristotle ignores this "ἐντελέχεια as movement"[18] and explains that movement can "only" be in the κίνησις and not in actuality (ἐνέργεια). Such an interpretation/reading has to see ἐνέργεια as a result that is completed, thus no longer in movement.

But when we take what is said in Aristotle – and meant "so obviously" in a fresh way – when we look at it anew, when we rethink it, based on hearing the word anew and away from the inherited translations – then (a) movement is not limited to the κίνησις of the crossing but is a part of the entire dynamic from δύναμις to ἐντελέχεια, (b) δύναμις is never inert, passive potentiality, but always an inborn active tendency, (c) ἐνέργεια is not the name for a finished actuality that from now on stands "without movement," but continues to work and to unfold, (d) ἐντελέχεια is in no way a finished completeness, but an ongoing being-at-work in the τέλος. Thus (e) ἐνέργεια and ἐντελέχεια are phenomenologically the same, and all three of them (δύναμις ἐνέργεια ἐντελέχεια) are always and continually active and dynamic movement: they are all of them always "at-work," that is, dynamically and in movement.[19] All is movement.

The Story of Heidegger's Influence on English Translations of Aristotle

Jacob Klein, who has been described as one of Heidegger's "star graduate students," heard Heidegger's lecture course in 1924,[20] where Heidegger showed how to rethink Aristotle's Greek in today's language. Klein knew Greek very well, and he knew Aristotle. Klein took Heidegger's wisdom regarding Aristotle as a guide for redoing the English ways of translating Aristotle's Greek. He understood well Heidegger's question: How does one translate the Greek in Greek philosophy?

Both Jacob Klein and Joe Sachs taught at St John's College in Annapolis, Maryland. Sachs tells how, along with Heidegger, Klein was an "outstanding reader" of Aristotle who

> led me [Sachs] to see that a new way of translating him [Aristotle] was necessary and possible. Jacob Klein, in his extraordinary brief essay "Aristotle: An Introduction,"[21] helped me begin to encounter Aristotle's thinking directly and genuinely.[22]

Sachs writes a remarkable paragraph about translating Aristotle into English:

> At all the most crucial places, the usual translations of Aristotle abandon English and move toward Latin. They do this because earlier translations did the same. Those earlier translators did so because their principal access to Aristotle's meaning was through Latin commentaries. The result is jargon, but that seems not to make most of the professional scholars uncomfortable; after all, by perpetuating such inaccessible English texts, they create a demand for interpreters that only they can fill. I have criticised the current state of Aristotle-translating at length in the introduction to a recent translation of my own. There it seemed necessary to explain to those familiar with other translations the many departures they were about to encounter. Here a briefer justification may suffice: My aim is to give you in translation an experience as close as I can make it to reading the original. The original is written not for specialists but for generally educated people of any sort who are willing to think hard. Where Aristotle exploits the resources of the Greek language to capture his meaning, the translation will be in bad English; where he departs from Greek usage to coin new words and novel ways of saying things, the translation will be in worse English. From the point of view of a classicist, a good English translation of a classical author is one that finds, for every word or phrase in the original, some equivalent expression that reads smoothly in our language. This may be a good practice with some kinds of writing, but philosophic meaning cannot be captured in habitual uses of language. The point of view of a professional philosopher may, however, pay too much heed to the linguistic choices that have become habitual in modern philosophy and in the secondary literature, at the expense of faithfulness to the original.[23]

I would say that – in connection with Klein's important essay, with Heidegger's putting existing translations of Aristotle into question, and with Klein's own overall understanding of Greek and of Aristotle – Sachs revolutionized the translation and study of Aristotle in English.

Sachs went on to translate many texts of Aristotle, including *Metaphysics*, *Physics*, *Nichomachean Ethics*, and *De Anima*. These translations are the backbone for retranslating Aristotle into English and thus **retrieving the thought in Aristotle's "said."** I will point to a few texts in Aristotle's *Metaphysics* where this fresh and "less Latin" way of translating Aristotle fits in with what Heidegger calls the "return" to the Greeks.

First, a chart of key words: first the Greek (in Greek letters and then transliteration), then the traditional, "received" English translation, and finally the "retrieving" translation:

Keywords from *Metaphysics*, Book Θ (IX)

Greek	Transliterated	"Received" Translation[24]	"Retrieving" Translation
δύναμις	*dynamis*	passive, inert potentiality	innate, active tendency
ἐνέργεια	*energeia*	actuality, static result	being-at-work
ἐντελέχεια	*entelecheia*	completedness, static end	being-at work-in-the-*telos*
κίνησις	*kinesis*	motion, movement	being-at-work-staying-itself dynamically
ἀρχή	*arche*	principle, beginning	active source/origin
μεταβολή	*metabole*	change	change-over, transformation
οὐσία	*ousia*	substance	thinghood

Using passages from Book Θ of the *Metaphysics*, I will compare the "received," traditional English translations with the "retrieving" translations. Notice how the "received" translations (both in my chart and in the various traditional translations of Aristotle) use words that are static and disconnecting – with the obvious exception of κίνησις and μεταβολή, which are words of motion – whereas the words in the "retrieving" translations are more dynamic. The sources for the various translations are as follows:

> Sachs, Joe, trans. *Aristotle's Metaphysics* (Green Lion Press, 2002).
> Ross, David, trans. *Aristotle's Metaphysics* (Oxford University Press, 1924).
> Loeb Classical Library, *Aristotle: Metaphysics*, Books I–IX (Harvard University Press, 1933).
> Furth, Montgomery, trans. *Metaphysics: Zeta, Eta, Theta, Iota (VII–X)* (Hackett, 1985).

In the examples of translation that follow, please keep in mind the difference between dynamic movement and static potential or static completedness, between static substance and concrete thinghood, between ἐντελέχεια as τέλος in completion/completedness and ἐντελέχεια as being active within the end/τέλος, between ἐνέργεια as "complete reality" and ἐνέργεια as being-at-work. Note here the startling juxtaposition of the traditional, "received" translation and the "retrieving" translation. Before looking carefully at the various translations, I summarize here:

Received translation:

> "Potentiality" (δύναμις) is "passive, inert potentiality." "Actuality" (ἐνέργεια) is derived from "activity" and has the meaning of "complete reality" or points to the completed reality (ἐντελέχεια). When complete(d), it is static, a static "result."

Retrieving translation:

> The τέλος/end is work (ἔργον) and work is being-at-work (ἐνέργεια) and "the phrase being-at-work is meant by reference to work and extends to being-at-work-staying-complete" – so that in ἐνέργεια the activity of things forms a **continuous state of being-at-work** and their "completion" or ἐντελέχεια is a **being unceasingly at-work**.[25]

1. **1045b27   οὐσία/ousia**

    SACHS: What concerns being of the primary sort, toward which all the other ways of attributing being are traced back, has been discussed, namely what concerns *thinghood* [οὐσία].
    ROSS: [O]f that which is primarily and to which all the other categories of being are referred – i.e., *substance*.
    LOEB: We have discussed being in the primary sense – that is, *substance*.
    FURTH: That which primarily is ... – that is, substance.

2. **21045b32   δύναμις/dynamis ... ἐντελέχεια/being-at-work-in-telos ... ἔργον/at-work**

    SACHS: ... but in another way in virtue of potency and complete being-at-work and of a doing-something.
    ROSS: ... in another way distinguished in respect of potency and complete reality, and of function.
    LOEB: ... in accordance with potentiality and actuality and function.
    FURTH: ... in another way with respect to potentiality and completedness, and with respect to function.

3. **1046a10&15   ἀρχή/source/start of change ... δύναμις/dynamis**

    SACHS: [S]ource of change ... these potencies in turn are spoken of either as only acting or being acted upon.
    ROSS: [T]he originative source of change ... these so-called potencies are potencies either of merely acting or being acted on.
    LOEB: [O]ne primary sense of potency ... all these potentialities are so called, either because they merely act or are acted upon.
    FURTH: [O]rigin of change in another or [in itself] as qua other ... these potentialities are said [to be] either of acting or being acted-upon.

Note how Sachs' translation shows δύναμις/dynamis as active and in movement. The word ὕλη, as "capable of being-worked-on," says active readiness; the "stillness" of δύναμις/dynamis is a movement. In his glossary Sachs writes that δύναμις/potency is:

> The innate tendency of anything to be at work in ways characteristic of the kind of thing it is: the way of being that belongs to material. (1050a18)[26]

A potency in its proper sense will always emerge into activity, when the proper conditions are present and nothing prevents it. (1047b35-1048a21)[27]

Ἐνέργεια is always in movement, as well:

4. 1048b18   ἐνέργεια/energeia ... ἐντελέχεια/being-at-work-in-the-*telos*

> SACHS: [O]f the actions that do have limits, none of them is itself an end, but it is among things that approach an end.[28]
>
> LOEB: [S]ince no action which has a limit is an end, but only a means to the end.
>
> ROSS: [O]f the actions which have a limit none is an end. But all are relative to the end.
>
> FURTH: [A]mong actions that have a limit [πέρας], none is a completion [τέλος], but each is the sort of thing relating to the completion.

In his glossary Sachs writes that ἐνέργεια is being-at-work. There he says:

> Activity comes to sight first as motion, but Aristotle's central thought is that all being is being-at-work ... Since the end and completion of any genuine being is its being-at-work, the meaning of the word [ἐνέργεια] converges (1047a 30–31, 1050a 22–24) with that of the following: **Being-at-work-staying-itself** (ἐντελέχεια). A fusion of the idea of completeness with that of continuity or persistence. Aristotle invents the word by combining ἐντελες (complete, full grown) with ἐχεῖν (=ἕξις, to be a certain way by the continuing effort of holding on to that condition), while at the same time punning on ἐνδελέχεια (persistence) by inserting τέλος (completion). This is a three-ring circus of a word, at the heart of everything in Aristotle's thinking, including the definition of motion. Its power to carry meaning depends on the working together of all the things Aristotle has packed into it. Some commentators explain it as meaning being-at-the-end, which misses the point entirely, and it is usually translated as "actuality," a word that refers to anything, however trivial, incidental, transient, or statice, that happens to be the case, so that everything

is lost in translation, just at the spot where understanding could begin.[29]

5. **1047a30 (ἐνέργεια/energeia) connected to ἐντελέχεια/being-at-work-in-telos**

   MALY: [T]hat which is named "at-work" (ἐνέργεια/energeia), which is connected to being-at-work-in-telos (ἐντελέχεια), belongs to movements. (ἐνέργεια *is* κίνησις!)

   SACHS: [T]he phrase being-at-work, which is designed to converge in meaning with being-at-work-staying-complete, comes to apply to other things from belonging especially to motions.

   LOEB: [T]he term, with its implication of "complete reality," has been extended from motions.

   ROSS: The word actuality, which we connect with "complete reality," has, in the main, been extended from movements.

   FURTH: [T]hat which is named "actuality" [ἐνέργεια], which is connected to completedness [ἐντελέχεια], has been extended [lit. "has proceeded"] from chiefly [applying to] the movements.

6. **1047a37 γένεσις/genesis = coming-to-be, birthing, emerging**

   SACHS: [W]hile not actively being, they would have to be in activity. For of the things that are not, some are potentially; but they are not, because they are not at-work-staying-complete.

   LOEB: [A]lthough these things do not exist actually, they will exist actually; for some non-existent things exist potentially; yet they do not exist, because they do not exist in complete reality.

   ROSS: [W]hile they do not actually exist, they would have to exist actually if they were moved. For of non-existent things some exist potentially; but they do not exist, because they do not exist in complete reality.

   FURTH: [T]hough they aren't in actuality [and thus can be thought as desired?]. For of things that are not, some are, potentially; but [still] they are not, because they are not in completedness.

I come now to the last example for comparing the two ways of reading, thinking, saying, and translating Aristotle. It is a kind of gathering of all that we have witnessed up to now. I quote the entire sentence:

7. 1050a21 τὸ γὰρ ἔργον τέλος, ἡ δὲ ἐνέργεια τὸ ἔργον, διὸ καὶ τοὔνομα ἐνέργεια λέγεται κατὰ τὸ ἔργον καὶ συντείνει πρὸς τὴν ἐντελέχειαν.

> MALY: For the ἔργον [being-at-work] is the τέλος, and ενέργεια is the ἔργον hence even the name ἐνέργεια is said with respect to the ἔργον and aims at [moves to/within] the ἐντελέχεια.
>
> SACHS: For the end is work, and the work is a being-at-work, and this is why the phrase being-at-work is meant by reference to work and extends to being-at-work-staying-complete.[30]
>
> LOEB: For the activity is the end, and the actuality is the activity; hence the term "actuality" is derived from "activity," and tends to have the meaning of "complete reality."
>
> ROSS: For the action is the end, and the actuality is the action. And so even the word actuality is derived from "action" and points to the complete reality.

Notice how the "received" translations (both in my chart and in the various traditional translations of Aristotle) use words that are static and disconnecting:

- δύναμις: passive potentiality, "mere" potency (no indication of anything "dynamic" or a "being-in-movement" as part of its being).
- ἐνέργεια: actuality, static result, complete reality.
- ἐντελέχεια: complete, static reality, completedness.

We now turn to Heidegger's own reading-thinking-saying. Retrieving or calling up Greek thinking and putting into question all of the inherited, received translations, Heidegger has shown both the limits of traditional translations as well as a rich possibility for translating and thinking anew. In his manner of retrieving Greek philosophy, Heidegger emphasizes what is ownmost in the deep sway of that which Aristotle says from within δύναμις and κίνησις and ἐνέργεια = ἐντελέχεια. Instead of reading these from any dualistic perspective, Heidegger reveals the experience-based thinking: Here everything is a dynamic one:

> If we were first to stand, spontaneously branched
> in the boughs of beyng,
> free to the wind, which keeps its secret from us,
> everything stays one.[31]

Let me finish our reading of Aristotle in translation by hearing Heidegger as he "retrieves" what Aristotle says about δύναμις and ἐνέργεια and ἐντελέχεια as names for being and "ways of being-in-movement." The "starting" for this mindful thinking comes from the final pages of Heidegger's GA 33, *Aristoteles, Metaphysik Θ 1–3. Von Wesen und Wirklichkeit der Kraft* (216–24).* To start, I quote Heidegger:

> [T]he right way of distinguishing δύναμις and ἐνέργεια can only happen with a prior and continual adhering to κίνησις. What does that mean? Nothing less than: both the presence of capability itself [δύναμις as *Vermögen*] and what is actually there [ἐνέργεια as *Wirklichkeit*, in the sense of carrying-it-out, *Vollzug*] are [both] *equally ways of being-in-movement*. (216)

As a kind of gathering – comparing the various traditional translations of Aristotle with the "retrieving" translations of Sachs and inspired by Heidegger's groundbreaking work on thinking and translating (or translating and thinking) Aristotle – I now do a reading/commentary of the last pages of Heidegger's *Aristoteles, Metaphysik Θ 1–3*. This offers a kind of gathering of this entire work up to this point, as well as a kind of transition to the last moment: time-space as ab-ground.

1. As one of the manifold ways of saying being, the interactive dynamic of δύναμις-κίνησις-ἐνέργεια/ἐντελέχεια merges in a rich inseparable dynamic. (Reminder of the non-dual inseparable way of beyng.)

---

* Numbers in parentheses in this section refer to this text.

2. What holds these three together in their inseparability is κίνησις, movement. And then δύναμις and ἐνέργεια = ἐντελέχεια show, each in its own way, two ways of being-in-movement or what we have called the dynamic. All is movement, dynamic at-oneness. For example, as Heidegger says above, "capability itself [δύναμις as *Vermögen*] and what is actually there [ἐνέργεια as *Wirklichkeit*, in the sense of carrying-it-out, *Vollzug*] are [both] *equally ways of being-in-movement*" (216).
3. The dynamic of δύναμις is called "the starting moment [*Hinausführen*, leading out] of the power [*Vermögen*, capability] itself into that to which it, as itself power, surges" (218). Heidegger gives the example of a runner in the 100 metre run. Right before the race, the runner is on the starting blocks, poised to run. We might say that the runner is not yet in motion, but we see the loose open hands, the fingers touching the ground almost pushing off. The face and eyes are tensed toward what lies ahead.

   The runner is poised to start running. This poise is already filled with readiness. So one can say that the runner's pose is far removed from a pose without movement, the runner's pose is an active anticipation "away from the position." I might say that the runner is in active anticipation. Its way of being is as full preparedness and as leading-out (as the dynamic "start").[32]
4. We are called to think Aristotle's words here "beyond any abstract deliberation." We are called to think-say "what is said by bringing it forth from out of what shows itself to the truly philosophizing look/glance" (221). The true philosophical look is to the phenomenon, which becomes manifest in *empeiria*: experience. This is non-conceptual.
5. Ἐνέργεια says: being-at-work (*am-Werke-sein*). That is its way of being. Its way of being is being-in-movement as actualizing.
6. Ἐντελέχεια says: holding itself in staying complete (*Sich-in-Fertigkeit-halten*). Being actively adroit and ready.[33] Here movement shows itself "as that whereby something is in

motion [in full gear], something is at work, something is going on, happening" (218).

The dynamic of movement is everywhere. Everything is inseparably interconnected, a onefold. We do not say this conceptually or dualistically. Rather we heed what shows itself and learn how to say-think it.

This is the inseparable intertwining of δύναμις and ἐνέργεια, held together by κίνησις/movement, that is, in such a way that all three are of one piece as the non-dual inseparable dynamic of being/beyng/radiant emptiness. Being is as movement and is there in the same manner.

7. If we hear all of these words as saying beyng, then we highlight how these words do not name things, beings, or concepts. Rather they say the no-thing non-dual dynamic of radiant emptiness.

We are now ready to look at and work with the fifth groundbreaking moment: time-space – and eventually timing-spacing – as ab-ground. It names a radiant dynamic that is no-thing, nothing whatsoever, and that can be experienced and worked with – as it itself is at work. This dynamic, which we have also called the dynamic of radiant emptiness, is a non-dual, non-conceptual, no-thing dynamic. This is at work as we learn to think-say timing-spacing.

This provides a useful and fitting transition: Moving from reading Aristotle and his thinking-saying the non-dual dynamic aspect of the way things are, we tackle the question of timing-spacing (progressive verb forms, participial-gerundive) as a way to say beyng/Ereignis/*logos* as gathering – all words that say the no-thing whatsoever even as it emerges, no-thing whatsoever even as it is dynamically at work, no-thing whatsoever even as we can experience "it": the non-dual dynamic of radiant emptiness that we learn to experience in a thinking-saying that is non-conceptual.

Before we turn to the last and longest – and most exciting! – chapter (on the Fifth Moment: Time-Space as Ab-ground: Ab-grounding and Timing-Spacing), I want to share a short sentence that I ran across while preparing the final version of this text. It goes like this:

Finding the words is another step in learning to see.[34]

This is at the core of this writing project, namely finding the language/words that match the thrust of the thinking here, "after" Heidegger, is a step in learning to "see" or experience what is at stake in this work.

Within the mettle of what is possible, let me apply this statement and try a few words that say/show the keenness that belongs to the pursuit of the Fifth Moment. One could say that the non-dual dynamic of radiant emptiness as a name for Ereignis/*Seyn-beyng* is like space – not space but *like* space – in its boundlessness, with no limit. Not a physical space, but like the boundlessness of space. It is like light in its having no border and there being no line to draw where the light ends. For example, when dusk falls, different eyes experience different moments when the light is "gone." The "boundary" is open-ended. It is like energy (ἐν-ἐργον) – not measurable energy and not physical energy – in its being simply "at work," without any form. The non-dual dynamic of radiant emptiness (as a name for Ereignis/*Seyn-beyng*) is *like* energy, not as a unit but as a quality of movement, intensity, a radiating, a swaying or … ἐνέργεια, ἐν-ἐργον – a dynamic quality that is no-form and nothing. All three word-images mirror the dynamic emptiness,

All three of these word-images open our thinking up to the dynamic that is no-form and that has no perceivable line to limit the sway of radiant emptiness. As Cicero says, all comparisons limp.[35] And how true that is for poi-etic language, which is at work here!

> It is courage, courage, courage,
> that raises the blood of life
> to crimson splendor. Live bravely …
> Horace

Chapter Eight

Fifth Moment: Time-Space as Ab-ground – Ab-grounding and Timing-Spacing

Time-space. Why is this unique and massive breakthrough semi-hidden[1] toward the end of the section "'Grounding': Time-space as Ab-ground"? My own insight tells me that, when thinking/saying moves beyond the inherited meanings of time and space – both inner and outer space and time – the language itself is uniquely non-dual, non-conceptual and dynamic – as in the dynamic of radiant emptiness that is no-thing but works and that we can experience. Therefore it is strange to our ears. It is not easy to think-say this dynamic. I will try a thinking/saying in which this will show itself ... from out of itself, its non-dual and non-conceptuaizable dynamic.

This requires that we first pay attention to the "style" of the saying/showing. For sure it is not direct or immediately transparent. For sure it must needs stay within the realm of hinting, as well as within the realm of no place to "stop" or stay put.

These dynamics of language, of thinking, of going the way, remain obscure and non-revealing even as they open up and show the radiant dynamic that shows what is no-thing whatsoever as it emerges, what is no-thing whatsoever even as it is at work, what is no-thing whatsoever even as we can experience and work with it.

As we go beyond the limits of language as dualistic (subject–predicate, subject–object, substance–accidents), as we go beyond the limits of concepts and conceptual language, as we go beyond the limits of the metaphysics of presence – we dwell within the region of radiant emptiness, the no-thing dynamic that unfolds beyond real and not-real, beyond subjective and objective, beyond inner and outer world. This is where Heidegger's thinking/saying takes us, which he names being, beyng, Ereignis, timing-spacing, λόγος, ἀλήθεια, ἐόν, φύσις, among other words.

Inner time consciousness (Husserl), inner time and space intuition (Kant), external curved space and time as the fourth dimension of space (Einstein) – all are gone beyond, even as these manifestations are included in this beyond, both metaphysically and epistemologically. Whereas they belong within the radiant emptiness of non-dual and non-conceptualizable being, now named beyng – in order to think/say what is gone beyond – they do not encompass that beyond to which they do not go. We are moving in a dynamic that they do not know and cannot say.

a. Setting the Stage: Marking Time-Space in Heidegger's Thinking

The fifth joining in *Beiträge* is named "Grounding" and has the following parts:

1. Da-sein and Projecting Being Open
2. Da-sein
3. The Deep Sway of Truth
4. Time-Space as Ab-ground
5. The Deep Swaying of Truth as Sheltering

In situating the phenomenon of time-space in Heidegger, we first note that it focuses on Da-sein, in a way that ensconces Da-sein within the non-dual dynamic of Ereignis, beyng, *Unverborgenheit*, αλήθεια, φύσις, ἐόν – however the question is named. If we try to illuminate or elucidate or shed light on[2] how to embed the word and the dynamic of "time-space," its focus is Da-sein. But as we have already seen, Da-sein is the open expanse of the Da ... always already opening out to and inseparable from beyng. In truth, Da-sein as the open expanse is how it is only within the non-dual and non-conceptualizable region of the *onefold* dynamic radiance of beyng as emptiness, as enowning.

In paragraph 205, "The Deep Sway of Truth," the part before "Time-Space as Ab-ground" and titled "The Open," Heidegger writes:

> The open:
>
> as the *free* of the boldness of accomplishing [*Schaffen*],
> as the *unsheltered* of the carrying out of thrownness; both belonging together of themselves as the *lighting-up of self-sheltering*.
> The *Da* as en-owned in enowning.*
>   *Marginal note: Truth and being. (328)**

The Da, enowned within the dynamic enowning of which it is deeply part and parcel and itself the free – as it boldly accomplishes the opening of the "free" in the unsheltering that bursts out from being thrown within the non-dual one dynamic of Er-eignis – is the lighting-up of self-sheltering. The name of this radiant dynamic at this point in *Beiträge* is: time-space.

Why is the language of time-space uniquely non-dual? Why is it uniquely non-nonceptual? And why is the word *timing-spacing* unique in saying/naming the radiant dynamic that shows what is no-thing whatsoever even as it emerges, what is no-thing whatsoever even as it is at work, what is no-thing whatsoever even as we can experience it?

Thinking creatively, I suggest that the move from time-space to timing-spacing mirrors other wordings in Heidegger – in such words as *Wesen*, *Ereignis*, *Zeit*, and *Raum* (or better: *Zeit-Raum*) – namely, that Heidegger's saying/thinking at the edge (of what is possible to think/say, of what is still to come) is always about the dynamic no-thing, rather than a static thing. One could say that *Wesen* says *Wesung*, *Ereignis* says *Ereignung*, *Zeit* says *Zeitigung*, *Raum* says *Räumung*, and *Zeit-Raum* says *Zeitigung-Räumung*.

At the beginning of this chapter, I asked the question: Why is it that the unique and massive breakthrough that is thought/said in this section of *Beiträge* emerges in semi-hidden fashion toward the end of the joining "'Grounding': Time-Space as Ab-ground"? And

---

** Unless otherwise indicated, all numbers in this chapter refer to *Beiträge zur Philosophie (Vom Ereignis)* (GA 65).

I suggested that, when thinking/saying moves beyond the inherited meanings of time and space, the language is itself uniquely non-dual and non-conceptual, in its hinting mode from within self-sheltering or reservedness. Thus, perhaps this section on time-space as ab-ground moves at the very margins of what is possible to think-say. Because of that, it appears in a semi-hidden point in Heidegger's lifelong venture.

With a healthy reticence I suggest that "Time-space as Ab-ground" belongs to the five groundbreaking moments in Heidegger's thinking because the word itself (and with the hyphen it *is* one word) – *Zeit-Raum*, time-space, leading to *Zeitigung-Räumung* – opens out onto the one-ing dynamic of Da-sein and beyng, simply so. Beyond the dual, beyond the conceptual, and beyond the metaphysical way of defining everything in the universe as substance.

Let us look at the dynamic wording of *Er-eignis/en-owning*. Beyng as enowning says how enowning is the non-dual dynamic (a) of the throw of/from enowning to Da-sein, (b) of Da-sein's being enowned and then (c) throwing open this dynamic of owning and being enowned, and (d) this whole dynamic that is being experienced and said in words is: En-owning. From a propositional perspective, the first "en-owning" is not the same as the second "en-owning." But phenomenologically and as we can experience it, there is no duality here. It is all one dynamic. Even so, in the way that the words are being used here, there is the temptation to make "dualistic" distinctions that do not exist in the experience of the non-dual and inseparable dynamic of Er-eignis. This same thing happens with the words *time-space* as they are named *timing-spacing*. What is named in this way can only be a non-dual and no-thing dynamic. I will try to let this become manifest.

Remembering that Heidegger's Er-eignis-thinking is always preparatory, a preparatory thinking – given that the language does not exist to say it, even as the deep swaying of beyng as enowning affords to thinking Da-sein the opening to think/say "it" – the question becomes: How then to say it, as a preparatory way of saying, on the way to thinking/saying the dynamic radiance of beyng as no-thing? In "Time-Space as Ab-ground" Heidegger takes the names and concepts for time and for space beyond their traditional limits.

And on the way he thinks time-space. And that thinking opens onto saying timing-spacing as the one-ing of Dasein and beyng. This thinking opens onto the dynamic field where timing-spacing points to and says the one-ing at-oneness (*die einigende Einheit*) in the work/play of Da-sein within the work/play of the radiant emptiness that sustains and surrounds all things, while including all things, even in their metaphysical sway and even as they cannot experience or think/say the non-dual dynamic of radiant emptiness. The same wording of timing-spacing belongs to Da-sein and to radiant emptiness. And when we can *experience* this non-separation, this at-oneness of all phenomena – is this perhaps a step closer to saying "it"? (Note that in this paragraph it is all about Dasein and being – or beyng – but by not using this pair of words I want thinking/saying not to yield to the temptation to limit everything here to the "usual" way of saying the issue with the words Dasein and being/beyng – because of the dualistic connotation. Thus I have said it here as "the work/play of Da-sein within the work/play of the radiant emptiness," as in "timing-spacing belongs to Da-sein and to radiant emptiness" as non-dually one. Dasein is the flashpoint for hearing and saying this non-dual dynamic. In this way I hope to say what is the same and is non-dual in this discussion.)

Heidegger pointed to this one dynamic, claiming that timing and spacing are *gleichursprünglich*: equiprimordial, equally originary. But wherein lies this "equally originary"? It is in the *einigende Einheit*, the one-ing at-oneness, the one non-dual dynamic that is no-thing and non-conceptualizable. This is our path. Perhaps one can say that it is in the "enowning" of timing-spacing.

How aware was Heidegger that the word *timing-spacing* might have this unique ability to say the non-separation of subject–object (already named in Da-sein) or the non-separation of being-beings (already named in moving beyond the ontological difference)? As we think "after" Heidegger (thinking after Heidegger did his thinking, a thinking that calls on us to think "after Heidegger" the dynamic "to be thought" as it emerges from what calls on us to think), is it possible that the word *timing-spacing* is uniquely capable of pointing to and saying/showing the non-dual and the non-conceptualizable and non-static = dynamic radiance of emptiness and its power?

Giving attention to those things that Heidegger left somewhat shrouded in silence, I dare to go there, sustained, not by some arrogant notion of "being right," but out of respect for the said and the to-be-said that hovers within the revolutionary thinking on Heidegger's way ... way, not works. I remind us of his words about going "beyond" the wordings of the original thinker:

> But, that a thinker can be understood "better" than he understood himself – this is in no way a flaw [lack, *Mangel*] that could be attributed to him afterwards, but rather a sign of his greatness. For only the originary thinking hides in itself that treasure that can never be thought through completely – and can each time be understood "better," i.e., other than what the immediately meant wording say. (GA 55:64)

I dare to attempt to let this dimension be shown.

This last groundbreaking moment becomes explicit in section 238, "Time-space," and especially in section 242, "Time-Space as Ab-ground." Close to the end of this text we will delve directly into those two sections of *Beiträge*. However, there are several pages between here and there!

It is the intent of this chapter on timing-spacing as ab-ground to let be shown how, within these pages from *Beiträge*, there hovers the possibility of hearing and experiencing and saying the non-dual dynamic of radiant emptiness that is at the core of Heidegger's thinking throughout. "Throughout" says here the way in which Heidegger continued to press forward throughout his life and to break through barriers, methodically and honestly, in his thinking search for the "meaning of being." That is, the matter at issue that calls for thinking is the no-thing non-dual dynamic that is at work and that we can experience: not a being, not dual, not conceptual, sayable but not definable, thinkable but not intellect-wise, sayable but not propositional or logical. This matter for thinking I have called: the non-dual dynamic of radiant emptiness.

In working through *Beiträge*, Heidegger is moving the goalposts, as it were, to a field or dimension or a lighting-up (*Lichtung*, at least in one of its senses) of what is a dynamic but not a thing, not a being, doing this in the way of thinking/saying the dynamic of being/beyng that is non-dual. This trajectory is a continuation of the matter for thinking in *Sein und Zeit*. But this matter sometimes gets lost in the wording that takes us from beings to being – including its being named as ontological difference. But how to think-say in a way that is not trapped in dualistic language? The clue that has guided me in my thinking here is to say and resay the key issue as radiant emptiness – or the dynamic of radiant emptiness – that shows what is no-thing whatsoever even as it emerges, what is no-thing whatsoever even as it is at work, what is no-thing whatsoever even as we can experience it. And then to hang out in this dynamic, to see what comes up.

It is my sense that the dynamic that is named with these words – and especially with the word *emptiness* – is one with rich possibilities for moving us from our old goalposts to the new ones. Not that the matter for thinking has changed, but that we have learned to grow into it.

From our traditional way of intellectual reasoning, this dynamic is paradoxical if not contradictory. From that same point of view, we are dwelling in a kind of darkness or a shroud, but we are in the realm of the withdrawing that belongs to beyng. We are called to pull away from the light of reason and transparency in order to dwell in this newly emerging realm and to hear what self-shows and is being said. The no-form and no-thing of this dynamic – even as it includes and encompasses form and things – is the richness and freshness of possibility that affords to us at this juncture/joining.

For sure we are called upon to engage in this thinking with subtlety. More nuance than logic. Hinting rather than seeking transparency. Going beyond intellect, or using intellect to go beyond intellect. Above all: experience, experience-based critical thinking.

These are deeply hidden matters, both because we in this epoch put more confidence in the empirical, in what can be measured or calculated by reason, and because the dynamic itself is hidden in a self-sheltering.

Empirical science and its mathematical certainty have increased our knowledge of the universe. But another thinking is called for to reach to the vastness of dynamic, radiant emptiness. This calls for another way (the second beginning or the "timeless" "starting"), an experience of knowing awareness that is non-conceptual and non-dual in its non-logical revealing. If we do not make this leap, the matter to be thought here remains closed to us. But then experience can show us that this knowing awareness brings clarity.

This pathway calls for a look at the way and how we are on it. But first a brief sojourn in the word-images that serve as guidelines for this endeavour.

b. Word-Images Marking the Non-Conceptual Experience of Knowing Awareness (Knowing Awareness as Experience) of the Non-Dual Dynamic of Timing-Spacing as an Enriching Way of Saying the Truth of Beyng

All is one. While we approach Heidegger's time-space from several important angles, it is one dynamic. And it is inexplicable. This is its joy and its challenge.

All is one. It is non-dual. It is non-conceptualizable. It is dynamic. It is no-thing whatsoever. How to say it?

Time-space as ab-ground. Ab-ground as time-space. Ab-ground is the staying away of ground – no foundation, no substance, no-thing, not a being. Time-space: no form, no thing, sustaining even as it is no-thing. Finally, time-space in its no-thing is named dynamically: timing-spacing. And to where does timing-spacing, in its mirroring, take us in our thinking experience?

I will now look at two word-images that say/show the richness and power of the dynamic time-space (timing-spacing) as the name for beyng, emergent emerging, Ereignis, the non-dual dynamic of revealing and self-sheltering. Names that Heidegger focuses on as he unwaveringly pursues the question of being and beyng. They are:

> emptiness, the empty, *die Leere*
> the open, *das Offene, die Offenheit*.

These words point to and say the same non-dual and non-conceptualizable dynamic of what is in question. And it is my sense that the dynamic that is named with these words – and especially with the word *emptiness* or the *empty* – carry the richest possibilities of moving us from our inherited and traditional and metaphysical ways to this newly emerging realm (from the first beginning to the "other" or "second" beginning, which I name the "start").

The word-image *empty, the empty*. If indeed what is named in the words *being, beyng, enowning,* φύσις, ἐὸν ἔμμεναι is what is no-thing whatsoever even as it emerges, what is no-thing whatsoever even as it is at work, what is no-thing whatsoever even as it we can experience it, then the word *empty* or *emptiness* offers a richness, one that opens our thinking onto the dynamic of beyng.

I find that these two word-images – the open and emptiness – are among the most compelling ways to think/say/show/name what is at stake in the dynamic no-thing of being, beyng, Ereignis/enowning. For it is most obviously non-dual. And as Heidegger unfolds the words, it is beyond a doubt a dynamic that is at-work. Finally, what is at stake in these word-images and what is named in this dynamic cannot be conceptual. The dynamic of emptiness is simply non-conceptualizable.

In the Oxford English Dictionary (OED), the Old English word was *aemett*,[3] which over time changed to *aemet* and then to *empt*.[4] Among the many meanings of the word *empty* as given in the OED are the following: leisure, freedom, opportunity (possibility), formlessness, with nothing (no-thing) inside, unbounded expanse, not holding anything, lacking solidity or physical existence (i.e., no thing). Unoccupied, unfurnished, free, not tied down, unimpeded, unhampered, unburdened (with form, with concepts), foundationless, indeterminate – unbounded or open expanse (*die offene Weite*).

A very curious use of this word, which is now quite rare[5] – usually in the plural form of *emptyings, emptins,* or *emtins* – means: a leavening agent, for example, a sourdough starter. In this sense the "empty" is above all dynamic and about possibility – says something about how things "start."

In the *Grimms Wörterbuch* the German word *leer* says: *gehaltlos* or *inhaltlos, ohne das zu haben, was ein Gegenstand haben soll*: without substance, insubstantial and without content, not having that which an object should have.

Leer: empty, blank, vacant, void. Then: unfurnished, unformed. And *die Leere* is: vacuum, emptiness, vacancy. Vacancy in English means: Devoid of all material contents or accessories; containing, or occupied by, nothing; unfilled, empty, void (all from the OED).

If beyng – or timespace as the truth of beyng – shines with radiance but has no existing being or is not an existent being, if "it" is not, if it is unlimited by the usual time-space designation, if it is therefore free and not held in any direction (has no direction) – in this sense radiant with unlimited possibility – then the dynamic of the empty is a useful way to say the truth of beyng as time-space and then as timing-spacing.

Beyng does not depend on anything, is itself no-thing, is beyond any property of things – colour, size, weight, extension – "is" not but is at work or in play, has no comparison and is sheer (sheerly there, beyond space and time). "The empty" says this.

All experience, all things, all experience of things, is within beyng, whereby beyng is more than these, in a non-dual dynamic. The empty says this.

Conventional and conceptual ways do not reach this dynamic. Metaphysics of presence or unity cannot touch "it." It is beyond any frame of reference. It is free of all references. It has no properties. It is not the way of intellect or of concepts. We cannot find it because it is not a thing.

The word-image *empty* or *emptiness* lights up our knowing awareness as we heed the dynamic of time-space as the truth of beyng, as it self-shows. Beyng of the empty; the empty of beyng.

As indeterminate, the empty is originarily empty. As such the empty is the same dynamic as the opening of the open.

We will soon focus our attention on the strange and estranging word *Ab-grund*/ab-ground. Heidegger says that *Ab-grund*/ab-ground says "the staying away of ground." (More on this later.)

When Heidegger ties this "staying-away" with "the empty," he shows how the two word-images work as one – and then includes opening:

> Ab-ground [as] staying-away; as ground in self-sheltering/hiding [is] a self-sheltering/hiding in the manner of the staying-away [*Versagung*] of ground. But staying-away is not nothing [is no-thing, even as it is not

nothing, not nihilistic], but rather an excellent and originary manner of letting be unfulfilled, of letting be empty; in this way an excellent manner of opening. (379)

Gathering some of what we have been saying, we can say that the empty that rises here is not a lack of anything, as if something should be present and is not. Nor is it an emptiness that we could never gain access to – a purely and simply empty. The unfulfilled that is "let" in the empty of the staying-away of any ground proves itself to be the deep swaying lighting-up of this hesitation or staying away (holding back, withdrawing, self-withholding) that shows itself precisely in the empty.

The empty that opens up in the staying away is the dynamic empty of that showing (or showing up) that draws thinking to it as a staying-away that pushes at thinking. The staying-away that opens up is the withdrawal (*Ent-zug*) that is also called ab-ground (*Ab-grund*) – being pulled into the open of the "absent" of ground. This opening says/shows the empty. The question then becomes: If the empty is dynamic, then what is the dynamic that is named here?

- In *Nietzsche II* (GA 6.2)* there is a subheading "Being as Emptiness and Richness" (220). Heidegger writes:

> The uniformity of this used-up and at the same time unspent-fresh word "is" hides – behind the sameness of the wording and its expression – a richness that has barely been considered. (221)

This has to do with the fact that the words *being* and *is* are "in themselves undefined and empty" (223).

> The so-called "generic" [universal, general] meaning of "being" is not the tangible emptiness of a giant container [i.e., empty "of things"]. (223) [But rather] being is the most empty and simultaneously the richness from within which all beings – both the known and experienced and the unknown and yet to be experienced – emerge ... (224)

---

* Numbers in parentheses in this short section refer to this text.

Thus Heidegger says:

> Being does not offer us any ground or foundation, as do beings to which we turn, on the basis of which we build and to which we adhere. (225)

Along with being empty and at the same time rich, "being" is the most spoken and at the same time the most concealed and undisclosed. From these musings Heidegger comes to a kind of culmination:

> Being reveals itself to us in a manifold otherness, one that for its part can again not be accidental, because merely stringing together these opposites points to their inner connection: Being is both the most empty and the richest. (226)

Being is therefore more than something empty of "content." Rather in its emptiness is its richness of possibility.

- In *"Das Ding"* Heidegger says that what is own to the jug is not at all its being a thing or the form that it has as a jug. Rather what is at the core of the jug is its "emptiness." That is, the emptiness which carries the possibility of containing, of being filled. It is the dynamic unfilledness of the jug. Emptiness is not about the absence of liquid or anything that would fill its volume. It is the dynamic empty that is an open expanse of possibility: It is letting the pitcher emerge as what it is in its truth, to "know" what it is for, its core, i.e., to receive, to hold and to pour out. This is the work of the empty that is the deep sway of the jug. "The empty is the jug's holding. This empty, this nothing of the jug, is precisely what the jug as a container that holds is" (GA 7:170).

Heidegger says: "The thinging [*das Dinghafte*] of the jug in no way consists in the stuff or material of which it is made, but rather in the empty that holds" (GA 7:171). The empty is the no-thing of the jug by which it grasps, holds, and pours.

The empty is the dynamic emptiness in and through which things appear – beings. And the empty, which is itself not a thing, no-thing, carries within it this appearing as well as what appears. Empty is thus the open.

- In *"Aus einem Gespräch von der Sprache"* Heidegger has his Japanese dialogue partner say:

> Still today we [Japanese] are astounded how the Europeans could come to the conclusion that the nothing that is discussed in the lecture ["Was ist Metaphysik?"] means something nihilistic. For us *the empty* is the highest name for what you want to say with the word *being* [*Sein*]. (GA 12:103)

Earlier in the dialogue there was a discussion of the Japanese word *ku*, where the word says "the empty, the open, the sky" and "names the empty and open," while saying something other than what is only "beyond the senses" (GA 12:97). Thus:

> This empty requires an unusual gathering. (GA 12:101)

How does the empty function? How is it at work? The Japanese partner says:

> In a gazing that is itself invisible, it [the gazing], itself as so gathered, encounters [comes up against, *sich entgegentragen*] the empty …

And Heidegger's response:

> The empty is then the same as the nothing, namely that deep swaying that we are trying to think as what is other than everything that emerges and withdraws. (GA 12:103)

A dynamic no-thing – or a no-thing dynamic – is actively holding sway, even as it is no-thing. We can now better understand the marginal note in *Sein und Zeit*, referring to the words in the text: "a being (Da-sein) with reference to its being [*hinsichtlich seines Seins*]." The note then says: "Da-sein: as being-held into and within the nothing of beyng [*Seyn*], held as a relation [held relationally, *Verhältnis*]" (GA 2:10).

What changes from the words in the original text to the words of the marginal note? Allow me to suggest that the word *hinsichtlich* or "with reference to" is more static and less dynamic than the "new" word *Verhältnis*. Also, the word *Seyn* carries a dynamic aspect in a way that the original *Sein* did not. Indeed, in his book *Hermeneutische Phänomenologie des Daseins*, von Herrman notes that the word *Seyn*, with the *y*, shows how being is thought here as deep swaying (*Wesen*) and holding sway (*Walten*) as what is own to the word *being* as *beyng*.[6]

And this dynamic in/of/from within beyng is one of no-thing but is at work, no-thing but we can experience it, no-thing and is non-dual and non-conceptual. Thus sways the empty in the work that it does.

- In *Beiträge* – and specifically in paragraph 242 in the section "Time-Space as Ab-ground" – Heidegger shows how the dynamic no-thing of time-space, "originarily," "is" not, but rather sways deeply (*wesen*), that is, is the core dynamic of beyng as enowning. Heidegger: "time-space, the staying away [*das Ab-gründen*] of the ground: the deep swaying of truth" (385–6). "But time-space belongs to truth in the sense of enswaying [*Erwesung*] of being as enowning" (372). (Again, more on this later.)

Note how in each of these three namings of time-space – *wesen*, *ab-gründen* and *Erwesung* – it is all about the dynamic, what is actively at work in each case, the no-thing that is dynamic and actively an emergence:

- *wesen* = there is a happening, a dynamic;
- *ab-gründen* = stressing the verbal, the staying away; and
- *Erwesung* = participle = verbal, the active and dynamic enswaying of being as enowning.

I do not know to what extent Heidegger was explicitly aware of these "action words" to say/show the non-static dynamic of coming forth, emerging, unfolding. But for sure this dynamic aspect is there in the wording and the saying of the words.

With these remarks as a backdrop, we listen in on how Heidegger says the dynamic aspect of "the empty" in paragraph 242:

> Enowning attunes and sets the pace for the deep swaying of truth. The open of the clearing/lighting-up of self-sheltering is thus originarily not

a mere emptiness of being unoccupied, but is the attuned and attuning empty of the ab-ground [no-thing and no-form, but rich in possibility].

The "empty" is also not merely the dissatisfaction or annoyance when an expecting and a wishing is not fulfilled. It [the empty] *is* only as Da-*sein*, i.e., as [the dynamic of] being reserved [restraint, *Verhaltenheit*], the holding back in the face of the staying away or self-withholding[*Sichversagung*], by which time-space grounds itself as the flashpoint [*Augenblicksstätte*] of decision.

The "empty" is likewise and actually the fullness of what is not yet decided and remains to be decided, [namely] what has the character of the ab-ground [staying away of ground], pointing [a "dynamic" *weisend*] to the ground, the truth of being.

The "empty" is the suffused unsettledness [*die Not*] of the abandonment of being, but this [as] already shifted into the open and, with that, related to the uniqueness of beyng and its inexhaustibility.[7]

The "empty," not as what comes with a lack and its unsettledness, but rather the unsettledness of being-reserved, which in itself is the throwing open that is a breaking open and starting of something – the grounding-attuning of the originary belonging-together. (381–2)

The dynamic of radiant emptiness, emptiness that radiates out – flashes from, rises out from – an "unsettled emptiness" whose dynamic allows coming-forth and emerging as no-thing, cannot be dual.

The word-image *opening, open. Das Offene, die Offenheit.* As with the word-image of *ground*, which Heidegger makes into "grounding" – as ab-grounding – a dynamic is at work, so too is the open a dynamic work: open as open-ing.

In a sense the dynamic of opening goes hand in hand with the dynamic of the empty. Compare the words of Heidegger just quoted above with a quotation from earlier in *Beiträge*:

> The "empty" is the suffused unsettledness of the abandonment of being, but this [as] already shifted into the open and, with that, related to the uniqueness of beyng and its inexhaustibility.
>
> When Da-sein emerges as Da-sein, at the same time the shifting into the open is achieved. (68)

The non-dual dynamic that is named here says the bearing that the truth of beyng has to the deep sway of human Da-sein. In *"Einleitung zu 'Was ist Metaphysik?,'"* Heidegger says why the word Dasein was chosen for this thinking:

> In order to say, together and in one word, the bearing of being to the deep sway of humans as well as the core relation of humans to the opening [*Offenheit*] ("Da") of being as such, the name *Da-sein* was chosen for the deep [essential] realm in which human being stands as human. (GA 9:372)
>
> When *"Existenz"* is thought appropriately, the "deep sway" of Dasein can be thought, in whose opening being announces and hides itself, grants and withdraws, without exhausting this truth of being in Dasein ... the exposing of the opening of being itself is still to be thought. (GA 9:373–4)

The open or opening takes place here in a hidden way. We could say that this dynamic open or opening is furtive, that is, sheltered and hidden. Whenever we say the "is," in terms of being or beyng, this "is" – as a onefold in the non-dual sense – shows the open or the lighting-up.

> The word inabiding [*Inständigkeit*] could name most beautifully what is to be thought in the name *"Existenz"* – when the word is used within the thinking that thinks unto and from out of the truth of being. But then we must for sure think the inabiding [*Innestehen*] in the open of being ... (GA 9:374)

The move in the wording – from *Existenz* to *Inständigkeit* – is crucial here. We could say that both the "Da" of *Existenz* and the "is" of being come together in the radical possibility of inabiding (*Inständigkeit/Innestehen*) or dwelling non-dually in an open expanse, namely the non-dual *no-thing* dynamic of beyng. This open expanse withdraws from transparency and concept. It is nothing physical, it is not in space, it is not in time. These just-named ways of thinking – transparency and concept – take what is in deep sway in the opening as "something" or "some thing," thus hiding the no-thing dynamic that belongs ownmost to the open.

(The dynamic of the open will come up again later, in section d, "Time-Spacing as Way."

As we now "read" as carefully as we can and "listen" to what is being said-thought, here are several more word-images – alongside *empty* and *open* – that, in some way or another, say the dynamic empty of opening:

- the clearing,
  die Lichtung;
- the onefolding of hesitating not-granting, self-withholding,
  das zögernde Sichversagen;
- as the clearing-concealing/hiding,
  als lichtende Verbergung;
- the hinting, *der Wink und das Winken;*
- Da-sein as the flashpoint for the manifesting and appearing of non-dual and non-conceptual beyng,
  Da-sein als Augenblicksstätte für das Scheinen und Erscheinen des nichtdualistischen und unbegrifflichen Seyns.

When we come to "reading" Heidegger's text on time-space and then timing-spacing, we will try to let these word-images come to a saying.

All of these "angles" point to and say the same non-dual and non-conceptualizable dynamic of what is in question. And it is my sense that the dynamic that is named with these words – and especially with the word *emptiness* or *the empty* – is the one with the richest possibilities of moving us from our old goalposts to the new ones. And they all point to the possibilities of reading and thinking and saying the dynamic of timing-spacing, here taken as an enriching way to say the non-dual and non-conceptualizable dynamic of radiant emptiness – now heard as a rich way to say beyng, *Ereignis, Unverborgenheit, aletheia, physis, eon.*

c. The Way and How to Go It

Before I turn to reading the sections from *Beiträge* where Heidegger tries to hear and "say" what is at stake in his life work of thinking – as he turns to "time-space" for the opening that this word offers – I want to do a kind of gathering of the way of this whole book. It may appear that this gathering is a looking backward and looking forward, that is, in the usual way of chronology or of separate events. But we are called, by the matter for thinking here, to avoid this usual sense of things. For it is a non-dual experience. Thus the looking back and then forward is in the experience within the timelessness of the here and now – in terms of what is in front of us.

As I see it, the thinking-saying of time-space is one of the most significant moves that Heidegger's thinking makes – a move, as I see it, in which Heidegger continues to seek the wording that can say-show the most core dynamic that he pursued throughout his life, beginning in the 1920s: the question of being, beyng, *physis, logos, aletheia, eon*, Ereignis-enowning … now said with the word time-space.

How can we ever get there? How can we keep up with the pace of unfolding of Heidegger's thinking – always driven by the haunting question of that which is no-thing, not a being, but is itself a dynamic unfolding of … radiant emptiness?

Somehow this dynamic of being as beyng, beyng as radiant emptiness, no-thing and no-form, non-dual – this *dynamic* motivated Heidegger from early on. Da-sein names the non-dual dimension of the oneness that collapsed the subject–object distinction. Ereignis names the non-dual onefold dynamic of Dasein and beyng. Here it is named the radiant emptiness that is mirrored in the language of timing-spacing.

***

Excursus: Before returning to the question of the "way," it is important to look at how we think/say *the way things are*: From seeing things as fragmented – and then as dynamically one, in emptiness.

Let us start with Western metaphysics and its paradigm for thinking. We in the West traditionally divide things into smaller units in order to analyse them better. We do the same with our logic, trying to take things apart, until we can order everything into the most detailed way: in categories, definitions, propositions, discrete particles and substances – generically, concepts – because from the perspective of the onefold dynamic of radiant emptiness (also known as beyng/Ereignis) the discrete and static character of things is itself a concept. Separate and distinct substances that are static, independent, and dualistic include: subject–object, soul–body, internal–external (mind and the world), beings–being. (Remember that this way of seeing the world is incorporated non-dually within radiant emptiness.)

In a significant sense, this dualistic approach works very well and has many benefits. But it also has a shortcoming, namely it gives the impression that all "reality" is fragmented and can be analysed in its separateness.

Now, what about Eastern thinking? In Daoism and especially in Buddhism? For Heidegger turned to these Eastern ways of thinking and saying in order to find the words to say at-oneness, connectedness, and emptiness.

In Eastern thinking in general, things have their being in mutual interdependence and are nothing in themselves. Whatever shows itself does so by being ensconced with many conditions, which are always changing. Everything as related and everything as one. And therein lies the dynamic of emptiness.

In the non-philosophical language used in our culture, this dimension/dynamic is called: energy, force, cosmic force, space, the infinity of space, cosmic consciousness, quantum mind, noogenesis, universal mind, a quantum communion with universal oneness.

In Buddhism what is own to things/beings is *sunyata* or emptiness. It is also called *dharmakaya*, which is in everything that is, including the human mind. *Dharmakaya* is the unmanifest aspect of buddha mind, beyond substantial existence and beyond concept (free from the limits of concept and empty of inherent existence), radiant and beyond duality. Everything is related, connected as one with the no-thing and non-dual dynamic radiant emptiness. And everything that emerges and "is" in the world is a manifestation of this no-thing radiant emptiness. This manifesting is part of radiant emptiness, called buddha mind. The enigma here is: How can a dynamic that is completely free of limitation in its emptiness, how can this also include what gets manifest? It is this coming-together of the no-thing of radiant emptiness and the something of what manifests from within the no-thing – the non-dual and non-conceptualizable one dynamic – that is the incomprehensible of/in the dynamic. Asked in another way: How can we understand and think the "how" in the coming-together of the unmanifest, no-thing, non-dual and non-conceptualizable dynamic of radiant emptiness *and* the phenomena that appear from within this emptiness, the world of time and space and of things/beings? From the Buddhist notion of emptiness, the manifesting phenomena are more "conditions" than they are "things."

To be clear, there are at least two meanings of emptiness in Buddhism. The one refers to phenomena, everything that arises. Here we can say that they are "empty of essence," that is, in their own-being they are "empty," that is, not separate entities. As manifestations and conditions, their "own" nature as separate is empty, that is, there is no own nature in entities. The second meaning of emptiness is with reference to buddha nature or the qualities of enlightened mind. There is a richness of space and bliss, of spontaneity. And this dynamic emptiness is no-thing and non-dual and non-conceptualizable. And when the phenomena/appearances, the manifested separables of duality, are part of and emerge from within the no-thing non-dual dyaminc of radiant emptiness – well, then how is this? And how are these distinguishable aspects not two, but a non-dual at-oneness? This way of seeing the way things are may be helpful in our own search here.

Daoism names the dao as movement, way-making. Dao is about harmony and the always changing inner dynamic of seeming opposites. Thus the opposites, whatever they are, are never static and never dual. And just as with the emptiness of *dharmakaya*, the dao is no-thing but grants everything, a dynamic emptiness that moves all things on the way. And it is inaccessible to conceptual thinking or dualistic language.

Whether it is *dharmakaya* or dao, what it is in its nature – what is own to it – is … empty! It is beyond denotative words. During all of his life of thinking, Heidegger tries to find a language (a) that goes beyond language's usual limitations in saying-showing this dynamic or the way of language that can say-show it, poi-etically, and (b) that can say this ineffability! Following Heidegger, I call it poi-etic saying.

It is a dynamic stillness. And all is preparatory. We in thinking need to learn how to go this path. We are by far not yet there. And if and when we are there, this ineffability will not bother anyone!

Said rather simplistically, the Western way of seeing the world fragments everything, while the Eastern way unifies everything.

In his ongoing pursuit to find a language that could say this non-dual dynamic of emptiness – what I call the non-dual dynamic of radiant emptiness – Heidegger took every opportunity that he had to pick the brains of his Asian students – mostly professors – who were versed in the Daoist (Chinese) and the Buddhist (Japanese) languages and ways of thinking. Heidegger was not a Daoist or a Buddhist. His intention was not to *become* Daoist or Buddhist, but rather to find a language that allowed an opening to the non-conceptual saying of the non-dual dynamic of Ereignis, here named in *timing-spacing*.

In the language of Daoism and Buddhism he found openings for the words/wording that say this dynamic. This way of thinking-saying the question of being/beying as no-thing, non-dual and non-conceptual, was always already in Western thinking, but got covered over by substance metaphysics and Christianity and rationalism. (Chapter 7 of this book, "Fourth Moment," showed examples of how what Eastern thinking has held on to through the ages is *also* embedded – still hidden – in Western, Greek thinking.)

In a sense these Eastern and Western ways have been two different worlds. But they are coming together in Heidegger's thinking and in quantum physics. While Heidegger was pursuing his quest to name this non-dual and non-conceptual dynamic, contemporary Western quantum physics was ever so surely moving in the same direction. As we shall see, both quantum physicists and Heidegger turned to Eastern ways of thinking and saying in order to find the words to say non-dual at-oneness, connectedness and emptiness.

So now we turn to quantum physics, to see how what this contemporary Western way of seeing the way things are moves ever so near to the Eastern way of seeing. One could say that now, after two plus millennia of Western dualistic and fragmentary thinking,

Western quantum physics is coming to an understanding of the world – and the way things are – that was already present two and a half millennia ago in Eastern thinking. We see Heidegger doing something similar.

Remembering how the dao cannot be named and how *dharmakaya* is inexpressible, we see how both Buddhism and Daoism show us the ungraspability of the dynamic that is at play here.

What happens when we add quantum physics? Emptiness is at the centre of the New Quantum Physics,[8] where the "vacuum" has a dynamic that allows tiny particles to appear and then to disappear into the space of … emptiness. Emptiness is the dynamic at work in the emerging and the withdrawing from emergence. That is its power, its dynamic work – how emptiness is at work. (Remember Mas Planck from earlier: "Matter comes from a force that sets into motion [starts] and holds together. Behind this force is an ungraspable dynamic.")

Let us now turn our attention to the cutting edge of today's science.[9] Heisenberg's uncertainty principle says that we can never know simultaneously the exact position and momentum of a particle. The incompleteness theorem says that we can never prove the final coherence of a mathematical system. Chaos theory says that the world is so complex, with so many conditions, that we cannot predict how the world or universe will evolve – for these are dynamic systems sensitive to changing conditions, non-linear things that are effectively impossible to predict or control.

All three of these principles or theories show that what is at the core of things (of what is "real") is inaccessible. Regardless of how we try, we can never eliminate the mystery at this core. The same is true of *dharmakaya* and of the dao. What things really are is a fantastic indescribable mystery, inscrutable and obscure.

If we look at the Eastern modes of thinking in terms of the non-dual dynamic that they mirror, we see a dynamism, an ongoing non-dual dynamic changing. Buddhist *samsara* says never-ending movement or impermanence, and the dao says the dynamic of opposites moving to the non-dual way-making that is the no-thing dynamic from which things manifest. They are cousins to quantum physics.

Now look at relativity: energy and mass are the same thing; they just look different, depending on which state they are in – or which state we observe them to be in. In quantum physics something can be both a wave and a particle. Simultaneously? Or in the timeless dimension? The universe is dynamic. And space and time are connected.

Perhaps the most dramatic phenomenon of all is what is called entanglement. Entanglement says that, depending on the conditions, particles communicate with one another instantaneously, that is, not needing any "time" to do this. They also ignore the "limits" of space. Regardless of how far apart two particles are, when one moves or changes in a certain way, the other instantaneously responds, that is, outside the passage of time. What does this say? That things have invisible connections and are related to one another, that material things have an inherent organization that is not limited to the physical. And what carries the information from one particle to the other is a no-thing dynamic, non-extended and not physical.[10]

Here are some quotations from quantum physicists:

Erwin Schrödinger:

- Quantum physics thus reveals a basic oneness of the universe.[11]
- The world is given to me only once, not one existing and one perceived. Subject and object are only one. The barrier between them cannot be said to have broken down as a result of recent experience in the physical sciences, for this barrier does not exist.[12]
- The plurality that we perceive is only an appearance; it is not real.[13]
- The great revelation of the quantum theory was that features of discreteness were discovered in the Book of Nature, in a context in which anything other than continuity seemed to be absurd according to the views held until then.[14]
- The really/objectively existing world does not exist.

Werner Heisenberg:

- The atoms or elementary particles themselves are not real; they form a world of potentialities or possibilities rather than one of things or facts.[15]
- There is a fundamental error in separating the parts from the whole, the mistake of atomizing what should not be atomized. Unity and complementarity constitute reality.[16]
- We will have to abandon the philosophy of Democritus and the concept of elementary particles. We should accept instead the concept of elementary symmetries.[17]

Niels Bohr:

- Everything we call real is made up of things that cannot be regarded as real.[18]

Let me end this meditative look at how Western science of today and Eastern thinking of 2,500 years ago are coming to very similar conclusions about the world and the way things are. I do this by quoting from Buddha's poem the Prajnaparamita:

> Empty and calm and devoid of self
> Is the nature of all things.
> No individual being
> In reality exists.
>
> There is no end or beginning,
> Nor any middle course.
> All is an illusion,
> As in a vision or a dream.
>
> All beings in the world
> Are beyond the realm of words.
> Their ultimate nature, pure and true,
> Is like the infinity of space.[19]

End of excursus. We now return to "The Way and How to Go It."

***

Heidegger's thinking moves in the same direction as Eastern thinking and contemporary physics, namely in heeding the matter for thinking in its inaccessibility and its no-thing, non-dual, dynamic radiant emptiness, which can be reached only beyond the limits of intellect, even as we can think it.

Inaccessibility and incomprehensibility. Among Heidegger's notes in connection with the last of the Zollikon seminars (18–21 March 1969), we find these words:

> All words of thinking are *starting* words [*an-fangende Worte*, words that "start" thinking, that get thinking going on the way, i.e., words of the "second beginning"] … As words that get thinking started, they remain unfailingly starting words – not *final* words, not definitive – rather they open up what is in question [as a question]. (GA 89:623)

Then these words:

> *Das Unver-ständliche – den Verstand verabschieden …*
> The unintelligible – letting go of intellect … (GA 89:624)

If we play with these three German words, letting their many nuances emerge, then we hear a panoply of word-images:

Der Verstand: intellect, comprehension, intellectual comprehension, intellectual understanding, reason, rational mind – understanding in these senses.

Das Unverständliche: incomprehensible, unintelligible, non-conceptualizable and inconceivable, inarticulable, unfathomable, non-transparent, not graspable, impenetrable, inexplicable – in the sense of not comprehensible by the intellect.

Verabschieden: say goodbye to, take one's leave of, move away from, let it fall away, get distance from, move beyond – beyond *Verstand*/intellect.

Heidegger continues:

> Thinking means to honour [zeroes in on honouring, *heißt anerkennen*] the inconceivable as such. If one wanted to make it [*das Unverständliche*] conceivable-comprehensible [*verständlich*] and to take it *back* to something known, it would be destroyed. But how honour and how is this honouring as a thinking? An impossible undertaking – according to the words of Lichtenberg: "When philosophy speaks, it is always compelled to speak the language of nonphilosophy."[20] (GA 89:624)

Or:

> Unintelligible [inconceivable, *unverständlich*] – not yet intellectually understood, or what is in contrast to all understanding = wanting-to-understand intellectually – something that is other.
> Honouring [zeroing in on] ... *acknowledging* – letting it be said. (GA 89:624)

Honouring the ungraspable in Heidegger's thinking fits within the overall and more general ways of Eastern thinking and Western quantum physics. Whatever the name is for this dynamic, in all these cases the core issue that is pursued is no-thing, is non-dual, is non-conceptualizable and hidden within or beyond the concept, is beyond denotative words – is beyond the limits of intellectual conceptuality, even as it is available to thinking as knowing awareness.

In these ways Heidegger's thinking pursues its aim.

For Heidegger the being of Da-sein emerges as inabiding in the open expanse that is beyng/Ereignis. This is the site that Heidegger's thinking pursues, in response to this no-thing, non-dual dynamic. The matter for thinking by Heidegger calls on us to honour this, acknowledge it, and let it be said.

Non-dual dynamic of radiant emptiness. Let us ask the question again: How to go the way? I invite you to try the following exercise in thinking and awareness. We have a pretty good understanding of the dynamic and the radiant aspects. What about the non-dual and the emptiness?

- Start with the image of a pregnant mother with child. For sure not static. Dynamic movement is clearly shown, with the robust development of the fertilized egg. There are two beings, yes, which are a non-dual oneness, in full interdependence. So far so good. But mother-with-child is not without form. We want to come to formlessness.
- So then, take the image of clouds in the sky. There are no clouds without the sky. The clouds and the sky are fully non-dual. Dynamic, but still form, although less so.
- So then, take the image of a rainbow in the sky. It is non-dually with the sky. No sky, no rainbow. Virtually formless. We see the rainbow, but it is not really a thing at all. The only things that we can measure are the different light waves. But the rainbow? Without form or almost so. We cannot touch a rainbow. We can photograph a rainbow, but it is still not a thing! Seeming to have a form, but it is no-thing. Almost formless? Virtually formless?
- Finally, we come to the "image" of emptiness … where all form disappears.

We remind ourselves of some of the word-images from the physicists, quoted above:

- Quantum physics reveals a basic oneness of the universe.
- The barrier between subject and object cannot be said to have broken down as a result of recent experience in the physical sciences, for this barrier does not exist.
- The plurality that we perceive is only an appearance; it is not real.
- The really/objectively existing world does not exist.
- The atoms or elementary particles are not real; they form a world of potentialities or possibilities rather than one of things.
- Everything we call real is made up of things that cannot be regarded as real.

Try this. Simply be aware of the things that come and go in mind – thoughts, emotions, sensory experience, concepts, phantasies. Staying as aware as possible, let all these things go. Stay in awareness as you experience their going away. What remains? Awareness. Be aware of the mind's letting go of these limitations. Let this awareness expand, as much as possible, as such. All else disappears. Whatever and however, this is awareness of emptiness!

We are usually not used to this dynamic state of our mind, that is, empty of concepts and intellectual thinking but simply aware and open. And we are used to thinking of emptiness as something like nihilistic nothing. In order to have an experience of emptiness, take into account how Heidegger says that the empty or emptiness is the same as openness and freedom. Here is an example of how we have to take the definitions and labels off from words. Or move from definitional to poi-etic hearing.

The more we are able to let go of all the "stuff" in our mind-awareness, the closer we get to the experience of emptiness, of what the non-dual dynamic of radiant emptiness is. Remember that it is no-thing, no-where, and no-when. That it is a dynamic that works and that we can experience it.

Remember also that the concepts and sensory experience, and so on, do not disappear. It is as if our awareness expands out beyond the usual. It is as if we learn to add this dimension of emptiness to our experience. As an "add-on," emptiness is a name for the no-thing no-form dynamic that is named beyng or Er-eignis or beyng as Ereignis, what I am calling the non-dual dynamic of radiant emptiness. Radiant emptiness does not replace everything else, rather it shows itself as that formless dynamic from which everything manifests. Everything that is – things, concepts, the metaphysics of the first beginning – are ensconced within radiant emptiness, non-dually. This non-dual dynamic is perhaps the hardest thing to envision, let alone experience in our thinking.

This gives us a fuller picture of what all is there in our being-in-the-world within beyng. We can know this in experience but we cannot grasp it (= conceptually).

How can doing this still be philosophy? Moving from "philosophy" to thinking. Moving philosophy *to* thinking. Taking knowing awareness to the edges of what we think we know. And which "language" can "say" it?

"Thinking" in knowing awareness of the boundlessness of Anaximander's ἄπειρον. Perhaps the peak experience of Heidegger's five groundbreaking moments?

d. Timing-Spacing as Way

Heidegger describes *both* the changes of being-underway in thinking *and* what is experienced in the way gone, namely, the open expanse that is beyng, as "way":

> In saying this now, I do not mean to imply that, as I was working out *Being and Time* in 1925/26, I ought to have known all of this as clearly as I describe it now [written in 1964].
>
> But whoever knows what it means to be underway in a deep, necessary sense knows how the view of the way-to-go that opens out in front of him is constantly changing, just as is the view of the way just gone – especially when this being-underway is not meant personally or biographically, but is experienced in the historical unfolding of Dasein.[21]

Heidegger calls his *Gesamtausgabe*: ways, not works (*Wege, nicht Werke*). We are on the way. And the very point of beyng/Ereignis is the way itself. All is way. Beyng is way-making.

Dao is Way. Yes, we are on the way. But more than that. Dao is the "principle" of all that is. Dao "as such" is no-thing, as everything arises through/from within the dao. The dao is "way" and "way-making." It *is* as dynamic unfolding. It is formless, as it is that which gives rise to all form. It is "itself" dark/obscure/withdrawing, even as it manifests light – as part and parcel of the one dynamic of no-thing radiant emptiness. Dao is that from where things arise as well as that to which – or within which – everything returns. This dynamic shows dao for what it is. I am reminded of Heidegger's statement in *Sein und Zeit*:

> Philosophy is universal phenomenological ontology, proceeding from the hermeneutic of Dasein, which as analytic of *Existenz** has affixed the

end of the guiding thread of every philosophical questioning *there from where it **arises** and to where it **returns***.
    *Marginal note: i.e., directed to the truth of being itself, and only this! (GA 2:51)[22]

When we take the marginal note as Heidegger's pointing to the deep sense of his lifelong question (one that he perhaps could not yet say in 1927 but says in this marginal note), the whole question of being/beyng has to do with the "from where it arises and to where it returns." For Heidegger this from-where and to-where is first being, then beyng, then *physis*, then Er-eignis ... and now timing-spacing – all names for the non-dual, "timeless" one dynamic.

Here we can add the dynamic of way-making. Since all of these words name the non-dual and incomprehensible dynamic of radiant emptiness for the opening that it is, way becomes both the way of going and the very dynamic of radiant emptiness, in a non-dual dynamic at-oneness. I stress here: The oneness in which and from within which all phenomena manifest is not a concept but is experienceable.

If we now return to the word *dao*, in order to gather some of the nuances of the way and way-making as we prepare to read Heidegger's text on timing-spacing, we can let the word-image of the *dao* inspire and enrich us. For this I now turn briefly to the description of the word *dao* in the translation of the *Daodejing* by Roger T. Ames and David L. Hall.[23]*

There the authors tell us that *dao* is "primarily gerundive, processional, and dynamic: 'a leading forth'" (57). Following this statement, they say that they "can identify three overlapping and mutually entailing semantic dimensions" to the word *dao*:

1. momentum: "sense of *dao* as unfolding disposition" as in "'life' or 'history' that resists resolution into familiar dualisms such as 'subject/object,' 'form/function' or 'agency/action' and so on" (58).
2. way-making: "Making our way includes making productive adjustments in the direction of the lived experience by

---
* Numbers in parentheses here refer to this text.

manipulating the more fluid and indeterminate opportunities that come with the unfolding of experience" (58).
3. decidedly verbal: "The swinging gateway – opening and then closing – is where and when dao spontaneously 'opens out' to provide creativity a space through which to make its 'entrance,' qualifying the processive nature of dao with the immediacy and specificity of the creative act." Here the image of non-dual movement of all that is named in the *dao* shines in its ongoing waying, way-making movement, with words like "the swinging gateway" that "spontaneously 'opens out'" or "the pervasive 'birthing' sense of an emerging world" (59).

This way-making – dao, the unfolding from within the hidden – is open and dynamic. Heidegger says that our task in thinking beyng is to have an experience of this:

To experience something means: to gain access to something while underway or on a way. (GA 12:167)

Waying and making-way [*Wëgen und Be-wëgen*] as preparing the way and the way as letting-come-forth belong in the same realm of wellspring and stream as the verbs: *swaying* and *venturing* and *surging* [*wiegen und wagen und wogen*]. Apparently the word *way* is an ur-word of language that speaks to minding humans. The key word in the poi-etic thinking of Laotse is *dao* and "in fact" signifies way. (GA12:187)

Perhaps hidden in the word *way, dao,* is the secret of all secrets of thinking saying, provided we let these names return to what is unspoken in them and are capable of this letting. Perhaps the enigmatic force of the modern-day dominance of method also and precisely arises from the fact that these methods, notwithstanding their efficiency, are actually the wastewater of a vast and hidden stream, that of the way that makes-way for everything and that carries everything along. All is way. (GA 12:187)

To be on the way says the way-making movement within radiant emptiness or beyng/Ereignis. How do we gain access to this?

One way in which Heidegger tries to respond to this question is to think through the German word *Gegend* and its cognates *das Gegnende, gegnen,* and *die Gegnet*. In this endeavour Heidegger moves from the normal meaning of the word *die Gegend* to the broader meanings in use and then to the senses of the word and its cognates that he gleans from their usage going back to the fourteenth and fifteenth centuries.

Die Gegend is defined as neighbourhood or vicinity and then, more generally, as region or area. If we look at these English words, we learn that "neighbourhood" has the meaning of area or open space, from the Latin *area*: vacant or open place, clear/free space. The English word *region* says a field or domain, an open expanse. Region is without boundaries and is expansive. With that we might say that regioning says "in the region of." The English words *expand, expansion,* and *expansive* point to opening and opening out. Expansion is opening out from a smaller area; expansive is tending to open out; expansive thoughts are thoughts opening out to a wider range.

Let us now follow Heidegger's thinking in hearing the words *die Gegend, gegnen,* and *die Gegnet*. As I translate these passages, I take into account the meanings and nuances of the English words *area, region,* and *expand* or *open expanse*.

From his essay "*Das Wesen der Sprache*" we read:

> For mindful thinking ... the way is what we call the region [dynamic expanse, *die Gegend*]. Said intimatingly, as regioning [*das Gegnende*], the region or dynamic expanse is freeing clearing/lighting-up, in which what is lit up attains the free, along with the self-sheltering. The releasing/uncovering-sheltering of the open expanse is that way-making [*Be-wëgung*] in which the ways that belong to the open expanse happen. (GA 12:186)

Here Heidegger joins way-making with regioning and with freeing – which is a core dynamic of the open:

> The regioning – as regioning or open expanse – first yields ways. It makes way [*be-wëgt*]. We hear the word *way-making* [*Be-wëgung*] in the

sense of: first and foremost to reveal and to found ways ... Way-making means: to provide the open expanse [*die Gegend*] with ways. (GA 12:186)

Let us now hear Heidegger from "*Feldweg-Gespäche*" (GA:77).* Heidegger says:

> the open is something like regioning [*Gegend*], through whose allure everything that belongs to it returns to the point where it resides. (112)

> ... we are looking for what the opening that encompasses us is in itself. Let us say that it is the open expanse [*die Gegend*, regioning] ... (113)

> The word "*gegnet*" means the free expanse ... The open expanse gathers anything to anything, and all each to each, into the abiding within the resting in itself ... Regioning is the lingering expanse [*die verweilende Weite*] ... (114)

> SCHOLAR: The open itself would be that which we can only merely wait for.
> RESEARCHER: But the open itself comes from the regioning [*die Gegnet*].
> SAGE: Into which we, waiting, are admitted when we think. (116)

> And what is own to thinking, namely releasement into the regioning, would then be the resolve to the deep swaying of truth [of beyng]. (144)

> The inabiding in releasement to the regioning or open expanse would then be what is genuinely own to the spontaneity of thinking. (145)

> It [the regioning or open expanse, *die Gegnet*] enowns what is own to humans into their own regioning expanse [a onefold dynamic of emptiness]. (146)

A dynamic way is named as regioning or the dynamic of the open expanse. Regioning as a dynamic that drives our experience and thinking as well as the dynamic emptiness itself, that is, beyng/Ereignis/*physis*/timing-spacing.

As we prepare to read Heidegger's text on time-space – leading to timing-spacing – let me meander along the pathway of the "way" that leads to timing-spacing and how it takes us "back" to its timeless core of the non-dual one in the dynamic of radiant

---

* All numbers on the next two pages are from this text.

emptiness. My intention is not to provide scholarly information to support what we already believe to know about Heidegger. It is an invitation to the possibility that shows itself in the opening saying.

Maybe this way is meant to unsettle us, as we move within the vast openness of radiant emptiness, which, I propose, is a way of marking or saying timing-spacing. Here, in part, we are using our intellect in order to point beyond intellect, to experience what cannot be reduced to logic or reflection. Heidegger's attempts – to think Da-sein, being, beyng, Ereignis, timing-spacing – are of this sort.

We must have some experience in order to understand what is not graspable by conceptual intellectual reflection. For this dynamic goes beyond the realm of the reflective. My strategy in a careful rendition of Heidegger's words – unto what is being said and the letting thereof – is simply to allow the insights and experience that I have to provide opening experiences, ones that will shine on and illuminate the texture of what emerges for the reader.

The dynamic of emptiness is … empty and thus unlimited and without form or concept. With the intellect alone we have no access to the rich source of intellect's many possibilities. Thus we are going toward the "start" for intellect's activities. This "start" includes the intellectual in the non-dual no-thing radiant emptiness, even though the intellectual as such cannot encompass or embrace the start.

This question of a fresh kind of thinking, including experiencing the non-dual no-thing dynamic, is a central aspect of the way Heidegger is going within the framework of Ereignis, being, or radiant emptiness. Its most significant moves here are a fresh, non-conceptual way of thinking and the *experience* that belongs to the dynamic. In the early pages of *Beiträge* Heidegger outlines this framework, including the central role of time-space in this unfolding.

In section 1 he writes:

> The time of "systems" is over. The time for enacting the shape that is own to beings from within the truth of beyng has not yet come. In between [these two "times"] philosophy in the crossing to another beginning [the second beginning as what "starts" the work] has to have

achieved something crucial: the throwing-open, i.e., the grounding opening of the freeplay of time-space of the truth of beyng. How is this one thing to be accomplished? ... Mere modifications of what we have up to now – even if they happened with the help of the maximum possible mixing and confusion of the known ways of thinking in history – get us nowhere. And every manner of scholastic worldview stands totally outside philosophy, because it can only exist as a result of denying that beyng is worthy of question. By honouring this question [of beyng], philosophy has its own irreducible and incalculable dignity ...

The other beginning of thinking is so named, not because it is simply different in form from all other philosophies up to now, but because it must be the only other beginning, from within its connection with the one and only first beginning. From within the allotment of the one beginning to the other, the style of a thinking mindfulness in the crossing is also already determined. The thinking in the crossing accomplishes the grounding throwing-open of the truth of beyng as *historical* [*geschichtlich*, something that happens, takes place] mindfulness. History is thereby not the subject matter and domain of observation, but rather that which awakens and triggers thinking questioning as the site of its decisions. The thinking in the crossing begins the dialogue between the first "having-been" [*das* Gewesene] of the beyng of truth and the most extreme "to-come" [*das* Zukünftige] of the truth of beyng; and, in that dialogue, thinking brings to word the deep sway of beyng, which has not been inquired into up to now. In the knowing awareness of thinking in the crossing, the first beginning remains decisively the first, but is overcome as beginning. For this thinking, the most distinct respect for the first beginning, which discloses its uniqueness, must coincide with the relentlessness of turning away from this beginning to an other questioning and saying. (5–6)

After listing the six joinings that make up the core text of *Beiträge* (echo, playing forth, leap, grounding, the ones to come, the last god), Heidegger says:

> This outline is not a series of various observations about various matters [items, *Gegenstände*], nor is it a preliminary ascent from something below to something above. It is a preliminary sketch of the freeplay of

time-space, which the historical happening of the crossing first opens up as its realm ... (6)

We can gather from these words of Heidegger the following:

- We can no longer think in terms of "systems," either in substance or in concept.
- The style of thinking is no longer conceptual, but a "thinking mindfulness," a mindfulness or minding that is historical, that is, something that happens – outside of conceptual thinking.
- History as historical happening "awakens and triggers thinking questioning as the site of its decisions."
- This thinking – as knowing awareness and not conceptual – "brings to word the deep sway of beyng, which has not been inquired into up to now."
- What is at stake here is "the freeplay of time-space, which the historical happening of the crossing first opens up as its realm."
- Finally, what is called for here is a thinking that is not conceptual but takes place in and as experience.

e. Thinking as Experience, Thinking-Experience

To clarify where we have now come to, I turn to a discussion of thinking as *experience*, which goes beyond conceptual thinking or logical proof. In January 1962 Heidegger gave the lecture "*Zeit und Sein.*" In September of that year he held a three-day seminar on this lecture. In the protocol of that seminar (prepared by Alfredo Guzzoni) we read:

> In the course of the seminar, we often spoke of experiencing. We said, among other things: The awakening to Ereignis/enowning must be experienced, it cannot be proven. One of the last questions raised concerned the meaning of this experiencing. The question came with a certain contradiction, lying in the fact that thinking is supposed to be the experiencing of the matter itself and, on the other hand, is only the

preparation for experience. Thus, it was concluded, thinking (including the thinking attempted in the seminar) is not yet the experience. But, then, what *is* this experience? Is it the abdication of thinking?

However, as a matter of fact thinking and experiencing cannot be set against each other in the manner of an alternative. What happened in the seminar remains an attempt at a preparation for thinking, thus for experiencing. But this preparation already takes place in *thinking* insofar as experiencing is nothing mystical, not an act of spiritual enlightenment, but rather [experience is] the entry into dwelling in Ereignis/ enowning. Thus, while the awakening to Ereignis/enowning remains something that must be experienced, as such it is precisely something which is primarily and necessarily bound together [non-dually] with the awakening from within the forgetfulness of being to that forgetfulness. Thus it remains primarily a happening [*Geschehnis*, thus within the dynamic of experience], which can and must be shown.

The fact that thinking is in a preparatory stage does not mean that the experience is of a different nature from preparatory thinking itself. The limit of preparatory thinking lies elsewhere. On the one hand, [the limit of preparatory thinking lies] in the possibility that metaphysics remains in the last stage of its history in such a way that the other thinking cannot appear at all – and nevertheless *is*. Then something similar would happen to thinking, which, as preparatory, looks ahead to Ereignis/enowning and can only point to it – that is, can give directives which are meant to make the direction of the entry to the site of Ereignis/enowning possible, similar to Hölderlin's poetry, which was not there for a century – and at the same time *was*. On the other hand, [the limit of preparatory thinking lies] in that the preparation for *thinking* can only be accomplished in a special way. It is also accomplished in a different way in poetry, in art, etc. – [for] in them a thinking and speaking also happens [*geschieht*, takes place, thus within the dynamic of experience]. (GA 14:63–4)

Here we can also gather a few important points:

- Thinking and experience go hand in hand, in such a way that even as preparatory, both are already a thinking and an experience.

- Thus this thinking is also experience. Experience is not an abdication of thinking.
- With reference to poetry and art, the thinking that is called for and *happens* there is accomplished in a special way. I call this special way of thinking *poi-etic*. We have to learn how to do thinking in this special way, in order to think-say the truth of beyng, Ereignis/enowning, and time-space as timing-spacing.

This "fresh way of thinking" coaxes our thinking out of the narrowness of constricted conceptuality, which is able to hide the very dynamic that we aim to understand, one that grows within our experience.

The experience is direct, but the manner of approaching it is indirect. We cannot get there by means of concepts. Within duality, beings-being and ground-abground are experienced as divided, specifically by and for our conceptual thinking. How do we learn to think/say such that the word-images show indirectly the non-dual nature of what traditionally but necessarily gets named as dual within the historical affordance of our age? It is like pulling the rug out from under our cherished assumptions.

(This is not about trying to convince the reader that what I say is correct. It calls for the reader's testing all of it. Checking it out.)

Intellect is central to our "thinking life" in this epoch. But it is also non-dually ensconced beyond intellect, in the dynamic of radiant emptiness – or beyng-Ereignis. To think this non-duality requires experience.

Albert Einstein said: "The intuitive mind is a sacred gift and the rational mind is a faithful servant." We have created a society that honours the servant and has forgotten the gift. Our work here is not an intellectual pastime, but pathways of possibility, pathways that open the mind to the dynamic of radiant emptiness as experience. This dynamic is something other than what we know intellectually and conceptually – or rationally. It is subtler than comprehension by intellect and concept. It goes beyond the merely cognitive.

This calls for a language that bears up life and lived experience. Language beyond mere words and mere facts and mere definitions. Language as non-conceptual, showing the non-dual dynamic of the no-thing and no-where and no-when of beyng – and said in timing-spacing. This calls for a poi-etic language because what is to be said is not sayable by denotative words, definitions, or logic.

From quantum physics we know that the observer is part of the world that shows itself. We do not know the world as it is in separation from us. The Dasein–*Seyn* dynamic is the same. Dasein's open expanse changes whatever "being" we think is there "on its own." Thus there is no being "on its own, without Dasein." And the dynamic of beyng/Ereignis includes the dynamic of Dasein.

Dasein-beyng is always the non-dual one dynamic. This mirrors the dynamic of the no-thing of beyng as Ereignis and timing-spacing, in which the beings of the world belong intrinsically and "of a piece." Da-sein is the flashpoint (*Augenblicksstätte*) for this dynamic, non-dual at-oneness. This always involves experiencing. "The awakening to Ereignis/enowning must be experienced, it cannot be proven" (GA 14:63). For experience takes place beyond concept, intellectual knowledge or logic. A fresh way of thinking is called for, one that is non-conceptual and experiential.

The thinking-saying called for here is marked with the hidden, with hesitancy, with the self-sheltering. What, then, is the style of thinking-saying that is called for? What applies here to time-space and then timing-spacing is what applies to Heidegger's whole work of thinking.

What is this hesitancy? In *Beiträge* Heidegger calls it, among other words, *Verhaltenheit*: the condition of being reserved or holding back. Why this holding back? Because the dynamic of radiant emptiness, which is the dynamic of timing-spacing, cannot be made transparent or comprehensible by concept. The flashpoint of timing-spacing abides in radiant emptiness. In section 14 of *Beiträge* Heidegger says it this way: Da-sein's condition of being reserved "rings true only as enowned belongingness to the truth of being" (35). Thus reservedness shines fully in the non-dual and non-conceptual dynamic of beyng and Da-sein – and then, the non-dual dynamic of Da-sein and beyng rings forth in the non-dual dynamic of timing-spacing, which is no-thing and no-where.

Verhaltenheit – said here as the condition of Da-sein as being reserved (withdrawn, reticent, evasive, hesitant) – plays a key role in thinking-saying timing-spacing as the truth of beyng:

- "as the origin of stillness and as the law of gathering. Gathering in the stillness and the sheltering of truth. Sheltering of truth and its unfolding into caring-for and dealing with."
- "as being-open [*Offenheit*] for the reticent nearness of the deep swaying of beyng, attuning to the most distant enquivering [*Erzittern*] of the hintings that are coming into their own, enowning, from out of the far away of the undecideable."
- "and seeking; the greatest find in seeking itself [is] the nearness to decision."
- "the self-restraining jut into the turning of Ereignis/enowning …" (35–6)

f. Words, the Word, the "Speechless" Dynamic Stillness

Given the condition that is named with the word-images above – stillness, sheltering, reticent nearness, enquivering, hintings, the undecidable, self-restraining – one is left "speechless," that is, left in the condition of not being able to speak or to say as we normally understand these words. And this is what belongs to the stillness in saying beyng and Ereignis, is what is own to Da-sein in its condition of being reserved.

Thus the subheading in section 13 of *Beiträge*: "*Verhaltenheit, Schweigen und Sprache* [Reservedness, Silence and Language]." Listen to Heidegger's words:

> One is left without the word; this, not as occasional occurrence – in which an accomplishable speech and expression remains unspoken, where the speaking and resaying of something already said and sayable merely does not take place – but originarily. The word simply does not get said at all, although it is precisely when one is left without the

word that the word takes its first leap. The condition of being without the word is Ereignis/enowning as the hint and yielding of beyng.

Being left without the word is the originary [starting, *anfänglich*] condition for the self-unfolding possibility of an originary – poi-etic – naming of beyng. (36)

It is only in being "speechless" that the poi-etic word jumps in, emerges, gets its "starting" leap. Inabiding in beyng *without language as we normally and commonly know it* is the condition for the self-unfolding of a poi-etic saying and originary naming of beyng. We continue to hear Heidegger's words:

Language and the great stillness, the simple nearness of the deep sway and the radiant farness of beings, when the word begins to work [function] again. When will this time come to pass? (cf. originary thinking as non-conceptual).

The condition of being reserved: the spawningly[24] [bringing forth, engendering] staying the course ["braving it out," enduring, holding out, dwelling, abiding] in the ab-ground. (36)

(Note that it is this same stillness, reservedness and poi-etic saying that gets revealed a few pages from now, when we turn our attention to "reading.")

Thus, as we have said – above all in the chapter on the Second Moment, non-conceptual languaging – there is no beyng without the dynamic of poi-etic saying-showing, which does not define or conceptualize but shows. No beyng as radiant emptiness without the word that shows (saying as showing, *sagen* as *zeigen*), no language without the experience of the no-thing, non-dual, non-conceptual dynamic of radiant emptiness. This way of language is part and parcel of timing-spacing – along with the way-making of timing-spacing as a way to say beyng in its non-dual dynamic. Thus timing-spacing is as way and as saying.

As Heidegger says on the first page of *Beiträge*:

Thus the proper title says *From Enowning*. And that does not say that a report will be given on or about enowning. Rather, the proper title tells of a thinking-saying that is en-owned by enowning and belongs to beyng and to beyng's *word*. (3)

Beyng and its *word* are inseparably one, a non-dual dynamic. And the last paragraph of *Beiträge* reads:

Language starts in silence. Silence is the most hidden-sheltered holding of measure. It *holds* the measure by first setting the measure. And in this way language is measure-setting in the most inner and the most expansive way [as dynamic opening, as way-making], measure-setting as the deep enswaying of the befitting and its joining (enowning). And insofar as Da-sein is embedded in language, the measuring lies within it [Da-sein] and in fact as the driving motive for the strife of world and earth. (510)

Language, way, Da-sein, beyng, radiant emptiness – or beyng, word, Da-sein, world – all one in a non-duality, a knowing awareness beyond the intellect and beyond concepts, sayable only in a non-conceptual, poi-etic saying, where this one dynamic contains and encompasses all concepts, differentiation, things, beings, dualities.

- Silence is speech, speech is silence, silence and speech inseparable.
- Stillness is language, language is stillness, stillness and language inseparable.
- No-word is word, word is no-word, no-word and word inseparable.

Being left without the word is the originary condition for the self-unfolding possibility of an originary – poi-etic – naming of beyng. (36)

g. Interlude: A Gathering of the Non-Dual, Non-Conceptual Experience of Dynamic Emptiness

The dynamic of emptiness includes and manifests from the dynamic stillness of beyng and what leaps from it, where both the stillness of beyng and its manifestations inabide within the one non-dual awareness, manifesting as timeless emergence of enowning (or timing-spacing). What manifests – as beings, as form, and even as concept – continually and timelessly manifests from within the holding and sustaining of beyng as radiant emptiness, already from within the first beginning, albeit in hidden and unthought fashion.

Let me repeat: Thinking in terms of beings stays bound to beings. This is why Heidegger abandoned the ontological difference as a tool or gateway to the question of being. But the experience of what is beyond the limitations of metaphysics (the first beginning) – the dynamic of "other than intellect, form, and beings" – leads to the non-dual and no-thing and non-conceptualizable regioning of beyng. We know this "beyond intellect and the world of things," even as beyng/Ereignis as radiant emptiness includes concepts, forms, and things/beings in its shelter.

There is no more validity to such a thing as beyng as such (even the no-thing dynamic) than the beyng that always already is one with human thinking. Since beyng always already contains humans and the world – and their dynamic changes – it is more accurate to say that the no-thing of beyng is not "other than" beings, which are sheltered within the no-thing of beyng or radiant emptiness. How does one say that?

Form is never separate from formless emptiness. Beings in the world and metaphysical being are never separate from dynamic emptiness. We must learn to collapse these "opposites" in order to think-say what all belongs non-dually to the radiant emptiness of beyng. Therefore dualistic and non-dual experience is to be thought within dynamic emptiness, and vice versa. In other words, the non-dual experience of emptiness of beyng includes the manifesting of dualistic thinking. If beyng and beings are non-dual, then the experience of radiant emptiness is connected with the emerging and withdrawing of beings. These phenomena of beings/things and concepts are a natural function of radiant emptiness. It is only that we must learn to think these phenomena within the hold of radiant emptiness. What seems a paradox – namely that non-dual emptiness somehow contains the duality of beings over against beyng – evaporates when we experience emptiness in its "timelessness" as containing all. Otherwise radiant emptiness taken "by itself" or "over against beings" is a form of dualism. Mere emptiness without beings' manifesting is as unnatural as human being filled with concepts and beings isolated from emptiness – as illogical as it sounds.

Within emptiness, beings and concepts can manifest and be thought beyond their limitations. Thinking concepts/beings within emptiness takes them out of their closed system and carries them beyond said limitation. Thus withdrawal and the obscure[25] provide the framework in which the experience of openness and emptiness has concepts and beings in its hold. The condition of Da-sein's being reserved, the self-sheltering/hiding that belongs to beyng as disclosing/unfolding, the showing forth of silence – all are like sparks belonging to the same fire.

We (a) dwell within the dominance of concept and substances until we (b) discover emptiness and then (c) turn to form and concept in order to (d) include both, non-dually and beyond limiting concepts, within the shining radiance of emptiness. In this way concepts become mollified and have less "glue" – we do not get rid of concepts, but they are reframed and refreshed within the dynamic whole of beyng/Ereignis. We lose our conventional limits in the experience of no-thing, no definition, with knowing awareness beyond concepts. This leads, not to discarding beings and concepts, but to a renewed and refreshingly new relation to them.

Within the non-dual dynamic of radiant emptiness – beyng, beyng as Ereignis – beings are distinguishable but not separate or separable. How can one go, in thinking, to what is the one dynamic in which manifesting things *and* the manifesting itself are contained, non-dually? How can one dare to go in thinking from beings, concepts, things, objects, to the inner movement of the dynamic of radiant emptiness – the dynamic in/of/from within beyng is no-thing even as it is at work, no-thing even as it we can experience it, a no-thing that is non-dual and nonconceptualizable dynamic? In the way that all things are one, all aspects of the dynamic are together as one, everything totally one-ing.

If the knowing and the known remain two, if Dasein and beyng are seen and thought as two, if beyng and beings are conceived as two – lying next to each other, as it were – where is the leap into their onefold dynamic oneness? In order to think-say this one-ing radiant dynamic emptiness, the thinker is called on to experience what holds sway beyond conceptual thinking. Heidegger commends to us a knowing that goes beyond conceptual understanding – even as we remain critical thinkers and even as the dualism of concept and form is contained within the non-dual dynamic of radiant emptiness.

When the dynamic of beyng/Ereignis shows itself within the open expanse of the Da, our poi-etic thinking and saying vouches for the collapse of opposites, which goes beyond the conceptual mind's ability to grasp. If this thinking/seeing, going beyond the pinnacle of reason, reaches what is unknown to intellectual understanding, there stands the dynamic of radiant emptiness, or beyng/Ereignis – unknown to and unknowable by reason. Beyng as the dynamic emptiness of timing-spacing can be thought/said/experienced only by going beyond opposites, that is, with the experiential thinking beyond dualism. It is at this point that the non-dual and one-ing dynamic of radiant emptiness can be experienced.

Referencelessness (from logic, from concepts, from beings) opens the vastness of the space of dynamic emptiness. Von Herrmann calls this: beyond reflective phenomenology (Husserl) to pre-reflective hermeneutic phenomenology (Heidegger).[26] Instead of "pre-reflective," here I might suggest the words "beyond the reach of reflection," that is, not a pre- that implies a post-, but rather "non-dual non-conceptualizable originary dynamic emptiness."

The dynamic from which phenomena and things appear is not solid, not permanent, not static, not separate, and not definable. With this understanding, we let go of our usual life experience of duality, of concepts, of things separate from thoughts. And we move beyond all those states, motivated and sustained by what shows itself in the experience of this non-dual timing-spacing.

When we, loosening the tight boundaries of conventional logic and conceptualization, trust experience, then the no-thing dynamic of radiant emptiness rises up in and sparkles through poi-etic words, which carry the power to undermine dualistic thinking. With that the no-thing dynamic of radiant emptiness parachutes us into the field of non-dual experience and non-conceptual poi-etic saying. Separated thoughts and mental gymnastics merge with – are inseparable from – emptiness and become one with the non-dual beyng of radiant emptiness. This experience is not available to conventional scholarship or merely intellectual understanding. Because of that, the demand for explanation is out of place, as is the urge for proof. Rather, it demands and invites a thinking-saying that radiates *all* possibility.

Hearing the dynamic of no-thing and non-conceptualizable emptiness also says that, whereas all things that are – beings (*das Seiende*) – appear to exist as static, separable beings and we thinkers/sayers appear to exist as separate, in a deeper sense there is always "more." Beyng as enowning/Ereignis – in which beyng enowns Dasein and enowned Dasein throws open this always non-dual dynamic – is the freeing and opening in which subject and object are not mutually exclusive and beings/things are more than merely static substances. Within radiant emptiness it is simply a non-dual dynamic.

The dominance of metaphysics and rationalism and conventional logic has given rise to ways of knowing (epistemology) in which duality reigns and conceptual thinking has priority and entities are discrete and definable. In hearing and responding, within non-conceptual thinking-saying, to the non-dual dynamic of radiant emptiness – also known as beyng, Ereignis and timing-spacing – duality, conceptual thinking, and the language of denotation and definition emerge within the at-one dynamic of emptiness. The question then is: What becomes of them then?

The dynamic one-ing of radiant emptiness can be described without being encompassed or wrapped in conceptualization. Thus the withdrawal. Thus the "way" that is "incomplete." The way is both the manner of going and the issue itself: beyng. When Heraclitus is named "the obscure," the same is true, namely his "method" is an obscure one, along with and partly because the matter itself is obscure. But it can be experienced as the emptiness of all phenomena.

The full thrust of Heidegger's openings needs preparation. Here too, preparation is both the way of going and the matter itself. It is as if the dynamic of radiant emptiness is essentially preparatory. How much of this preparation have we achieved or managed, let us say, since 1927 and *Sein und Zeit*?

Concepts are good and useful, but they cannot reach "there." Knowing awareness, the experience of thinking, goes beyond those limits. We know this, not through concepts and metaphysics, but by going there, radiantly and spontaneously (following the third joining in *Beiträge*, The Leap) – always checking with our critical thinking whether the experience is true. When we "exhaust" the limits of concepts and beings as beings, then we come to beyng-enowning – now named by Heidegger: "timing-spacing."

As we move in thinking as experience to this "regioning," paradox and tautology keep coming up. As do the self-sheltering of withdrawal and the various ways of the obscure. Why? Because traditionally paradox and tautology belong to logic, and the thinking of beyng-enowning/radiant-emptiness (timing-spacing as well) is beyond logic and concept. Yet we can learn to heed this dynamic and to experience it in knowing awareness.

This thinking goes from concepts to the simultaneous at-oneness of the emptiness of beyng to seeing the first beginning of thoughts and concepts within metaphysics as limiting – but carried along in the no-thing radiant emptiness, now as concepts within and inseparable from radiant emptiness. Now with no perch, no hold, non-dually. We can call this the vastness of emptiness beyond space and time – to time-space and then to timing-spacing. There is an abiding opening of radiant emptiness in the emergence of any phenomenon or concept. But how do they change in this abiding opening?

What happens in language? The sentence cannot start with the saying-showing that is called for. But as the sentence starts with the first word and moves on to the period, the saying-showing shines through by "starting" in between the words, as it were. So what looks like the dualistic language of subject–predicate – mirroring subject–object dualism – becomes the poi-etic language that emerges from within the non-dual, dynamic, radiant emptiness.

Again, we need to continually pay attention to what changes in the words and the language.

h. Traditional Words to Say Traditional Conceptual Understanding of Space and Time

As we move closer to reading and experiencing what Heidegger wants to say *from within* timing-spacing as ab-ground, it is useful to remind ourselves how the tradition thinks and says space and time.

What Heidegger says in *Beiträge* about time-space, yielding to timing-spacing as ab-ground, is a far cry from anything that philosophy has previously thought about time and space. Although these definitions and concepts of time and space are not my primary focus in this work, they are, all of them, part of and held within the non-dual dynamic of radiant emptiness (the words that I have chosen to help open thinking to the non-dual and non-conceptual work to which Heidegger's thinking has led me). For this reason let me now look briefly at the various ways that Heidegger describes the traditional words and concepts about time and space that belong to metaphysics, in which the tradition fails to take into account the dynamic in Ereignis, beyng, and timing-spacing.

In *Beiträge* it is the hesitating self-withholding that is at the core of the truth of beyng, which his thinking pursued in various ways throughout his philosophical work. His thinking works with the being-historical thinking of Ereignis and thus of time-space that goes beyond the inherited and traditional conceptual frameworks. These traditional wordings and concepts include:

- Representations of space and time (372).
- "The history of the first beginning (being as beingness – constant presence)," where space and time became representations for "'mathematical' calculations" including "time as lived-experience (Bergson et al.)" (373).

- "The ambiguity of space and time in Leibniz" and "in Kant, where both are simply attributed to the human subject" (373).
- "By retaining the familiar representations of space and time, it always seems as if something 'metaphysical' is piled onto these empty forms of *order* (and what?)" (373–4).
- The "legitimacy and source of these empty forms" is still a question. And their "truth has not yet been shown on the basis of their correctness and usefulness in the field of *calculation*" (374).
- The ordinary word and concept of *Zeitraum* (what we call in English "span of time") has nothing to do with space and is thus "an ordinary concept of 'time'" (378).
- Time-space as "simply a coupling of space and time in the sense that time, taken as the (t) of calculation, becomes the fourth parameter," which then "is made the four-dimensional 'space' of *physics*" (377).
- Time-space "is also merely a coupling of space and time in another somehow conceivable sense, for example, [in the sense] that every event in history would be somewhen and somewhere, with that, temporally and spatially determined" (377).
- "Only when something [*das Vorhandene*] is held fast and fixed does there arise the flow of 'time' that flows by it and the 'space' that surrounds it" (382).

All of these concepts and representations – as well as the world that is alluded to in them – are included in the scope and reach of Ereignis or the non-dual no-thing dynamic of radiant emptiness. Whereas they are included, they in no way encompass or even come close to the dynamic of emptiness or Ereignis or beyng.

How can we ever get there? How can we keep up with the pace of the unfolding of Heideger's thinking – always driven by the question that haunts Heidegger for the whole of his life of thinking – that which is no-thing, not a being, but is itself a dynamic unfolding of radiant emptiness and named as the question of being, beyng as Ereignis and timing-spacing? How do we stay with this, as it calls for thinking?

i. Reading Heidegger's Words on Time-Space as Ab-ground

In this section I will try to prepare our thinking for the last section of this work, "Fusing 'Saying the Non-Dual Dynamic of Radiant Emptiness' with 'Saying Timing-Spacing as Ab-ground' in Section 242." I do this preparing by presenting five aspects that call for thinking the dynamic, as I see it. They are:

1. Reading and "the Word"
2. Hinting as Hesitating Self-Withholding
3. The Da- of Da-sein Here
4. Truth as Ab-ground
5. Reading Section 239.

These five aspects are presented one after the other, but they are in truth non-linear. Thus they are to be seen as a kind of encircling.

1. Reading and "the Word"

First, I want to quote Heidegger on the difference between "words" and "the word":

> When do words [*Wörter*] again
> become word [*das Wort*]?
> When does the wind linger, turning and showing?
>
> When words [*Worte*], in their hidden bounty,
> say
>   – not signify by denoting –
> [but] when they show and carry
> to the point [*Ort*]
> of timeless [*uralt*, "age-old"] owning [*Eignis*],
>   – mortals owning into affordance –
> whither the peal of stillness calls,
> where what is thought early on
> joins and aligns itself to be-fitting attuning.
>   (GA 13:229)

In a letter of March 1976, Heidegger says about this poem that "the accompanying text is also a word against linguistics, which is spreading everywhere and which makes what is own to language [its *Wesen*] useful for the technologically determined world – for the computer – but which in truth is hastening the destruction of language" (GA 13:251).

What are the key points that Heidegger is making in these two quotations? On the one hand, words (*die Wörter*) "signify by denoting." That is, this way of speaking is about denoting, defining, conceptualizing – and ultimately also about linguistics. This way of speaking is dualistic and cannot reach the saying-showing that is poi-etic language and that takes place in the regioning of Ereignis/enowning and timing-spacing, the regioning of the non-dual dynamic of radiant emptiness. *This* takes place as word (*das Wort*).

In this regioning – and on the other hand – the word (as *Wort*) "shows and carries to the place of timeless [*uralt*, "age-old"] owning [*Eignis*]." Can we hear this word *uralt* as "time immemorial" as in "so primordial and going back so far in time that it is … timeless"? Reaching so far "beyond" what we know of as time that it is … timeless? I invite the reader to consider this possibility. If so, then timing-spacing as a name for beyng and Ereignis is part of a dynamic that reaches beyond time and space as we know it – just as beyng and Ereignis and the non-dual dynamic of radiant emptiness is a regioning beyond conceptualization and intellectual thought and, as what is own to timing-spacing, is beyond time-space as we know it. Reaching also beyond the being of metaphysics as well as the being over against beings in the ontological difference. But this says that how we read Heidegger's words on "Time-space as Ab-ground" must heed this shift, *from* linguistic and conceptual language *to* poi-etic language that says-shows.

In our thinking and our saying, which opens out to context beyond text in its usual sense, how shall we know when the word carries us to the region of sheer owning? When do words again become "word"?[27]

In this context – and before we take up the task of "reading" Heidegger's words on and from within "Time-Space as Ab-ground" – it is incumbent upon us to consider the very activity of "reading." The dynamic that is said in the way of using language that is central to this book, especially in this chapter, as well as in the way that Heidegger is working with words in his dauntless pursuit of the question of being – unfolding throughout his life and coming to an enriching possibility in *Beiträge* – is the dynamic that Heidegger is working with when he speaks of "reading" and what one "reads unto":

> What does reading call for? What is reading? What bears up and guides reading is the gathering. Unto what does the gathering gather? Unto the written, unto the said in the writing. Proper[28] [*eigentlich*, authentic, trustworthy, congruous] reading is the gathering unto that which has laid claim to us in what is own to us, sometime in the past, without our knowing it – regardless of whether we respond to it or refuse/deny it.
>
> Without proper reading we are also incapable of seeing what turns its gaze to/on us and of gazing on what emerges, appears, and shines [*das Scheinende*]. (GA 13:111)

The question becomes: How are we called upon to hear and then to think-say the non-dual dynamic of radiant emptiness, Ereignis/enowning, and timing-spacing as ab-ground? We hear and gather what has laid claim to us and what is own to us, within the dynamic of radiant emptiness, within the expanse of regioning in Ereignis/enowning – and here in timing-spacing. This calls for an understanding of the poi-etic word and wording as well as an understanding of how to "read" the text that is not text in the usual sense of the word.

We remember the "other, second" beginning that is *anfänglich*, that is, is within the dynamic of the "starting," what starts thinking. This starting is, of course, a no-thing, non-dual and rich dynamic – and "timeless." In this "other" beginning or start, the word shows and carries thinking-saying to the place of timeless [*uralt*] owning [*Eignis*], also named Ereignis/enowning, where Da-sein is the inabiding within the open expanse of beyng, which is sayable only within the poi-etic word.

How do we learn to listen to the words for what they open up in their saying, for what they say-show – poi-etically, that is, beyond the confines of constricted conceptuality, beyond the logic in the words, and within "the word" that says-shows poi-etically?

We are getting ready to read carefully from the section of *Beiträge* titled "Time-space as Ab-ground / *Der Zeit-Raum als der Ab-grund*" (371–88), while attending to the poi-etic language that shows in the saying. This reading is guided by the ways and directives that have emerged in this work of thinking.

When I take up the section of *Beiträge* titled "Time-space and Ab-ground" – in the final section of my book – I want to show how the words and wordings that I have used in this chapter and in this book mesh or merge with Heidegger's words and wordings.

2. Hinting as Hesitating Self-Withholding

Heidegger writes:

> *Der Wink ist das zögernde Sichversagen.*
> The hinting is the hesitating self-withholding. (383)

Der Wink: hinting, indirect, hardly noticeable, intimating, like a whisper, an inkling, alluding.
Zögerndes Sichversagen: hesitating self-withholding, self-refusal, self-concealing.

Heidegger thinks the experience of Ereignis/enowning as *hinting* (*der Wink*). It is the hesitating self-withholding in its non-dual one-ing dynamic of timing-spacing. Time-space is the region where the non-dual or "at-one" dynamic emerges. Hinting emerges as the dynamic, active happening of timing-spacing. As Heidegger tries to show how time and space and timing and spacing belong to the "one," he says: "the condition of being separate [*die Geschiednis*]" emerges "out of the oneing [*aus der Einheit*] of the *hesitating self-withholding*" (384).

He says how, in this originary dimension, time and space – read: timing and spacing – "'are' not, but rather hold sway or sway deeply" (385). This says the dynamic of the no-thing. Then Heidegger says:

> But the hesitating withholding itself has this originarily merging-into-one of the joining of self-withholding *and* hesitating from within the *hinting*. This [hinting] is the self-opening of the self-sheltering as such – and indeed the self-opening for and as en-owning [*Er-eignung*], as [beyng's] call to [Da-sein] and [Da-sein's] belonging to enowning [*Ereignis*] itself, that is, to the grounding of Da-sein as the region of settling decisively for beyng. (385)

In her book *Der letzte Gott als Anfang*, Paola-Ludovica Coriando focuses on the "hinting that guides the step back into the originarily experienced phenomenon of time-space."[29] There she says: "The hinting of beyng is the hesitating self-withholding as the ab-ground of time-space."[30] With that Coriando ties together the aspects named in hinting, hesitating self-withholding, ab-ground, and time-space into the onefold dynamic that is at issue in this section.

We will try to unravel for thinking what is at its core a one dynamic, the one also named as beyng and Ereignis.

From within itself, hesitating self-withholding opens up the dimension of time-space in its dynamic active way of timing-spacing. The hinting is the standpoint that embraces or holds Ereignis in its non-dual dynamic, in the thinking that is originarily *both* "of time" *and* "of space," non-dually. That is, this dynamic holding together as self-withholding names the non-dual dynamic of "one-ing" or the "one" dynamic.

This at-oneness, which says-shows the non-dual dimension that is at stake here, requires of language and saying a special way to "say" it. For, unlike signs that point to something, the hinting does not point to anything outside itself. Quoting Coriando,

> what is opened up in the hinting, what is 'meant' in the hinting is ... in a certain sense already 'there' and even 'nearer' than a sign is able to precipitate what it is a sign for – and with that equally such that hinting's pointing to what is meant opens up *in the hinting itself* and admits no

further 'deciphering' ... rather, hinting reveals the movement of hinting itself, which it [hinting] gathers into itself in its happening.[31]

In a footnote, Coriando explains:

... laid out in the being-historical dimension, the concept of hinting takes place *entirely* within the phenomenologically accessible array/scope of that which "shows itself from out of itself." [In other words] ..."behind" that which is experienced in the hinting of being ... there "hides nothing more" than that which is hinted to the experience of thinking. But that it is this way accords not only with the deep sway of Ereignis-thinking but also the very character of phenomenological thinking.[32]

And how do we learn to experience, to think, and to say this non-dual one dynamic?

3. The Da- of Da-sein Here

Da-sein is called here *die Augenblicksstätte*. Since what is at issue here is the "timeless" aspect of timing-spacing, especially as it belongs to one-ing at-oneness (*die einigende Einheit*) that is beyng as Ereignis, the word *Augenblick* does not say anything about a "moment in time."

I repeat what I wrote in an earlier footnote: I have chosen to translate *Augenblicksstätte* as "flashpoint." It is the "point" in which something bursts open, in which there is an outburst or bursting out. *To flash* is to break out into sudden action, to break out suddenly, to burst suddenly forth. Point: a decisive juncture or joining; the centre of something; the highest degree of something; a moment of decision; something that has a tapering tip, where everything comes to "a point"; *fig.* sharpness, wit, or penetrativeness of performance; a witty or incisive action. Point as acme: the point at which something is "at its best," here is the fullest, a full blossoming of something.[33]

As the hinting of beyng, hesitating self-withholding is the "starting point" for ab-ground. It is ab-ground that starts things moving.

Ab-ground lets the timing-spacing emerge "as such" or "in itself," simply for what it is or does. Thus the intimating hinting that belongs to beyng takes place as the ab-grounding timing-spacing of beyng as Ereignis.

This means the call of beyng to Da-sein (*Zuruf*) and Da-sein's being enowned – and Da-sein's throwing open (*Entwurf*) the dynamic of Ereignis. All in a timeless one. But ... and ... the Da- of Da-sein is the clearing/lighting-up of the truth of beyng. It is at this juncture-joining (this point) in *Beiträge* that Heidegger tries to say this dynamic of non-dual at-oneness of Dasein-beyng, in such a way as to say (a) hinting is the ab-grounding of timing-spacing of Ereignis and (b) Da-sein takes part in the deep sway (*Wesen*) of beyng in a non-dual happening (*geschichtlich*) and (c) hinting belongs to Da-sein as the flashpoint (*Augenblicksstätte*) that opens up the truth of beyng. How to say this non-dual no-thing dynamic?

Heidegger's being-historical thinking comes closest to the "point" in this way of saying: Timing-spacing, ab-ground, truth as ab-ground, truth of beying, Da-sein's being the flashpoint for this revealing in saying, held within the hesitating self-withholding – far from being anything negative – are all words that carry the timing-spacing dynamic of emptiness as possibility.

In this sense I take this section of *Beiträge*, "*Der Zeit-Raum als der Abgrund*," to say most clearly and decisively the experience of Ereignis as the dynamic of no-thing non-dual beyng, Ereignis, enowning – for which I use the word-images "the non-dual dynamic of radiant emptiness."

When we read carefully, when we hear the said in the reading, when we hear and say poi-etically – dwelling in the dynamic of hesitating self-withholding – then perhaps the language of *Beiträge* and especially of this section, which seems at first so dense and convoluted, hides within its seeming inaccessibility the utmost of boldness and the finest of phenomenological thinking ... if we can let go of concepts and duality and try simply to experience it, even in words.

In this section of *Beiträge* – "*Der Zeit-Raum als der Ab-grund*," the fourth part of "*Die Gründung*," the fourth joining – what is own to human being as Da-sein becomes thematic. Ground becomes grounding of the Da as the flashpoint (*Augenblicksstätte*) for the call of/from beyng. The call of beyng (*Zuruf*) is grounding as ab-grounding, in which call Da-sein's own participatory understanding reveals the truth of beyng. All of this, including the hinting and the hesitating self-withholding and the one dynamic of Dasein-beyng named just now, is "of one piece" and experienced dynamically and non-conceptually. It shows-says at one and the same time how the truth of beyng holds sway *as what it is* in the thinking that grounds it. That is, as thinking claims and is claimed by Ereignis (by the non-dual dynamic of radiant emptiness) *historically* – as an experience *within* the historical unfolding, as what *happens* – its *own* thinking (at the same time, all at once, along with) accomplishes the being-historical turning of the other beginning, of the "starting" (*Anfang* as that which starts something, gets it going: *das, was etwas anfängt*).

Beyng is Da-sein, Da-sein is beyng, beyng and Da-sein inseparable is the non-dual dynamic of radiant emptiness. This can only be experienced from within emptiness as freeing and opening. It can be said poi-etically, but it cannot be conceptually understood. Thus the power of Heidegger's hermeneutic phenomenology, which hones in on the "pre-reflective" or what is "beyond the reach of reflection." This is so, even as the dynamic of radiant emptiness holds within it all that came before within the metaphysics of beings *and* the duality of subject–object, since in the deep sway of timing-spacing there is no pre- or post- and in that sense the dynamic is timeless. Thus the dynamic of timing-spacing is not about "one" dimension among others, but the very dynamic of emptiness itself – in the one-ing at-oneness (*die einigende Einheit*) in which (*worin*) the dynamic of timing-spacing is held and where it does its work. "It" radiates as non-dual no-thing dynamic, thus called "emptiness."

Heidegger writes:

> In the shift to the other beginning [*zum anfangenden Anfang*] philosophy has to have achieved the crucial thing: throwing open [*Entwurf*],[34] i.e., the grounding opening-up of the freeplay of the time-space of the truth of beyng. (5)

Section 238 (371) opens the section on "Time-Space as Ab-ground." Heidegger starts by asking: in what leading question is time-space launched? Then he writes:

> Time-space as emanating [*entspringend*, springing-up, having its source] from within and belonging to the deep sway of truth [of beyng], as grounded in the interwovenness (joining) of the shifting away [*Entrückung*] and shifting unto [*Berückung*, with its nuance of enchanting, beguiling, engaging] of the Da. (371)

So Da-sein is the flashpoint (*Augenblicksstätte*) for the dynamic of emptiness, from which all phenomena and within which the whole matter for thinking takes place. The Da of Da-sein as the open expanse and Da-sein's opening to this expanse is the one non-dual and inseparable togetherness of the dynamic flash of beyng. Thus Heidegger writes:

> Time-space and the "facticity" of Dasein ... The in-between [*das Inzwischen*] of the turning and also, as historically *happening* [*geschichtlich*], expressly inabiding! It winds up as the here and now! The *uniqueness* [*die Einzigheit*] of *Da-sein*. (371)

4. Truth as Ab-ground

The turn of/in Ereignis to the belonging-together of originary truth, originary timing, and originary spacing is a dynamic bearing or tension that is at work in the no-thing and non-dual happening of the one-ing at-oneness, here named the dynamic of radiant emptiness.

Timing and spacing are equally originary (*gleichursprünglich*) in the joining (*Gefüge*) of the truth of beyng, the dynamic of no-thing, non-dual, non-conceptualizable but experienceable reigning of radiant emptiness.

If grounding says the *grounding* of the truth of being as ab-ground and if the joining of the truth of beyng is timing-spacing, then the grounding is *not* something "added to" the truth of beyng. Rather, grounding (as *Gründung* or *Gründen*, verbal forms, thus active and dynamic) *is* the *dynamic* deep sway or the way of *happening* of the truth of beyng. This takes place in *Geschichtlichkeit*, which here says the "historical" or dynamic *happening* of the truth of beyng and the being of this truth. This says the same as the being-historical (*seinsgeschichtlich*) dynamic happening of beyng.

The grounding is grounding as ab-ground or the staying away of ground. The *ab-* of ab-ground is staying away of ground, so that its staying away accords and is one with the dynamic of no-thing. It is refusal or self-withholding (*Versagung*). This self-withholding is primordial (timeless as in "outside of" any usual time as past, present, or future), and Da-sein is the flashpoint (*die Augenblicksstätte*) for the way of lighting-up beyng as radiant emptiness.

The *-ground* of ab-ground is the hesitating beyond ground. Thus truth as ab-ground is *zögernde Versagung*: hesitating self-withholding. Ab-ground is, then, the dynamic belonging together in the no-thing emptiness – also called the one-ing at-oneness (*einigende Einheit*) – of the truth of beyng and Da-*sein*. The call of beyng (*Zuruf*) as hesitating self-withholding is lit up only when Da-sein in its being (as the enowned throwing open of this dynamic) takes part in ab-grounding as flashpoint – Da-sein *as flashpoint*.

As ab-ground, as hesitating self-withholding, the happening of truth of beyng grounds in timing and spacing. These – timing and spacing – unfold dynamically (as happening, *Geschehen*) in the non-dual, no-thing dynamic of Ereignis – now heard and said as radiant emptiness.

The shifting away and being shifted-away of Da-sein (*entrücken* and *entrückt-sein*) in timing, and the shifting unto and being shifted-unto (*berücken* and *berückt-sein*) in spacing, are seemingly a two, which somehow "meet" as one dynamic. But the focus becomes *experiencing* the dynamic one-ing at-oneness as (a) a dynamic that is (b) no-thing, non-dual, and not conceptualizable (c) emptiness of opening, freeing up that (d) radiates out, thus is "radiant." Thus timing-spacing is nothing dual, but a dynamic at-oneness.

Since the spacing of Da-sein's possibilities in Ereignis is equally primordial with the timing of Da-sein's possibilities in Ereignis, this counter-resonating (*Gegenschwung*) opens up the *one*, non-dual opening of dynamic emptiness.

Placing the flash (*Augenblick*) alongside time and eternity (the forever), Heidegger then says:

> The ongoing lastingness [*Ewigkeit*] is not what lasts without ceasing [*das Fort-währende*] but that which can withdraw in the flash, in order to return at one time – what can return – not as the same [*das Gleiche*], but as transforming to something new [fresh], [namely] the one-only, beyng, so that in this openness it is not recognized at first as the same [*das Selbe*]. (371)

This is beyng/Ereignis, and Da-sein is the flashpoint (timeless in terms of our usual notions of past–present–future, thus "out of time") in which the Da as open expanse flashes up and gets known. Anticipating a bit, we can say that the one-ing whole of timing-spacing as the non-dual no-thing that functions and works, thus pointing to the deep sway of beyng/Ereignis, that is, flashes and lights up and emerges, affording to us *as* Da-sein to be witness to – and to come to know ourselves within – this is the non-dual no-thing timing-spacing of beyng.

5. Reading Section 239

The title of this section is "Time-Space" and is called "preparatory [*vorbereitend*]." One of the ways in which it is preparatory is that it "prepares for" the big move that happens when time-space is revealed as timing-spacing in its non-dual one with – and said as one with – ab-ground in section 242.

Heidegger says: "But time-space belongs to truth in the sense of the full coming-into-its-own as the deep enswaying of being as Ereignis [*Erwesung des Seins als Ereignis*]" (372). One could assume that this is one of the cases in *Beiträge* where Heidegger could have used the word *Seyn/beyng*. But if one stays with the dynamic unfolding in this way of saying, perhaps it makes sense to read this passage as a saying-showing how the dynamic of time-space is such that in its unfolding it moves *from* being/*Sein* to beyng/*Seyn* as Ereignis.

Neither the word *Erwesung* nor the word *Wesung* appears in any German dictionary that I am aware of. However, the verb *wesen* appears, with its usual meaning of "to be, to exist, to happen."

Going beyond the usual meaning, *Grimms Wörterbuch* suggests that the verb *wesen* says something like *verweilen* (dwells, lingers, abides) and *sich aufhalten* (tarries, dwells, sways, holds sway). Grimms also suggests a connection of *wesen* to *wirken* – as in *Die Welt west hier*: The world unfolds, happens, exists here: *wesen* = *wirken* = functions, is at work, takes hold … something is done or happens.

In *Beiträge* the words *Wesen* und *Wesung* emerge beyond the usual meaning of *Wesen* as a being or as essence. So for sure here Heidegger is not saying *essence*. Rather the words in this sentence are saying-showing. As I said above, when Parvis Emad and I translated *Beiträge*, we used the words *essential sway* and *essential swaying*. At that time we were encouraged not to use "deep sway" and "deep swaying" to translate these two words. But as I think through what is at stake in *Beiträge*, I am confident that the use of the word *deep* is consistent with the phenomenological unfolding of the matter for thinking here. Thus we need to move beyond the cautious avoiding of the word *deep*, as if afraid that it always says – dualistically – what is other than surface. Here the "deep enswaying" is in no way dualistic.

With this story in mind, I first translate these words above as "truth … in the sense of the deep enswaying of being as enowning." Aside from the fact that the word *enswaying* does not exist in English, does the prefix *en-* really say the fullness that is said in the German prefix *er-*? But then, how do we say in English the power of the German *er-* here?

Now, since it is clear that Heidegger used the word *Wesen* also to say "what is own" to something, I have chosen to bring out both of these meanings of the German *Erwesung*, namely "what is own" and the "deep swaying": "But time-space belongs to truth in the sense of the full coming-into-its-own as the deep enswaying of being as Ereignis."

Finally, if my sense of why Heidegger uses the more traditional *Sein* here – which in his way of saying names the being of metaphysics or the first beginning – and did not mean to say *Seyn*, then Heidegger is trying to say the dynamic move from being (first beginning, as over against beings) to Ereignis (which names beyng/*Seyn*). With this reading in mind, I open up the possibility of a fuller paraphrase of the German to say "truth ... in the sense of being's full coming-into-its-own as the deep sway of beyng as Ereignis," showing that truth here means the dynamic in which the question of being, when it fully comes-into-its-own, opens up as Ereignis or beyng. And since Ereignis or beyng names the no-thing non-dual dynamic of radiant emptiness – that which *is not* even as it functions, is no-thing even as it works, and is experienceable by us humans – this is precisely the non-conceptual way of thinking-saying the dynamic move from being to beyng.

One sentence later Heidegger says: "But the question is: How and as what does time-space belong to truth? What truth itself is cannot be said adequately in advance and apart from understanding time-space" (372). Another translation of this sentence: What truth itself is cannot be said adequately in advance and on its own, but rather only in understanding time-space:

> Time-space is the enowned full enjoining of the turning of the pathways of enowning/Ereignis, the turning between the belongingness [of Dasein to beyng] and the call [of beyng to Dasein], between abandonment of/by being and the originating [as the start] beckoning (the full quivering of the oscillating of beyng itself!) The near and the far, the empty and the bestowing, the spark of momentum and the holding back (hesitating) – all of this dare not be comprehended in terms of what time-space is from the usual representations of time and space, but just the opposite: within them lies the hidden deep sway of time-space. (372)

j. Fusing "Saying the Non-Dual Dynamic of Radiant Emptiness" with "Saying Timing-Spacing as Ab-ground" in Section 242

Each of the words in the phrase "the non-dual dynamic of radiant emptiness" adds a nuance or hint to the dynamic of beyng/Ereignis. Here let me address each word specifically – each one, as it were, shining its ray onto the one, one-ing that the whole phrase says. First let me shed some light on each of the nuances and then let them shine on the wording of Heidegger here in section 242, a shining that has freshness and possibility within its dynamic.

Emptiness. We have already taken a close look at this word and its connection to the "nothing" (no-thing) and to open/opening as well as free/freeing. Emptiness, openness, freeing in the no-thing nothing of the dynamic of beyng/Ereignis/enowning. I refer the reader back to those pages, while I offer here a gathering of word-images for "emptiness" and how *within that one word* the other three words in the phrase "non-dual dynamic radiant emptiness" are nuanced and hinted at:

- Formlessness, no-thing, lacking physical existence – a kind of leavening that "starts" things moving.
  Note the non-dual that is inherent in these images.
- Vacuum, devoid of contents, containing nothing.
- The staying away of ground (ab-ground), Heidegger says, is "an excellent and originary manner of letting things be empty; in this way an excellent manner of opening."
  Note the radiating of this dynamic: opening, radiating out from it, actively letting be.
- Being "is the most empty and simultaneously the richness from within which all beings … emerge …"
  The emptiness that carries possibility ("of being filled") is dynamic unfilledness, a dynamic empty that is an open expanse of possibility.
  "For us [the Japanese] the empty is the highest name for what you [Heidegger] want to say with the word *being/Sein*."
- The empty is that deep swaying as other than everything (every *thing*) that emerges and withdraws. Everything emerges *from* and withdraws *back into* the empty, inseparably. *Dynamic.*

Let me now simply offer again Heidegger's words on emptiness from section 242 of *Beiträge*:

> Enowning attunes and sets the pace for the deep swaying of truth. The open of the clearing/lighting of self-sheltering is thus originarily not a

mere emptiness of being unoccupied, but is the attuned and attuning empty of the ab-ground [no-thing and no-form, but rich in possibility].

The "empty" is likewise and actually the fullness of what is not yet decided and remains to be decided, [namely] what has the character of the ab-ground [staying away of ground], pointing [a "dynamic": *weisend*] to the ground, the truth of being.

The "empty" is the suffused unsettledness of the abandonment of being, but this already shifted into the open and, with that, related to the uniqueness of beyng and its inexhaustibility.

The "empty," not as what comes with a lack and its unsettledness, but rather the unsettledness of being-reserved, which in itself is the throwing open that is a breaking open and starting of something – the grounding-attuning of the originary belonging-together. (381–2)

Dynamic. From the Greek *dynamis*, power, might, strength, force, influence. Dynamic: vigorously active or at work; vibrant, vivacious, in movement. Dynamic is the opposite of static.[35]

I have tried to show how the words "the dynamic of radiant emptiness," in their poi-etic saying, can say-show beyng/Ereignis.

All ways to let the meaning of the deep sway (*Wesen*) of truth open up time and space take place within the core question of the deep sway (*Wesen*) of beyng. Heidegger says that *Wesen* here does not say *essentia* (*das Wassein*) but rather *währen* and *walten*.

Währen: performing, fulfilling, husbanding, pervading, endowing, gifting, providing, being in force, enhancing and expanding, enduring.

Walten: prevailing, being in force, enacting, carrying out, showing, extending, reigning, being active, running free.

These words are translated from *Grimms Wörterbuch* and show a dynamic happening. Beyng reigns in the open that is own to it, or the lighting-up (*Lichtung*). This lighting-up of beyng is the originary, dynamic deep sway or the showing-enacting of truth.

Radiant. From the verb *radiate* (Latin *radiare*, to shine or shine forth). Something radiates or emits, shines forth, shines out; is effulgent, refulgent (from the Latin *fulgere*, to flash forth), shining forth brilliantly, resplendent (from the Latin *resplendere*, to shine again and again); emergent, from the verb *emerge*, to rise out of; emanating (from the Latin *e-manare*, to flow out), coming forth, flowing out.

- In "*Zum Ereignis-Denken*," Heidegger writes:

  φύσις *aufgehendes Entstehen* | *ent-stehendes Aufgehen*
  physis rising emerging | e-merging rising

  Wie in ἀλήθεια | *"Werden" – sie selbst* **Ent-stehung!** *[als] aufgehendes Ent-stehen – aus Aufgegangenem Hinaus-stehen – (auf dem Grunde des Verborgenen, dann Ent-stehend und das Be-stehend!). Erscheinen –* **"Scheinen"** *– Leuchten – Aufglänzen … Erstellung der Offenheit als* **sich zeigende Helle** *–* | *Strahlung* |
  As in *aletheia* | "Becoming" – itself *emerging!* [as] rising emerging – from within the opening standing-out – (on the ground of the hidden/sheltered, then e-mergent and lasting!). Emerging/manifesting – "*shining*" – lighting/illuminating – gleaming … Generating out of openness as *self-showing brightness/shining/brilliance* | raidiance/flashing | (GA 73.1:122)

  So many ways to say "radiant" in both German and English! Becoming and coming out or coming forth, from within the hidden/sheltered. This "forth" and "out of" stresses what the word *radiant* says-shows – modifying the word *emptiness*, here named and said in *aletheia*, the hidden/sheltered and openness.

- In *Sein und Zeit* Heidegger refers to the radiant or *strahlend* in a discussion of two meanings of the German word *Erscheinung*. One is the normal way we use the word, to say "appearance" as in something that appears, what we call the phenomenon: what shows itself or the *what* that comes forward into view. But there is another "appearing," the dynamic of appearing as such, namely appearing as a not-self-showing. What does not show itself in this way is not a negative but a dynamic that can never appear fully – is always in the dynamic unfolding. What appears is only possible on the basis of the not-self-showing – which in the above quotation is the hidden/sheltered or what Heidegger has called the "hesitating self-withholding."

Thus Heidegger explains that the German word *erscheinen* is ambivalent, here used, not in the sense of uncertain or undecided, but in the more literal sense of "strong in two ways" or "two ways at once":

> That in which something "appears" [*erscheint*] says the wherein something [the phenomenon, *what* shows itself] comes forth [*sich meldet*], but does not show iself [*sich nicht zeigt*]; and in the words "without itself being appearance" appearance means *self-showing*. (GA 2:40)

A little later on the same page Heidegger clarifies:

> [There is] on the one hand *appearance* in the sense of self-announcing as not-self-showing, while on the other hand the announcing itself [*das Meldende*] – which in its self-showing announces something not showing itself.

Heidegger then distinguishes these two ways of "appearing":

> The announcing that is brought-forth [*hervorgebracht*] shows itself, for sure, in such a way that – as emanating/radiating-forth [*Ausstrahlung*] of that which it announces – [in the very radiating-forth] it keeps this veiled ... This self-showing (phenomenon in the really originary sense) is at the same time "appearing" as announcing radiating out [*Ausstrahlung*, emanating] of something that in the appearing *hides* itself [stays hidden]. (GA 2:41)

This radiating-out that stays hidden and is *not shown* – that which does not show itself in the announcing or appearing – is precisely what is named and said-shown with the words "radiant emptiness"

- where *emptiness* says hiding or sheltering of the dynamic that does not show itself, even as what does show itself is held within this non-dual no-thing dynamic of the empty, and
- where *radiant* says the coming-forth, emanating, radiating-out as that which in its radiating hides itself and stays hidden.

The non-dual one-ing. This is the name for the dynamic that is named in the no-thing and is non-conceptualizable, said in the words *beyng/Ereignis/Unverborgenheit-Verbergen* (revealing and self-withholding as of one piece, always non-dual), *aletheia, physis, eon* – and timing-spacing. It is not something that is unified or "brought into" a unity, because it is a dynamic that is always already, "timelessly and non-spatially," non-dual and at-one. It is never divided as such, even as it lets emerge (lets radiate forth) what does show itself, the phenomenon, including manifestation in duality of subject–object, beings–being–beyng, or metaphysics – all of which belong to the non-dual one, from which it springs and to which it returns. One could say that the emergence of duality itself is part and parcel of the non-dual one-ing dynamic of radiant emptiness. It is a non-dual at-oneness, the condition of being one. It is of one, in one, as one. Its oneness or being-one is own to it as non-dual *dynamic*. Undivided, forming a whole, in one. A kind of "one-ing" (OED), being dynamically non-dually a one. Holding sway in its at-oneness.

We are now almost ready to dive into the text of section 242, to let the "non-dual one dynamic of radiant emptiness" be mirrored in the words of Heidegger. On the way to this text (section 242 of *Beiträge*) we remind ourselves (a) of Heidegger's lifelong ongoing pursuit of the question of being as something other than beings or substances, something other than what *is*, a dynamic that is no-thing and non-dual, and (b) of how – when we encounter Heidegger's Ereignis-thinking – we first hear how Ereignis/enowning takes place. Heidegger says that beyng enowns Da-sein, and Da-sein, enowned, throws this enowning open; and this convergence of the enowning throw of beyng to Da-sein and the throwing open (into and within the open expanse) that enowned Da-sein does – this one dynamic is the *originary turning of en-owning*. The convergence is that from which the phenomenon springs and to which it returns. And far from being an after-the-fact, this convergence is a one-ing dynamic no-thing.

Before letting the text of section 242 shine light on the wording "the non-dual dynamic of radiant emptiness," and vice versa, let us listen to Heidegger on this matter, from earlier in *Beiträge*:

> *Da-sein* means en-owning within Ereignis/enowning as the deep sway of beyng. But beyng enters its truth only on the ground of Da-sein. (293)

> *Da-sein* is the turning point in the turning of Ereignis, the self-opening midpoint of the mirroring of the call [of beyng, to Da-sein] and the belongingness [of Da-sein, to beyng], the *ownhood* ... the exquisite midpoint of en-owning as owning the belonging-together [of beyng and Da-sein] to Ereignis/enowning, at the same time owning the belonging-together to *it* [Da-sein]: self-becoming. (311)

Here I want to stress the flashpoint of the one-ing at-oneness, named in the above quotation as the "self-opening midpoint." Midpoint is another name for flashpoint.

When Heidegger opens up the discussion about time-space and ab-ground – or time-space *as* ab-ground – he shows how time-space and ab-ground fit together in the same way. If we grasp time-space as ab-ground and, in a turning, get hold of ab-ground more precisely from the vantage point of time-space, we come to the ongoing turning-in-relatedness – one to the other and back – and the belongingness of time-space to the deep sway of truth.

Let me now present Heidegger's words from section 242:

> Ab-ground is the originary deep swaying of ground. The ground is the deep sway of truth. When therefore time-space as ab-ground is grasped and when, in the turning, the ab-ground is comprehended more precisely from time-space, then and with that the turning-in-relation and belonging of time-space to the deep sway of truth opens up.[36] (379)

When we think of the "two" aspects of this turning, we can imagine at first that they are actually "two," thus somehow a duality.

But then, when we focus on the words "turning-in-relation" and "self-opening oneness" as what holds them together, we get the sense that the seeming duality in this relatedness is in fact a one or one-ing at-oneness.

If we stay with the dynamic of the relatedness, we come to the experience that the relatedness as such, as it were, is non-dual – a non-dual dynamic. This no-thing dynamic is a being-at-one, a dynamic at-oneness. Again, Heidegger's words in this regard:

> The abground is the *originary at-oneness* of space and time, that one-ing at-oneness [*jene einigende Einheit*] of space and time that first lets them diverge in their separateness. (379)

How can we think this "originary" and "one-ing" at-oneness? If we now hear the words "non-dual dynamic of radiant emptiness," they mirror both the dynamic aspect and the non-dual aspect of what is at issue in Ereignis/beyng and the truth of being as ab-ground. The dynamic, vibrant, active dimension of emptiness, from within which the separateness radiates forth or emanates – emanates the duality of metaphysics, of subjectivity–objectivity, and so on – is non-dual, no-thing, even as it is at work, even as we can experience it, and even as we can think-say it poi-etically.

In the next sentence Heidegger emphasizes that this one-ing of the ab-ground is a *dynamic* at-oneness, using the verb or "action word" *gründen* to clarifiy what *Grund* means:

> But the ab-ground is also and primarily the originary deep sway of ground, of its ground*ing* [*seines Gründens*, the ground that *grounds actively*] *of the deep sway of truth.* (379)

And the deep sway of truth is the truth of beyng, also named Ereignis: the enowning call of/by/from beyng to Da-sein and its ongoing turning relatedness to Da-sein's throwing open the dynamic. Since Er-eignis is the name for this dynamic turning-in-relation, this originary Er-eignis too is a non-dual dynamic.

Let us now walk through the interwoven word-images of ab-ground as staying-away of ground as hesitating-withholding as sheltering/hiding that lights-up the open as emptiness:

> Ab-ground: staying away [of ground]; as self-sheltering/hiding, a self-sheltering in the manner of withholding [*Versagung*, not-granting, refusal] of ground. But withholding is not nothing, but rather an excellent and originary way of letting be unfulfilled, of letting be empty; in this way an excellent way of opening-up. (379)

This *letting* is dynamic, an active letting. And an "excellent way of opening-up." As we will see soon, this "letting" belongs to the dynamic of radiant emptiness – both emptiness as a dynamic of opening *and* radiant as a letting that radiates forth, certainly not static:

> But, as deep swaying of the ground, the ab-ground is not merely self-withholding as a simple pulling back and going away. The *ab*-ground is ab-*ground*. In its self-withholding, ground brings into the open in an excellent way, namely into the primary open of *that* emptiness that is thereby already a determinate one. Inasmuch as ground – even and precisely as abground – still grounds and yet does not really ground, it dwells in hesitating ... (379–80)

Ground is ab-ground. The ground is a grounding of staying away of ground, thus "not really grounding." As Heidegger says. the ab-ground is the withholding of ground. And in this withholding, the originary emptiness opens up. This originary emptiness happens as originary lighting-up, but lighting-up in such a way that the hesitating shows itself within it. Thus:

> The ab-ground is first and primarily the *sheltering/hiding that lights up* [*lichtende Verbergung*], the deep swaying of truth. (380)

Heidegger calls this the *ur-ground*. And "the ur-ground opens up as self-sheltering/hiding only in the ab-ground" (380). And "the ur-ground [*Ur-grund*], which grounds [*der Ur-grund*, **der Gründende**, ur-ground that is active grounding] is *beyng*, but always deeply swaying [*wesend*, a dynamic swaying, an action] in its truth" (380).

Then Heidegger shows the deep connection of beyng–ground–abground to emptiness, showing as well how this whole array of word-images points to and opens up and says the non-dual dynamic of radiant emptiness – highlighting all four aspects of what is at issue: non-dual, dynamic, radiant, emptiness. I quote:

> The more in-depth [*gründlicher*] the ground (the deep sway of truth) is grounded [*ergründet*], the more integrally does beyng hold sway.
>
> But the full grounding [*Ergründung*] of the ground must dare [*wagen*, venture] the leap into the ab-ground and take the measure of ab-ground itself and endure it.
>
> Ab-ground as staying-away of ground in the sense just mentioned is the first lighting-up of the open as "emptiness."
>
> But how is emptiness to be understood here? Not the not-being-occupied, in the sense that forms of ordering and frameworks for calculating what is extant of space and time are unoccupied, and not the absence of what is extant in space and time – but rather the empty of timing-spacing [*die zeit-räumliche Leere*], the originary gaping-open in hesitating self-withholding. But does this [hesitating self-withholding] not have to bump up against a claim, a seeking, an intention to go there, so that it can be a self-withholding? For sure, but both always hold sway as Ereignis, and now the only thing that is at stake is to determine the deep sway of emptiness [or what is own to the empty, *das Wesen der Leere*]. What that says is: to think the ab-ground character of the abground, how ab-ground grounds. In fact, that always needs to be thought only from within and out of the ur-ground, namely Ereignis, and in carrying out the leap into its turning. (380–1)
>
> The open of the lighting-up of sheltering/hiding is thus orginarily not a mere emptiness of being-unoccupied, but rather the attuned and attuning emptiness of ab-ground, which, in accord with the attuning hinting of Ereignis/enowning, is an attuned – and that means here enjoined – ab-ground. (381)

The journey of section 242 includes ab-ground, time-space, truth, emptiness – and timing-spacing. All of these markings in an intertwining one-ing and at-oneness dynamic.

First, a gathering of the aspects before the final turn:

- (the inherited backstory) Time and space as separate enties and/or concepts, including the entity and/or concept of *Zeitraum* in German and *span of time* in English.
- Heidegger's notion of time-space (*Zeit-Raum*) as ab-ground (*Ab-grund*), which opens up the dynamic of "staying away from ground" or dynamic and freeing emptiness and thus no-thing non-dual and non-conceptual dynamic.
- Heidegger's timing-spacing (*Zeitigung-Räumung*), which emphasizes the non-static, dynamic aspect of time-space as ab-ground and which emphasizes the turning-in-relation (*kehriger Bezug*) or self-opening midpoint (*die sich öffnende Mitte*) – also named counter-turning or counterplay (*das Gegenwendige*), where the *gegen* says the relationship or that which generally happens between the two and with the meaning of *entsprechend* or "corresponding to" or "correlative" and with the meaning of *gegeneinander* or "playing against" – one can say the dynamic relatedness, which stresses the movement between the two, a movement that indicates the oneness of the "two" within the dynamic, including
- the shifting away and being shifted away (*entrücken* and *entrückt-sein*) and the shifting unto and being shifted unto (*berücken* and *berückt-sein*), the point where Heidegger attributes shifting away to timing and shifting unto spacing – a seeming duality that is moved beyond and undone by the "one-ing that lets them spring up into [*entspringen*, have their source in] that inseparable pointing," to
- the one-ing at-oneness that holds the dynamic, the one-ing oneness or the non-dual oneness, which gets named emptiness. "The emptiness is also and in fact the fullness of what is not yet decided, what is to be decided – what belongs to ab-ground and shows or points to the ground, the truth of being" (382). It is "already shifted into the open" as the "'*originary at-oneness*,' which first *lets* [actively and dynamically, italics mine] space and time go apart into their separateness" (379). This originary at-oneness is also the originary emptiness and the originary

lighting-up and thus "as ab-ground is the first and primary lighting-up sheltering/hiding, the deep swaying of truth" (380), to
- Da-sein as the flashpoint (*Augenblicksstätte*), the point where this ab-ground as truth of beyng-Ereignis/enowning flashes forth in its non-dual dynamic of radiant emptiness, all of which must be
- experienced. Thinking and experience go hand in hand, in such a way that even as preparatory, both are already a thinking and an experience. Thus this thinking is also experience. Experience is not an abdication of thinking. The experience is direct, but the manner of approaching it in thinking is indirect. We cannot get there directly with concepts. It is experience by which we learn to think/say, indirectly, beyng-Ereignis/ enowning as the non-dual dynamic of radiant emptiness.

We now come to the final turn: letting this non-dual oneness dynamic be opened up. I will do this by presenting some quotations from section 242 in which this non-dual one dymamic is said-shown, which in turn ties beyng and Ereignis/enowning, hesitating self-withholding, timing-spacing, and ab-ground to radiant emptiness – in a kind of mirroring.

> The "staying away" of the ground, in its being without groundedness, is *attuned* from within the hesitating self-withholding, in timing and in spacing, especially as shifting-way and shifting-unto. The granting [*das Einräumen*, placing] grounds and is the point of the flash [*Die Stätte des Augenblicks*]. Time-space as the oneness of originary timing and spacing is orginarily itself the flashpoint [*Augenblicks-Stätte*] – and this as the ab-grounding owning time-spaciality of openness of sheltering/hiding, i.e., of the Da. (384)
>
> From where the juncture [*Geschiednis*] of timing and spacing? From out of the shifting-away and shifting-unto, which are extended in fundamentally different ways, from out of the *at-oneness* [*Einheit*] of the *hesitating self-withholding*. From where the juncture [*Geschiedenheit*] of shifting-away and shifting-unto? From within the hesitating withholding, and this [is] the *full hinting* [*Erwinken*] as the originary deep sway

of Ereignis/enowning, starting [*anfänglich*] in the other beginning. This deep sway of beyng [is] unique and once-only and thereby satisfies what is innermostly own to beyng; also *physis* unique and once-only. (384–5)

But the hesitating withholding itself has this originary one-ing joining of self-withholding *and* hesitating from out of the *hinting*. This is the self-opening of self-sheltering/hiding as such and indeed the self-opening for and as the en-owning [*Er-eignung*], as the call into belonging to Ereignis itself, i.e., to the grounding of Da-sein as the dimension of decision for beyng. (385)

When shifting-away proves to be gathering and shifting-unto proves to be an embrace, therein lies a counter-turning [*ein Gegenwendiges*, playing against each other, face-to-face, what is dealt with between the two, what happens in this "between"]. For shifting-away appears to be dispersal and shifting-unto appears to be embracing. This counter-turning is precisely what is ownmost and indicates the originary pointing of each to the other on the basis of their move. (385)

But they [space and time] also have nothing in common, like a unity [*Einheit*]; but rather what they [have, are] is [the dynamic of] their one-ing [*ihr Einigendes*] – which lets them spring forth *into* that inseparable pointing to [each other] – [namely] time-space, the staying-away of ground, the deep swaying of truth. But this springing-forth is no tearing-loose-from, but rather the opposite: time-space is only the unfolding that is own to the deep swaying of truth. (386)

The open of the ab-ground is not without ground. Abground is not the No to every ground – as in groundlessness – but the Yes to the ground in its sheltered/hidden expanse and breadth.

Thus the ab-ground is the flashpoint [*Augenblicksstätte*] – oscillating in timing-spacing – of the "between" [as the "timeless" site of the non-dual dynamic] as which Da-sein must be grounded. (387)

The ab-ground is as little "negative" as hesitating *withholding*; taken straightaway ("logically"), both [ab-ground and hesitating withholding] contain a "no" and at the same time the hesitating withholding is the first and utmost lighting-up [*Aufleuchten*, therefore a "yes"] of the hint.

> Grasped more originarily, a "not" does hold sway in it [hesitating withholding]. But it is the originary "not," which belongs to beyng itself and thus to Ereignis/enowning. (388)

In summary, this is my attempt to flesh out how the non-dual dynamic of radiant emptiness can say beyng or enowning/Ereignis as no-thing whatsoever even as it emerges, as no-thing whatsoever even as it is dynamically at work, as no-thing whatsoever even as we can experience "it."

Thus ends this venture in writing. And the true adventure just got started.

Notes

1. Setting the Stage

1 The German title of the lecture was *"Vollziehende Wiederholung des griechischen Denkens und die Bedeutung für die Praxis der Psychotherapie,"* published in *Daseinsanalyse. Jahrbuch für Psychotherapie, Psychosomatik und Grundlagenforschung* 33 (2017): 114–33.
2 Österreichisches Daseinsanalytisches Institut an der Universität Wien.

2. The Conditions in Which We Find Ourselves

1 I have decided not to italicize the word *Ereignis*. I do this with the awareness that, even though we have translated it as "enowning" – which is a viable way to say the word – it is not easy to translate; and thus I consider it similar to the word *Dasein/Da-sein*, a word that has become so common in English that it needs no translation. Or: Dasein and Ereignis have become English words.

3. Guideposts for This Work

1 *"Zunächst höre und sehe man, was vorgelegt wird, man gehe mit und sehe zu, wohin das führen mag und was damit getan werde."* E. Husserl, *Die Krisis der europäischen Wissenschaften und die transzendentale Phänomenologie* (The Hague: Nijhoff, 1954), App. 13:440.
2 See Friedrich-Wilhelm von Herrmann, *Hermeneutik und Reflexion. Der Begriff der Phänomenologie bei Heidegger und Husserl* (Frankfurt am Main: Vittorio Klostermann, 2000) translation by K. Maly, *Hermeneutics and Reflection: Heidegger and Husserl on the Concept of Phenomenology* (Toronto: University of Toronto Press, 2013).

3 Note that Heidegger's use of the German word *Seyn* over against *Sein* appears in this quotation. In this text I translate *Seyn* as "beyng" and *Sein* as "being." The difference between these two words, which are found in some of Heidegger's texts, will become a central theme later in this work.
4 From the Louise Bourgeois Archive, New York, LB-0021, undated loose sheet, as quoted in Ulf Küster, *Louise Bourgeois* (Ostfildern: Hatje Cantz Verlag, 2013), 16.
5 This wording of first and second/other beginning will become a key issue for the five moments.
6 As the reader will soon see, this text becomes central to all five moments that I am addressing in this work.
7 The following text is from *Brief über den Humanismus* (GA 9:327–8). Heidegger's marginal notes to this text are in braces {}, while my own additions here are in brackets []:

> But the full understanding and going along with this other thinking – that leaves subjectivity behind – is made difficult by the fact that with the publication of *Sein und Zeit* the third section of the first part, "Zeit und *Sein*," was held back (cf. *Sein und Zeit*, GA 2:39). Here everything {*marginal note: the what and the how of what is worthy of thinking and of thinking itself} turns around. The section in question was held back because thinking in the full saying {*marginal note: letting self-showing, *Sichzeigenlassen*} of this turning-around failed and, using the language of metaphysics, did not work. The lecture *Vom Wesen der Wahrheit*, thought and shared in 1930 but first published in 1943, offers a certain insight into the thinking of the turning from *Sein und Zeit* to *Zeit und Sein*: This turning is not a change of viewpoint {*marginal note: i.e., of the question of being} of *Sein und Zeit*, but in it the attempted thinking gets to the place of the dimension from within which *Sein und Zeit* is experienced – experienced from out of the grounding experience of the forgetfulness of being {*marginal note: forgetfulness – *lethe* – sheltering-hiding – withdrawal – dis-owning: enowning; *Vergessenheit* – Λήθη – *Verbergung* – *Entzug* – *Enteignis*: *Ereignis*}. [Maly: This was *experienced* from within *Sein und Zeit* but could not yet be *said* at that time. Why not? That is the question.]

From *Heraklit* (GA 55:63–4):

> Every translation that is taken for itself alone, made without the interpretation [*Auslegung*] that belongs to it, is open to all kinds of misinterpretations. For every translation is in itself always an interpretation. [I will take this up in the Third Moment, regarding

translation]. Implicitly [that is, unexpressed, *unausgesprochen*], it carries within itself all approaches, views, levels of interpretation from which it comes. Further, interpretation itself is simply the implementation of the translation that is still silent and has not yet entered the word that would accomplish this. Interpretation and translation are in their ownmost core the same. Therefore, since the words and writings in the native language often need interpretation, translating within the own language is also constantly necessary. Every saying, talking and answering is a translating. Thus, the fact that most of the time two different languages come into play is not what is ownmost to translating. For example, we have to translate Kant's *Critique of Pure Reason* every time anew, in order to understand it. That does not mean reducing the lofty language of the work into ordinary language. It means to *trans*late [*über*setzen] the thinking of this work into a dialoguing [*auseinandersetzend*] thinking and saying. With that, then, there sometimes arises the odd semblance that the interpreter "really" understands the thinker "better" than the thinker himself. For the empty vanity of minds that are merely clever, this semblance is dangerous. They conclude that in such a case Kant himself had not quite known what he really wanted and that now the interpreter who comes afterwards knows this precisely. But, that a thinker can be understood "better" than he understood himself – this is in no way a flaw [lack, *Mangel*] that could be attributed to him afterwards, but rather is a sign of his greatness. For only the originary thinking hides in itself that treasure that can never be thought through completely – and can each time be understood "better," i.e., other than what the immediately meant wording says. In the run-of-the-mill situation there is only what is understandable, and nothing of the kind that constantly requires more originary understanding and interpreting and that might itself call forth [evoke, call for, *hervorrufen*] the times that are necessary to recognize again what was supposedly known long ago and to translate it.

(Thus thinkers – and only they – also have the experience that they themselves one day understand better than what they had already thought. This has the consequence that everything that was built earlier suddenly collapses, even though they always think the same thing. But this same is not the boring emptiness of what is identical, which is only a semblance of the same. Then there are those who know nothing of the unrest of the same and are proud of the fact that they had already known as first-year students in high school what they are still thinking at 70.)

[Maly: How could one's own thinking *not* change over the years? In a private conversation, Paul Riceour – in response to a question about his saying one thing then and now something else now – said: "That was many years ago when I said that. My thinking has changed."]

Only what is truly thought has the good fortune again and once again to be understood "better" than it understood itself ["*besser*" *verstanden zu werden, als es sich selbst verstand*]. And this understanding-better is never the contribution of the interpreter, but the gift of what is interpreted.

8 Applying this to time-space (*Zeitraum*), which is the thrust of the Fifth Moment, Heidegger says: "Time and space (originally) 'are' not, but rather hold sway, emerge, unfold; *Zeit und Raum (ursprünglich) 'sind' nicht, sondern wesen*" (GA 65:385).

9 "*Die Zeit ist nicht. Es gibt die Zeit. Das Geben, das Zeit gibt, bestimmt sich aus der verweigernd-vorenthaltenden Nähe ... Wir nennen das Geben, das die eigentliche Zeit gibt, das lichtend-verbergende Reichen.*" "Zeit und Sein," in *Zur Sache des Denkens* (GA 14:20).

10 *Brauchen* from *bruchan*: to bear appropriately, to break or burst forth.

11 "*Deshalb nennen wir das erste, anfängliche, im wörtlichen Sinne an-fangende Reichen* {*marginal note: Brauchen*}, *worin die Einheit der eigentlichen Zeit beruht, die nähernde Nähe ...*" (GA 14:20).

12 These matters of lighting-up and opening and freeing are central to the Fifth Moment: Time-space as ab-ground. In that chapter they are intimately tied to emptiness.

13 *Heidegger Studies* 1 (1985): 1.

14 Orthodox literalists, reading Heidegger like a religion; existentialists, taking Heidegger's work to be about how to live as an individual; using the mirror of politics and seeing his connection with National Socialism as the key to his philosophy; the "leftist" reading, applying Heidegger to social-political matters without first understanding the thrust of his thinking; deconstruction, reading Heidegger as texts and traces in texts, finding in the grammar a "metaphysician" in Heidegger.

15 The "second beginning" is not at all like the first beginning. In German the noun *der Anfang* is used for both "beginnings." And Heidegger often uses the verb *anfangen* or the participial adjective *anfangend*. This leads me to understand that the static noun *start* covers over the dynamic here. Thus I will often use the word *starting* (let me call this "the gerund"), in order to stress and bring to bear its inherent dynamic.

16 This will become thematic in the Fifth Moment: time-space as ab-ground.

17 T. Sadler, *Heidegger and Aristotle: The Question of Being* (London: Athlone Press, 1996), 47.

18 Writing the Greek word in Greek characters helps us refrain from automatically thinking that we already know what the Greeks were saying with this word: ψυχή. As I will explain later, in the chapter on the Fourth Moment, when we see Greek words in Greek script, we experience a useful distance from the usual meaning or understanding what the Greeks want to say. There we will spend more time on this way of writing Greek words.

19 One of the more intriguing books that I have come across recently is *The Syntellect Hypothesis* by Alex M. Vikoulov (Estadelic Media Group, 2019). Where can mind's evolution lead us? From *Homo sapiens* to *Holo syntellectus*, Vikoulov says. I quote: "But biological minds reveal to us just a snippet of possible minds ... Digital Pantheism goes further and includes all other possible conscious observers such as artificially intelligent self-aware entities" (357).

4. First Moment: Heidegger and Non-Dual Thinking, Inseparable Phenomenon

1 When I say "all" here, I mean to say that already in *Sein und Zeit* he was pursuing this question, even as it could not be *said* there yet.
2 Heidegger, "*Gelassenheit*," in GA 16:517–29. Translated into English by J.M. Anderson and E.H. Freund as "Memorial Address," in *Discourse on Thinking* (New York: Harper and Row, 1966), 43–57.
3 Anticipatory only in the sense that Heidegger made it public for the first time in 1955. But the question of the first beginning and the other/second beginning – which I here call starting or the "start" – had already been worked out in *Beiträge* (written between 1936 and 1938), which Heidegger deliberately did not publish at that time. *Beiträge* was published in 1989 – only after the majority of his Freiburg lectures after the publication of *Sein und Zeit* had been published.
4 Heidegger's term here is *die Technik*. I explicate this issue in "The Translator's Workshop" in the Third Moment.
5 This marginal note by Heidegger shows very clearly that he wants us to understand that *Existenz* comes to mean far more than the transcendental phenomenology of *Sein und Zeit*, more than what *Sein und Zeit* was taken to mean and to say at first. One could say that this marginal note shows how, later, Heidegger himself saw how the other beginning (the starting) was operative already in *Sein und Zeit*.
6 Quotations in the last two paragraphs are from GA 2:71–3.
7 As Heidegger's thinking unfolds, from *Sein und Zeit* to *Beiträge*, the thinking-naming of his lifelong project changes from *Sein* to *Seyn* – from "being" to "beyng." Since this transformation cannot be pinpointed –

either logically or conceptually, let alone within the thinking-saying itself – it is hard to know at each point which form of the word, *being* or *beyng*, fits better. For one thing, they belong together even as each word says differently. In these early pages of my text I have not attempted any clear distinction between the two words. As I use the word *being* at this point, there are surely intimations of what the later word *beyng* wants to say. In a kind of *aporia*, how to understand these two words – and especially the word *Seyn/beyng* – should happen in the last chapter, the Fifth Moment.

8 Here a reminder of what Heidegger says about reading and thinking Kant's *Critique of Pure Reason* (see n7 in Chapter 3): "Further, interpretation itself is simply the implementation of the translation that is still silent, has not yet entered the word that would accomplish this." This applies to Heidegger's own way, or way-making, namely that Heidegger's own thinking "had not yet entered the word that would accomplish this."

Heidegger:

> They [the empty vanity of minds that are merely clever] conclude that in such a case Kant himself had not quite known what he really wanted and that now the interpreter who comes afterwards knows this precisely. But, that a thinker can be understood "better" than he understood himself – this is in no way a flaw [lack, *Mangel*] that could be attributed to him afterwards, but rather is a sign of his greatness. For only the originary thinking hides in itself that treasure that can never be thought through completely – and can each time be understood "better," i.e., other than what the immediately meant wording says.

One could say that the morphing of moving beyond the ontological difference shows how Heidegger himself "understood better," that is, other than what the earlier wording meant/says.

Dare we practise this kind of understanding of Heidegger "after" Heidegger? This leads me to a significant tangent to my project, namely how to understand why "the third section [*Abschnitt*] [of Part 1] of *Sein und Zeit – Zeit und Sein –* was held back" at the time and how to name this "missing section." Heidegger says that the ultimate business of philosophy is "to preserve the force of the most elemental words" (GA 2:291). Putting this sentiment in my own words, I would say that the philosopher/thinker has a deep love of words and language, caringly caring for words and how they are used. Even analytic philosophers love words! This brings me back to the question of how to name and describe what was "missing" in the *Sein und Zeit* of 1927. First let me simply "list" the parts and sections, as Heidegger describes them in *Sein und Zeit*:

Part One: The interpretation of Dasein in terms of temporality and the explication of time as the transcendental horizon for the question of being.
Part Two: Basic features of a phenomenological dismantling [*Destruktion* ... I use the word *dismantling* to keep clear that this project is nothing like what we today know as deconstruction]

The first part consists of three sections [*Abschnitte*]:

1. The preparatory fundamental analysis of Dasein.
2. Dasein and temporality.
3. Time and being.

The second part is organized in three [sections] as well:

1. *Kant's* doctrine of schematism and time as the preliminary stage of the problematic of temporality.
2. The ontological foundation of *Descartes' cogito sum* and taking over medieval ontology into the problem of *res cogitans*.
3. *Aristotle's* treatise on time as a way of discerning the phenomenal basis and the limits of ancient ontology. (GA 2:53)

There is some agreement that the three sections of Part Two of the whole project were dealt with in later lectures and texts of Heidegger. This means that it is the third section of Part One that is problematic here – namely, what was "held back" in 1927 and remains unfinished to this day? Or is somehow "finished" in a way different from how Heidegger conceived it in 1927?

(Please note that over the years this third section or "division" of Part One has often been named the "second half of *Sein und Zeit*" that was "held back.")

Here and there this "holding back" is called a failure. Heidegger "failed" to show how temporality is the sense of being as such – and this failure had to do with Heidegger's "overreaching." The book without the section that was held back is sometimes also named as "fragmentary." Failure and fragmentariness.

So my first observation here is that caring for language is compromised with these words: failure, fragmentariness, overreach. Setting aside whether the "task [*Aufgabe*]" of this section remained or remains unfinished, it was never seen by Heidegger as a failure or as fragmentary. We can verify this by looking at how Heidegger describes why the third section was "held back" in 1927, why it was/is not a failure, how it does not make *Sein und Zeit* a fragment, and why there is no overreach by Heidegger.

> For this latter task, not only are most of the words lacking, but above all the "grammar" is missing … and as we open up the area of being, way more difficult than what was afforded the Greeks to think, the complicatedness [enigma, intricacy, incomprehensibility – muddy, unfathomable, indecipherability, *Umständlichkeit*] of concept formation grows and the expression gets tougher. (GA 2:52)
>
> Accomplishing the thinking that abandons subjectivity was made more difficult when with the publication of *Sein und Zeit* the third section of the first part, *Zeit und Sein*, was held back. Here the whole thing turns around. The section in question was held back because the thinking fell short because of no sufficient way to say* this turning and so did not break through via the language of metaphysics.
> *Marginal note: *Sichzeigenlassen*: to let be shown. (GA 9:327–8)

Note that what "failed" here was nothing that Heidegger "failed to do"; rather, thinking did not have a sufficient way to say it, because of the limits of the language of metaphysics. This goes far beyond any failure by Heidegger.

> This turning is not a change in the perspective of *Sein und Zeit*, but rather, in the turning, the attempted thinking first arrives at the place of the dimension from within which *Sein und Zeit* is experienced, namely experienced in the grounding experience of the forgetfulness of being [*marginal note: Forgetfulness – Λήθη – hiding-sheltering – withdrawal – Enteignis: Ereignis]. (GA 9:328)

The marginal notes added to this quotation show quite clearly Heidegger's own rereading of *Sein und Zeit* showing just how the thinking and saying in *Sein und Zeit*, already carry the core dimension that belongs to the section that was withheld. It also shows how this clarity in the marginal notes was not available in 1927, because of the things mentioned above: no sufficient way to say it, the language and grammar of metaphysics, the necessity of the turning (which we humans do not control).

In summary, rather than calling *Sein und Zeit* a failure or something fragmentary, the language of Heidegger – both in the *Sein und Zeit* of 1927 and in the marginal notes added along the way after 1927 – shows the *promise* already there in *Sein und Zeit* as well as the timing that was necessary for a sufficient language that could say or let be shown the core theme of the third section of the first part of *Sein und Zeit*. More than that, it shows how thinking and saying unfold within the richness of Heidegger's single pursuit over his lifetime of thinking.

Let me end here by repeating a couple sentences of Heidegger's from the beginning of this note:

> But, that a thinker can be understood "better" than he understood himself – this is in no way a flaw [lack, *Mangel*] that could be attributed to him afterwards, but rather is a sign of his greatness. For only the originary thinking hides in itself that treasure that can never be thought through completely – and can each time be understood "better," i.e., other than what the immediately meant wording says.

Heidegger is referring to a thinker's being understood better by a thinker coming after. In this case it is also true that at a later point Heidegger could understand better what he himself attempted earlier. Better because the openings that are necessary come "after" what the immediately meant wording said "before." And this is a sign of greatness, not failure.

9 I have chosen to translate *Augenblicksstätte* as "flashpoint." It is the "point" at which something bursts open, at which there is an outburst or bursting out. *To flash* is to break out into sudden action, to break out suddenly, to burst suddenly forth. Point: a decisive juncture or joining; the centre of something; the highest degree of something; a moment of decision; something that has a tapering tip, where everything comes to "a point"; *fig.* sharpness, wit, or penetrativeness of performance; a witty or incisive action. Point as acme: the point at which something is "at its best"; here is the fullest, a full blossoming of something.

10 It is intriguing that already in the 1970s the Czech philosopher Jan Patočka saw this exciting and revolutionary move by Heidegger. See Patočka's

two essays "Der Subjektivismus der Husserlschen und die Forderung einer asubjektiven Phänomenologie [Husserl's Subjectivism and the Call for an Asubjective Phenomenology]," *Studia minora facultatis Philosophicae universitatis brunensis*, F series (1971): 14–15; and "Epochē und Reduktion – einige Bemerkungen [Epoche and Reduction: Some Observations]," in A. Bucher, H. Drüe, and th.M. Seebohm, eds., *Bewußtsein. Gerhard Funke zu eigen* (Bonn: Bouvier, 1975), 76–85. English translations of these two essays appear in L. Učnik, I. Chvatik, and A. Williams, eds., *Asubjective Phenomenology: Jan Patočka's Project in the Broader Context of His Work* (Nordhausen: Verlag Traugott Bautz, 2015), 1–54.
11 See n7 in Chapter 3.
12 See A. Hofstadter, "Enownment," in *Martin Heidegger and the Question of Literature: Toward a Postmodern Literary Hermeneutics*, ed. W.V. Spanos (Bloomington: Indiana University Press, 1979), 17–37.
13 Ibid., 29.
14 See Hofstadter, in his introduction to his translation of some of Heidegger's essays published in English under the title *Poetry, Language, Thought* (New York: Harper and Row, 1975), xix. The fourfold is "the *ereignende*/enowning mirror-play of the onefold of earth and sky, divinities and mortals" (Heidegger, "Das Ding," GA 7:181; translation in *Poetry, Language, Thought*, 179). En-owning/*Er-eignis* names the work of owning/*eignen* by which the fourfold is thought/said in the dynamic at-oneness and the dynamic at-oneness is said in the fourfold.
15 K. Maly, *Heidegger's Possibility: Language, Emergence, Saying Be-ing* (Toronto: University of Toronto Press, 2008), 111.
16 Even as this thinking is preparatory, it is already and still thinking. See the Fifth Moment.
17 W. Biemel, *Heidegger* (Reinbek bei Hamburg: Rowohlt, 1973), 129.

5. Second Moment: Heidegger and Non-Conceptual Language as Saying

1 Some parts of this section are a reworking of parts of chapter 2, "Own to Language: Word and Saying," from my book *Heidegger's Possibility: Language, Emergence – Saying Be-ing*. Note that in the current work I use the English word *beyng* instead of *be-ing*.
2 Heidegger, "*Rückweg und Kehre*," *Jahresgabe der Martin-Heidegger-Gesellschaft* (2000), 17.
3 Quotations in this paragraph are from F.-W. von Herrmann, *Die zarte, aber helle Differenz. Heidegger und Stefan George* (Frankfurt am Main: Klostermann Verlag, 1999), 55.

4 Heidegger, "*Das Wort: Die Bedeutung der Wörter*," in *Zur philosophischen Aktualität Heideggers*, vol. 3: *Im Spiegel der Welt. Sprache, Übersetzung, Auseinandersetzung*, ed. D. Papenfuss and O. Pöggeler (Frankfurt am Main: Klostermann Verlag, 1992), 14.
5 Ibid., 16.
6 Ibid.
7 In the dialogue the Japanese interlocutor remembers this course to have had the title *Ausdruck und Erscheinung* (Expression and Appearance). A marginal note added by Heidegger in his personal copy of *Unterwegs zur Sprache* reads: "richtig: Phänomenologie der Anschauung und des Ausdrucks. 1920 (correct: Phenomenology of Intuition and Expression. 1920)" See GA 12:86. This 1920 lecture course is published as GA 59.
8 *Logos als die Frage nach dem Wesen der Sprache.* (GA 38)
9 It might be useful here to remind ourselves once again of the ambiguity that Heidegger found in the word *Sein/being*. This has to do in part with the tie that the word *Sein/being* has with metaphysics, thus used in describing the ontological difference. Drawn along by the matter itself, within language, his thinking moved from using the word, to not using the word, to writing the word and then crossing it out – all attempts to think/say what the matter at hand is. Of course, in *Beiträge zur Philosophie (Vom Ereignis)* he introduced yet another word-image: *Seyn/beyng*.
10 There is an implication here of the dynamic tension of distinguishing and gathering, of moving apart while moving toward, of cutting apart to gather together, parting that yields the originary non-dual enowning. If we get a good sense of this "to and away and unto" of the beckoning here, we also get a better sense of what happens in *Beiträge*, in the section on "Time-Space as Ab-ground" (section 242, 264ff.), where Heidegger uses the words *Ent-rückung* (shifting-away) and *Be-rückung* (shifting-unto). Remembering that "ab-ground" is the staying-away of ground and that thinking needs to think *unto* the staying-away, the very "unto" is that whence the onefold of time-space first gets thought. This interlocking web of shifting-away and of shifting-unto opens up the space for thinking enowning, thinking beyng as enowning, thinking the deep swaying of beyng, in its beyng-historical sway. Another way to think this dynamic is to think how the unfolding, opening, deep swaying is outside the realm of any dualistic thinking (body–soul, night–day, metaphysics–non-metaphysics, being–beings). Can one dare to think that?
11 In a marginal note to this last sentence ("Saying ... the way/manner of enowning") Heidegger writes, "belongs into enowning" – "*in das Ereignis gehört.*" One could say, then, that *being* the *manner* or *way* of

enowning and *belonging/fitting into* enowning say the same from out of the same.

12 In the first paragraph of the lecture "*Georg Trakl: Eine Erörterung seines Gedichtes,*" published in *Unterwegs zur Sprache* as "*Die Sprache im Gedicht*" (Language in the Poem), Heidegger says:

> Here *erörtern* means first of all: to direct something into its place/site [*Ort*]. That means then: to heed that site/place. Both – directing into and heeding the place/site – are preparatory steps in a discussing that opens [*Erörtern*]. And yet, we already venture enough if in the following [lecture] we limit ourselves to the preparatory steps. The opening discussion ends – corresponding to any pathway of thinking – in a question. That question inquires into the siting of the place/site [*nach der Ortschaft des Ortes*: into the placeness of the place, the site-hood of the site] …
>
> Originally the word *place/site* means the tip of the spear. Everything comes/runs together in it. The place/site gathers to itself, in the highest degree. The gathering permeates and sways through everything. The site/place, the gathering, takes-in to itself, preserves what is taken-in – but not like a capsule that closes off, but rather such that it [the site/ point] shines through the gathered, lights it up, and thereby first releases it into its own. (GA 12:33)

In normal German usage *erörtern* means "discuss or explicate." That is, discuss in order to explicate. It is interesting how in English there are several synonyms for "explicate" that are etymologically about "light": elucidate/shed light on, illuminate, clarify or be lucid. So the word *erörtern* – lighting up or shedding light on – here may seem to be about discussing, but for Heidegger it immediately goes deeper, being about unfolding and elucidating. Grimms says that *erörtern* says: *in ort ermessen*: to gauge, calibrate, fathom in site/place. I imagine that the opening line of this essay emerged after Heidegger himself checked *Grimms Wörterbuch*.

13 When Heidegger wrote this dialogue, "*Aus einem Gespräch von der Sprache,*" he gave it a subtitle: "*Zwischen einem Japaner und einem Fragenden.*" Thus he names the two dialogue partners as a "Japanese" and an "Inquirer." The text was written in 1953–54 after a visit from the Japanese Germanist Tomio Tezuka. This is Heidegger's thinking, not a transcription of an actual dialogue. Thus "a Japanese" is more than Professor Tezuka; and although one can justify taking "an Inquirer" to mean Heidegger, in some sense "an Inquirer" is also more than

Heidegger – namely, anyone who questions and thinks in this way. There is a lot of subtlety here.
14 What follows here is my summary of this part of the dialogue, see GA 12:134–6.
15 Note how the one word *Sage* says all three of these aspects as a non-dual dynamic.
16 The Japanese word *iki* is traditionally translated as something like "aesthetics." But earlier in this dialogue there was discussion about that word (GA 12:131–3). In summary:

> (a) *"Iki, ein Wort, das Ich auch jetzt nicht zu überzetzen wage,"* (b) *"Iki ist das Anmutende,"* and (c) *"Iki ist das Wehen der Stille des leuchtenden Entzückens."*
> (a) *"Iki*, a word that even I at this point do not dare to translate." (b) *"Iki* is erupting." (c) *"Iki* is the gentle breeze of the stillness of radiant delight."

17 *"Das Wesen der Sprache,"* GA 12:188.

6. Third Moment: Heidegger and the Symbiosis of Translation and Thinking, from Saying

1 The first three points mentioned below are explicitly named in my book *Heidegger's Possibility: Language, Emergence – Saying Be-ing* (Toronto: University of Toronto Press, 2008), 165ff. The last three points follow from these first three and are implicit in that book. Here I draw them out.
2 The word *true* is in quotation marks here, in order to avoid the seemingly automatic assumption that a "true" translation means "fully equivalent," which is impossible. Rather I want to suggest that a "true" translation is one that is "true to" its proper measure. In this case that means: true to the saying word, true to the saying of beyng as emergence, including the saying that humans enact in response.
3 P. Emad, "Thinking More Deeply into the Question of Translation: Essential Translation and the Unfolding of Language," in *Reading Heidegger: Commemorations*, ed. J. Sallis (Bloomington: Indiana University Press, 1993), 337.
4 Reminder: When speaking another language or translating anything from one language to another, nothing is really "automatic." This is even more true for Heidegger.

5 • Heidegger, GA 32, *Hegel's Phenomenology of Spirit*, trans. K. Maly and P. Emad (Bloomington: Indiana University Press, 1988).
  • H.W. Petzet, *Encounters and Dialogues with Martin Heidegger*, trans. K. Maly and P. Emad (Chicago: University of Chicago Press, 1993).
  • Heidegger, GA 25, *Phenomenological Interpretation of Kant's Critique of Pure Reason*, trans. K. Maly and P. Emad (Bloomington: Indiana University Press, 1996).
  • Heidegger, GA 65, *Contributions to Philosophy (From Enowning)*, trans. K. Maly and P. Emad (Bloomington: Indiana University Press, 1999).
  • F.-W. von Herrmann, *Hermeneutics and Reflection: Heidegger and Husserl on the Concept of Phenomenology*, trans. K. Maly (Toronto: University of Toronto Press, 2013).
6 Heidegger, *Die Technik und die Kehre* (Pfullingen: Neske Verlag, 1962). Now published in GA 79.
7 Heidegger, "The Turning," trans. K. Maly, in *Research in Phenomenology* 1 (1971): 5–6.
8 Ibid.
9 Heidegger, *The Question concerning Technology and Other Essays*, trans. W. Lovitt (New York: Harper and Row, 1977), 38.
10 Ibid., 37.
11 Note that, whereas Heidegger makes this distinction very clearly in *Beiträge*, he himself is not always consistent in his usage. However, once we know the distinction between *Sein* and *Seyn*, we are able to think *Seyn*, even when the word Heidegger has used is *Sein*. A prime example of this is toward the end of 1962 essay "Zeit und Sein," where Heidegger shows that with the thinking of Ereignis we futurally retrieve the oldest of the old, named *A-letheia*. He says there that the task of that essay was "to think being [*Sein*] into what is own to it, from within and out of *Ereignis*, without considering the relation of being to beings." This means, he says, "thinking being [*Sein*] without considering metaphysics" (GA 14:29). But in *Beiträge* any "being" that is not determined by its relationship to beings is named *beyng/Seyn*. When one thinks about the thinkable and the sayable in this essay, it is clear that, when Heidegger wrote "thinking being [*Sein*] without considering metaphysics," he could have used *Seyn* instead of *Sein*.
12 For what I say here regarding *Technik* and *Ge-Stell* I have drawn on my translator's notes to the translation of H. Padrutt, "Heidegger and Ecology," in *Heidegger and the Earth: Essays in Environmental Philosophy*, ed. L. McWhorter and G. Stenstad (Toronto: University of Toronto Press, 2009), 43nn13–14.

13 Cf. the earlier discussion of *Gelassenheit*.
14 See the discussion on "thing" toward the end of Chapter 3.
15 Professor Emad and I had translated *das Wesen* as "deep sway" in the first draft of our translation of *Beiträge zur Philosophie (Vom Ereignis)*. However, at that time, among the reviewers of the translation, there emerged the fear that the word *deep* could not be used, because it always says and means something that is the opposite of surface. In negotiations with Indiana University Press, Professor Emad and I agreed to change our translation of *das Wesen* from "deep sway" to "essential sway" – aware of a certain enigma in the word *essential*. From where I sit today, I would opt once again for our original translation: "deep sway" for *Wesen* and "deep swaying" for *Wesung* – confident that the German word *tief* and the English word *deep* neither only nor always says what is opposite to surface. Rather the word *deep* says what is at the heart of anything, at its core. Thus the tip of the arrow, where everything is focused – where everything comes together – is indeed "deep."

7. Fourth Moment: Heidegger and Engaging in the Retrieval of Greek Thinking-Saying

1 My next project is to take up this question of retranslating and rethinking Greek philosophy in greater detail. It is truly a work of *retrieving* the freshness and possibility in Greek thinking. Let's see what happens.
2 It would be a study in itself to research how, in seventeenth-century England, philosophical works were translated from the original Greek text. Before that time all English translations used Latin sources for the Greek. In our context here the known translations of *dynamis* and *energeia* were through the Scholastic Latin: *potentia* and *actualitas*. Thus, when the translators translated directly from Greek to English, they used Latinate words (English words that derived from the Latin), without rethinking the original Greek words, instead using the known translations of key words: *potentiality* and *actuality*.
3 One wonders why this lecture (from 1941) does not use the word *Seyn/beyng*, which is at the centre of *Beiträge* (written between 1936 and 1938). We will go into this difference between *Sein/being* and *Seyn/beyng* in the next chapter.
4 "Andenken" in *Erläuterungen zu Hölderlins Dichtung*, GA 4:84.
5 P. Jaeger and Rudolf Lüthe, eds., *Distanz und Nähe. Reflexionen und Analysen zur Kunst und Gegenwart. Festschrift für Walter Biemel* (Würzburg: Königshausen + Neumann), 20.

6 From this point onward, to the end of this chapter, it will often be obvious how putting the Greek word in Greek script is useful, meaningful, and freeing – freeing us from jumping too quickly to the conclusion that we *already* know what the Greek word is saying.
7 I have chosen here to leave the German words *Unverborgenheit* and *Wahrheit* untranslated. *Unverborgenheit* is a Heideggerian word and means "disclosure, non-concealment, coming out of hiddenness." *Wahrheit* is normally the German word for "truth" and is usually applied to propositions or ways of speaking (truth versus falsehood). It also has the meanings of "trueness" and "truthfulness" and "actual fact." In these senses one can "speak the truth, hide the truth, stretch the truth." The usual senses of the German *Wahrheit* and the English *truth* get nowhere near saying what ἀλήθεια /*Unverborgenheit* wants to say in Heidegger.
8 I will address this issue in the next chapter, namely how quantum physics starts to understand the basic "elements" as not necessarily physical – or even "real."
9 Quoted in Simplicius, *Phys.* 24, 13; DK 12 A 9, and Hippolytus *Ref.* 1, 6, 1–2: DK 12 A 11. From G.S. Kirk and J.E. Raven, *The Presocratic Philosophers* (Cambridge: Cambridge University Press, 1957), 105–10. The following quotations are from these pages.
10 Kirk and Raven, *The Presocratic Philosophers*, 107.
11 Ibid., 108.
12 This quotation is from the entry on Anaximander, in *Handwörterbuch der Philosophie*, ed. W.D. Rehfus (Göttingen: Vandenhoeck & Ruprecht, 2003).
13 Nietzsche, *Die Philosophie im tragischen Zeitalter der Griechen*, Sections 9–10.
14 Read here beyng (*Seyn*), even though Heidegger writes "*Sein.*"
15 Kirk and Raven, *The Presocratic Philosophers*, 267.
16 See, for example, the translation provided by Kirk and Raven, *The Presocratic Philosophers*, 270: "That which can be spoken and thought must be; for it is possible for it, but not for nothing, to be."
17 These words naming what is not pure are from a text by Goethe that Heidegger quotes here.
18 A little later I will delve into this issue by looking at several Aristotle texts and watching how they get translated. For now let me mention how Joe Sachs translates and reads *entelecheia*. He translates the Greek word in Aristotle as "being-at-work-staying-itself" and says that the word is a "fusion of completeness with that of continuity or persistence." If continuity means change and movement, then within the core of *entelecheia* is movement. See Sachs, *Aristotle's Physics: A Guided Study*

(New Brunswick: Rutgers University Press, 1995), 245. We will return to this issue later, in more detail.
19 In a preliminary way we can say that Aristotle sees the phenomena in ἐντελέχεια and ἐνέργεια as convergent. See Aristotle, *Metaphysics*, Book IX (1047a, 30–1 and 1050a, 21–3) as well as Sachs, *Aristotle's Physics*, 79. We will look further into this matter when we spend time on the texts from the *Metaphysics*.
20 *Platon: Sophistes*, GA 19.
21 In Jacob Klein, *Lectures and Essays* (Annapolis: St John's College Press, 1985).
22 Joe Sachs, "Introduction," in *Aristotle's Metaphysics*, trans. J. Sachs (Santa Fe: Green Lion Press, 2002), xxxv–xxxvi.
23 Ibid., xxxiv–xxxv
24 A very useful book is F.E. Peters, *Greek Philosophical Terms* (New York: NYU Press, 1967). He goes both ways, namely toward the "received" as well as the "retrieving" translation of these words. For example, δύναμις is: active and passive capacity, hence (1) power and (2) potentiality; ἐνέργεια is: functioning, activity, act, actualization. But then: ἐντελέχεια is: state of completion or perfection, actuality; ἀρχή is: beginning, principle, ultimate underlying substance (*Urstoff*); οὐσία is: substance.
25 Words in quotation marks here are from Sachs. In the following pages, check example no. 7 and the footnote there.
26 Joe Sachs, "Glossary," in *Aristotle's Metaphysics*, trans. J. Sachs (Santa Fe: Green Lion Press, 2002), lvii.
27 Ibid.
28 Ibid., li. Sachs continues the translation: "(such as losing weight, for the thing that is losing weight, when it is doing so, is in motion in that way, although that for the sake of which the motions take place is not present), this is not an action, or at any rate not a complete one; but that in which the end is present is an action." One can read this as: Among things that *are approaching*, the progressive form inherently showing action, movement, dynamic activity.
29 Ibid., li–lii.
30 Sachs puts in a footnote (179): "That is, beings do not just happen to perform strings of isolated deeds, but their activity forms a **continuous state of being-at-work**, in which they achieve the completion that makes them what they are. Aristotle is arguing that the very thinghood of a thing is not what might be hidden inside it, but a definite way of **being unceasingly at-work**, that makes it a thing at all and the kind of thing it is." Bold by me.

31 *Stünden wir erst, rein verzweigt*
   im Geäst des Seyns,
   frei zum Wind, der uns verschweigt,
   bleibt alles Eins. (GA 81:63)
32 I have provided here a summary of what Heidegger describes in much fuller detail in GA 33:217–18. What Heidegger does in this passage is an excellent example of phenomenological seeing and interpretation or laying out – of a *dynamic* and not something static at all.
33 Sachs: being-at-work-staying-complete.
34 Robin Wall Kimmerer, *Gathering Moss: A Natural and Cultural History of Mosses* (Corvallis: Oregon State University Press, 2003), 168.
35 *Omnis comparatio claudicat.*

8. Fifth Moment: Time-Space as Ab-ground – Ab-grounding and Timing-Spacing

1 In one sense semi-hidden. On the other hand, already on the third page of *Beiträge* it is announced as crucial to the work of thinking:

> The time of "systems" is over. The time for building the shaping that is own to beings from within the truth of beyng has not yet come. In between [these two "times"] philosophy in the crossing to another beginning [the second beginning as what "starts" the work] has to have achieved something crucial: the throwing-open, i.e., *the grounding opening of the freeplay of time-space* of the truth of beyng. [Italics mine] (GA 65:5)

And in section 10 *time-space* is included in a list of where to look in order to uncover how beyng and Ereignis hold sway in the "starting" of the second beginning (GA 65:30).
2 Note that all three of these words refer to light, lighting up – or *Lichtung-clearing*. *Elucidate* from the Latin *lux/lucis* and *illuminate* from the Latin *lumen/luminis*.
3 "The original form of the stem of the noun in Old English is *ǣmett*, but simplification of the geminate (to *ǣmet-*) and syncopation of the medial *e* is frequent both in the noun and the derived adjective, giving *ǣmt-* as a common form. Already in Old English, the development of an epenthetic glide consonant *p* in the resulting consonant group *-mt-* is attested for the adjective and its derivatives" (OED).
4 "The long initial vowel ǣ of the adjective is subject to shortening in late Old English and early Middle English, both in its trisyllabic form and in its disyllabic form (before the consonant cluster). The resulting

short vowel regularly gave forms in ă and ĕ in Middle English; while the former type is not recorded after 1500, the latter is reflected by the modern standard form" (OED).
5 Interesting that the OED lists several usages of the word in 1971, 1984, and 2005.
6 F.-W. von Herrmann, *Hermeneutische Phänomenologie des Daseins. Eine Erläuterung von "Sein und Zeit,"* vol. 1 (Frankfurt am Main: Klostermann Verlag, 1987), 74.
7 Note the direct and intimate connection of the empty to the open. See below.
8 See, for example, https://futurism.com/measurements-cern-new-physics.
9 Disclaimer: I am not an expert in quantum physics, especially not in the mathematics that is its foundation. Thus this brief excursus into these theories or principles is intended merely to offer signposts or markings with connotations for what is at stake here.
10 Note that for Einstein the space of space-time remained something physical. Entanglement casts doubt on this physicality and points to a no-thing, something like the emptiness of space – or space as emptiness, the dynamic of radiant emptiness as space/spacing.
11 https://www.brainyquote.com/quotes/quotes/e/erwinschro304795.html.
12 Ibid.
13 https://en.wikiquote.org/wiki/Erwin_Schr%C3%B6dinger.
14 https://todayinsci.com/S/Schrodinger_Erwin/SchrodingerErwin-Quotations.htm.
15 http://www.azquotes.com/quote/515874.
16 http://www.azquotes.com/quote/570933.
17 http://www.azquotes.com/quote/1251771.
18 http://www.azquotes.com/quote/30754.
19 *The Buddha Speaks: A Book of Guidance from the Buddhist Scriptures*, ed. Anne Bancroft (Boulder: Shambhala, 2000), 33.
20 Quotation is from G.C. Lichtenberg, *Schriften und Briefe*, vol. 2 (Hanser Verlag, 1971), 200.
21 Heidegger, *"Zum Einblick in die Notwendigkeit der Kehre,"* in *Vom Rätsel des Begriffs: Festschrift für Friedrich-Wilhelm von Herrmann zum 65. Geburtstag*, ed. Paola-Ludovika Coriando (Berlin: Duncker and Humblot, 1999), 1–3.
22 As we have seen, what Heidegger here calls *Existenz* he later calls *Inständigkeit/Innestehen*: inabiding, dwelling.
23 Roger T. Ames and David L. Hall, *Daodejing "Making This Life Sigificant": A Philosophical Translation* (New York: Ballantine Books, 2003).

24 "Apparently for *spaund, < Anglo-Norman *espaundre*, = Old French *espandre* (modern French *épandre*) to shed, spill, pour out < Latin *expandĕre* expand" (OED).
25 I reiterate what I said earlier: *Das Unverständliche*: incomprehensible, unintelligible, non-conceptual and inconceivable, inarticulable, unfathomable, non-transparent, not graspable, impenetrable, inexplicable – in the sense of not comprehensible by the intellect.
26 See Friedrich-Wilhelm von Herrmann, *Hermeneutik und Reflexion. Der Begriff der Phänomenologie bei Heidegger und Husserl* (Frankfurt am Main: Vittorio Klostermann, 2000); *Hermeneutics and Reflection: Heidegger and Husserl on the Concept of Phenomenology*, trans. K. Maly (Toronto: University of Toronto Press, 2013).
27 See my book *Heidegger's Possibility*, 79.
28 *Proper*: fitting, belonging, appropriate, congruous ... or what is own to. In this case, the reading that is "proper" is a reading that fits within the poietic way of languaging, the way of saying-showing of that unto which the gathering gathers.
29 P.-L. Coriando, *Der letzte Gott als Anfang: Zur ab-gründigen Zeit-Räumlichkeit des Übergangs in Heideggers "Beiträge zur Philosophie (Vom Ereignis)"* (Munich: Wilhelm Fink Verlag, 1998), 59.
30 Ibid.
31 Ibid., 65.
32 Ibid., 64.
33 Cf. OED under, *flash*, *point*, and *flash point*.
34 Here, at the very beginning of *Beiträge*, Heidegger shows so clearly how the meaning of the word *Entwurf* (as belonging to the being of Da-sein in *Sein und Zeit*) has "morphed" into *Entwurf* as a throwing-open that grounds the truth of beyng.
35 Note that the traditional English translation of *dynamis* in Aristotle says: *potential* and *static*. Cf. the Fourth Moment above.
36 Grammatically there are two subjects to this verb and therefore it should be plural: "the turning-in-relation and belonginging of time-space to the deep sway of truth open up." But the text has a singular verb: "the turning-in-relation and belonginging of time-space to the deep sway of truth *opens* up." One can ponder however one wants; I decided to leave the singular verb "opens," as it is in the German. The next paragraph in the text tries to think this phrase "phenomenologically."

Index

affordance (*das Geschick*), 20, 92–3, 96–7, 174
aletheia / a-letheia, 8–9, 18, 29, 31, 43, 45, 48, 64, 81, 153–4, 181, 201, 203, 226n11
Aletheia (goddess), 107
ἀλήθεια / ἀ–λήθεια, 102–3, 109, 118–22, 138, 228v7
Ames, Roger T., 166–7
Anaximander, 48, 101–2, 108–9, 112, 114–18
Anaximenes, 112
apeiron, 116
ἄπειρον, 112, 115–18, 165
aporia, 218n7
ἀπορία, 103
arche, 127
ἀρχή 115–18, 127, 129, 229v24
Aristotle, 25–7, 101–2, 105, 108–16, 123–35
awareness, xix, 8, 27, 30, 35, 38, 45, 56, 59, 97, 164–5, 179; knowing awareness, 57, 144–5, 162, 171–2, 178, 180, 183; thinking awareness, xvii
awe (*die Scheu*), 38–9

Biemel, Walter, 51
Bohr, Niels, 160

Borman, Karl, 116
Bourgeois, Louise, 14, 87
Buddhism, 15–16, 155–8; buddha mind, 155–6; Buddhist view, 156–8

calculating thinking (*das rechnende Denken*), 34–6
chaos theory, 158
Cicero, 136
crossing, 16, 29, 33–4, 37–9, 110, 124–5, 171–2, 230n1

dao, 78, 156–8, 165–7
Daodejing, 166–7
Daoism, 15, 155–8; Daoist, 15, 157
Dasein or Da-sein?, 96
deconstruction, 3, 15, 216n14, 219n8
Democritus, 112, 160
Descartes, 27, 219n8
dynamis, 26, 127–35, 200, 227n2, 232n5
δύναμις, 109, 123–35
dualism, 32, 37, 41, 180–3; dualistic, 28, 32, 99, 113–14, 137, 140–1, 143, 155–7, 179, 182–3, 187, 223n10

eignen, vii, 46–8, 72, 75, 77, 222n14
Einstein, Albert, 19, 113, 138, 174, 231n10

Emad, Parvis, 21, 30, 83, 90–1, 94, 197, 227n15
energeia, 26, 123–35
ἐνέργεια, 102, 109, 123–36, 229n19, 229n24
entanglement, 159, 231n10
entelecheia, 123–35
ἐντελέχεια, 123–36
eon, 150, 153–4, 203
ἐόν, 102, 121–2, 138
eon emmenai, 76
ἐὸν ἔμμεναι, 121, 145

flashpoint (*Augenblicksstätte*), 43, 141, 151, 153, 175, 191–6, 204, 209–10, 221n10
Furth, Montgomery, 127–31

Geschick, das. See affordance
Ge-stell/Gestell, das, 88–9, 91–2, 95

Hall, David I., 166–7
Hegel, 25, 27
Heidegger Studies, 25, 90
Heisenberg, Werner, 19, 158, 160
Heraclitus, 27, 29, 48, 52–3, 58, 102, 108, 110–11, 118, 182
hermeneutics, 24–5, 59–6, 69, 73
Higgs boson particle, 158
hint/hinting (*der Wink, winken*), 15, 68, 74, 137, 140, 143, 153, 186, 189–93, 207–10
Hofstadter, Albert, 46
Horace, 136
Husserl, Edmund, 13, 15, 138, 181

information technology, 28, 35, 89, 91–2, 94
intimating (*die Ahnung*), 38–9, 50, 101, 168, 189, 192

Kant, Immanuel, 9, 15, 26–7, 49, 107, 138, 185, 215n7, 218n8
kinesis, 127
κίνησις, 123–35
Kirk and Raven, 115–16
Klein, Jacob, 125
koto ba, 67–8, 71

leap, the, 23, 32–3, 53, 144, 171, 177, 181, 183, 207
Leere, die, 50–1, 144, 146, 207
lichtende Verbergung, die, 153, 206
Lichtung, die, 18, 51, 142, 153, 200
logos, xv, 18, 25, 27, 29, 41, 55, 58, 61, 64, 75, 105, 110–12, 135, 154
λόγος, 101–2, 105, 109, 110–12, 138
Lovitt, William, 89–91

Memorial Address (*Gelassenheit*), 34–7
metabole, 127
μεταβολή, 124–8
Merleau-Ponty, Maurice, 44
mindful/minding thinking (*das besinnliche Denken*), 34–6, 133, 168

Nietzsche, Friedrich, 118

obscure, the, 44, 110, 137, 158, 165, 182–3
ontological difference, 31, 42–5, 90, 141, 143, 179, 187, 218n8, 223n9
ousia, 25–6, 127–9
οὐσία, 127–9, 229n24

Parmenides, 48, 101–2, 107–9, 115, 118–22
phenomenology, 9, 13, 21, 24–5, 41, 59, 64, 181, 193
physis, xv, 31, 43, 45, 153–4, 166, 169, 201, 203, 210

φύσις, 101–2, 109, 112–14, 138, 145
Plato, 26, 102
poiesis/poi–etic, xviii–xix, 10, 22, 25, 56, 58–9, 71, 81–2, 86, 110, 136, 156–7, 164, 167, 174–5, 177–8, 181–3, 187–9, 192–3, 200, 205
psyche, 26–7
ψυχή, 27, 102, 113, 216n18

quantum physics, 113, 155, 157–9, 162–3, 175, 228n8, 231n9

reading, 155, 177, 186–9
region/regioning (*die Gegend, die Gegnet, gegnen*), 47, 76, 83, 85, 109, 117, 137–8, 168–9, 179, 183, 187–90
reservedness (*die Verhaltenheit*), 38–9, 63, 69, 140, 175–7
rift (*der Riß*), 8
Ross, David, 128–32

Sachs, Joe, 125–33
saying (*die Sage*), 49, 55, 58, 64–78, 81–4, 86, 106
Schrödinger, Erwin, 159
startled dismay (*das Erschrecken*), 38–40, 50
stillness (*die Stille*), 55, 76–7, 225n16

Taoism. *See* Daoism
technicity (*die Technik*), 27, 32, 35–7, 88, 91–5, 217
technology, xix, 7, 35, 89, 91
telos, 127–31

τέλος, 123–35
Thales, 112
thinking as experience, 172–6
timeless (*uralt*, "timeless"),16, 23, 33–4, 104, 143, 159, 166, 169, 179, 186–8, 191–6, 210
translation, intra- and interlingual, 83, 86

übersetzen and *über*setzen, 9, 83, 86, 100
uncertainty/uncertainty principle, 39, 158
underway thinking, 17, 20–2, 73, 79, 115, 165, 167
Unverborgenheit, 18, 24, 29, 31, 41, 43, 45, 109, 120–2, 138, 153, 203, 228n7

von Herrmann, Friedrich-Wilhelm, 21, 30, 57, 90, 181

way-making, 17, 20, 34, 58, 73, 76–8, 84, 156–8, 165–9, 177–8, 218n8
withdrawal/self-sheltering, 17, 29, 47, 50, 53, 62, 69, 74, 139–40, 143–4, 146–7, 150, 168, 175, 180–3, 190, 199, 206, 210, 214n7, 220n8, 23–4, 38
Wesen, das, how to translate, 93–5, 196–7, 227n15
word (*das Wort*), 49, 58, 186–7

zögernde Sichversagen, das, 43, 153, 189, 195

New Studies in Phenomenology and Hermeneutics

General Editor: Kenneth Maly

Gail Stenstad, *Transformations: Thinking after Heidegger*
Parvis Emad, *On the Way to Heidegger's "Contributions to Philosophy"*
Bernhard Radloff, *Heidegger and the Question of National Socialism: Disclosure and Gestalt*
Kenneth Maly, *Heidegger's Possibility: Language, Emergence – Saying Be-ing*
Robert Mugerauer, *Heidegger and Homecoming: The Leitmotif in the Later Writings*
Graeme Nicholson, *Justifying Our Existence: An Essay in Applied Phenomenology*
Ladelle McWhorter and Gail Stenstad, eds., *Heidegger and the Earth: Essays in Environmental Philosophy*, Second, Expanded Edition
Richard Capobianco, *Engaging Heidegger*
Peter R. Costello, *Layers in Husserl's Phenomenology: On Meaning and Intersubjectivity*
Friedrich-Wilhelm von Herrmann, *Hermeneutics and Reflection: Heidegger and Husserl on the Concept of Phenomenology*, translated by Kenneth Maly. Published in German as *Hermeneutik und Reflexion. Der Begriff der Phänomenologie bei Heidegger und Husserl*
Richard Capobianco, *Heidegger's Way of Being*
Janet Donohoe, *Husserl on Ethics and Intersubjectivity: From Static to Genetic Phenomenology*
Miles Groth, *Translating Heidegger*
Graeme Nicholson, *Heidegger on Truth: Its Essence and Its Fate*
Kenneth Maly, *Five Groundbreaking Moments in Heidegger's Thinking*

www.ingramcontent.com/pod-product-compliance
Lightning Source LLC
Chambersburg PA
CBHW030313080526
44584CB00012B/550